DICTIONARY

OF

PAGAN RELIGIONS

Dictionary
of
Pagan Religions

by

H. E. WEDECK
and

WADE BASKIN

THE CITADEL PRESS · SECAUCUS, NEW JERSEY

First paperbound printing, 1973
Copyright © 1971 by Philosophical Library, Inc.
All rights reserved
Published by Citadel Press
A division of Lyle Stuart Inc.
120 Enterprise Avenue, Secaucus, N.J. 07094
In Canada: George J. McLeod Limited
73 Bathurst St., Toronto 2B, Ontario
Manufactured in the United States of America
ISBN 0-8065-0386-6

"The world is not divided into good Christians and bad pagans, but into good people and bad people. And God knows there are few enough of them, in either rank."
— *Dagobert D. Runes*

In Biblical phraseology, pagans were described as 'the nations,' as 'the gentiles,' that is, 'the heathens.' In the early Christian period, during the third, fourth, and fifth centuries, the Church Fathers, among them Tertullian, Lactantius, and St. Jerome, used the Latin term *ethnici* — derived from the Greek *ethnos,* a nation, *ethnicoi,* heathens — to denote pagans.

It should here be noted, however, that pagan philosophy and pagan theological speculation as represented, for instance, by the Neoplatonist Plotinus and his pupil Porphyry, often coincided, in many respects, with Christian thought, and that it was not difficult, or rare, to convert from paganism to Christianity. As an instance, it is not yet certain whether the philosopher Boethius was a complete Christian or whether he retained pagan concepts in his philosophical expositions. For pagan philosophy, notably among the Greek and Latin writers of the fifth century, elaborated, by dialectic argumentation, the same themes that involved Christian metaphysical and theological issues. And ultimately, there was a confrontation between pagan philosophy and Christian doctrine. The latter became the established and triumphant faith. Paganism, however, did not die out completely with the rise and expansion of Christianity. It went underground to a large extent, retaining its hold for several centuries in the form of mystery cults, in the Mediterranean littoral, in Egypt, Syria, Persia, in Northern and Eastern Europe. Despite the slow disintegration of pagan beliefs and practices, rites and ceremonials and liturgies, pagan concepts and certain vestigial traditions persisted far into the Middle Ages. They did not pass into total oblivion or historical obscurity. They were absorbed in many directions and incorporated into modern philosophical and religious systems.

In the context of this book, the terms of reference relate to the less known religious cults of the ancient world, including the mystery cults of Egypt, the Middle East, and the Mediterranean area, as well as to cults which have evolved in other parts of the world.

In addition to names, relevant items have been included relating to religious systems, temple sites, ancient religious texts, and similar matter.

H. E. W.

DICTIONARY
OF
PAGAN RELIGIONS

A

AAHLA In Egyptian religion, one of the divisions of the Ament, or lower regions. The word means 'field of peace.'

AARU In Egyptian religion, the abode of the blessed dead. The celestial field, encircled by an iron wall, is covered with wheat. The dead are represented as gleaning this wheat, which is the symbol of Karma, the law of retribution.

AATS In Egyptian religion, the fourteen or fifteen Aats or domains constituted the Elysian Fields. Each Aat was presided over by a different deity.

ABADDON The Hebrew name of the angel of the bottomless pit or the destroying angel, called Apollyon in Greek. Medieval demonographers regarded him as the causer of wars.

ABADIR In the Punic language, this name denotes *mighty father*. This title was bestowed by the Carthaginians on their principal deities.

ABARIS A mythical hyperborean priest of Apollo said to have been endowed with the gift of prophecy.

ABASTOR In classical mythology, the name of one of the horses of Pluto, god of the underworld.

ABATUR In Gnosticism, the father of the Demiurgus, corresponding to the third Logos in the esoteric teachings of antiquity.

ABBA AMONA In the Cabala, the occult names of the two higher Sephiroth of the upper triad. Sephira or Kether

1

stands at the apex or head of the Sephirothal Tree. The Hebrew words mean 'Father-Mother.'

ABELLION In Celtic mythology, a divinity who was identified with the Roman god Apollo.

ABERIDES In classical mythology, a variant name for the ancient Roman god Saturn.

ABHISEKA A term used by Buddhists for the tenth stage of perfection. It is also used to designate the ceremonial bathing in sacred waters as practiced by many Hindus.

ABLANATHANALBA In Gnosticism, a term similar to 'Abracadabra.' It reads the same from either end and was used as a charm in Egypt. It may mean 'thou art a father to us.'

ABO TANI According to one legend preserved by the Apa Tanis, a primitive tribe of the eastern Himalayas, the first man was Abo Tani. He was created by Hilo.

ABODE OF GODS In Norse religion, the abode of the gods was made from the head of the giant Ymir.

ABORIGINAL SOCIETIES Among Australian aborigines, men are grouped, with regard to birth, locality, and so on, into 'societies.' These societies maintain certain cults associated with totemism.

ABORIGINES Australian aborigines conceive that human beings, in groups, are linked to a particular species of animal such as the kangaroo, the iguana, the emu, or to a phenomenon such as rain. These species form the totems of each human group.

ABRACADABRA A symbolic word first used in a medical treatise by Samonicus. It is supposed to be a corruption of the sacred Gnostic term 'Abraxas,' a magic formula meaning 'Hurt me not.' It was attached to an amulet and worn on the breast.

(ABRASAX) ABRAXAS Variant of *abraxas,* a symbolic word traced back to Basilides of Alexandria, who used it as a title for the divinity. In Greek numeration, the seven letters total 365, the days of the solar year, which represents a cycle of divine action.

ABRAXAS This mystic term was in vogue among the Gnostic sect that was founded by Basilides in the second century A.D. In Greek numerology Abraxas denoted the number 365, the number of days in a year. Also, this was the sum total of the spirits who emanated from God.
Among occultists the word Abraxas, engraved on stones or gems, was held to have a mystic significance.

ABSU In Chaldean mysticism, the name for Space, the dwelling place of Ab, the Father or Head of the Source of the Waters of Knowledge.

ABSYRTUS In Greek and Roman mythology, a brother of Medea, who killed him and cut his body into pieces in order to detain their father as she fled from Colchis.

ABYDOS The ancient holy city of Osiris, god of the dead. It lies two hundred miles north of Luxor and was the sanctuary of an even older mortuary god before Osiris came to dwell there. Kings delighted to honor the place, and people came from all over Egypt to lay their bones in its sanctified ground, hoping thereby to win greater glory in the next world. The exact location of the tomb of Osiris was known to the devout.

ABYSS In Egyptian religion, the Abyss was a descriptive name for the underworld of the dead. In Babylonian thought it was the primeval chaos from which the universe evolved. In Gnosticism it was personified as the first principle of the infinite deity.

ABZU In Sumerian religion, the watery abyss that is the abode of the god Enki, the Lord of Wisdom.

3

ACAVISR In Etruscan religion, a deity whose functions were subsidiary to those of the major divinities.

ACCA LARENTIA An ancient Italic deity. She was worshipped as the protectress of crops. A festival in her honor was held on December 23.

ACERSECOMES In Greek religion, a descriptive term applied to the god Apollo. It denotes the uncut hair on the head of the deity.

ACESTES The son of the Sicilian river god Crimisus.

ACHELOUS In Greek religion, a river god. In Etruscan art, he is represented as a bull with a human face. In popular belief, swift, foaming water is often identified with horses or bulls. The Etruscans used masks of Achelous to protect from evil the objects or buildings they adorned.

ACHERON In Greek mythology, Acheron was one of the rivers of Hades. It is mentioned by Homer, in his epic poetry.

ACHORUS Among the inhabitants of ancient Cyrene, the god of flies. Sacrifices were made to this god for deliverance from the insects.

ACMON In Greek mythology, a deity who existed before the creation of heaven.

ACNA She is the moon goddess of the Mayas.

ACOSMISM A type of pantheism which denies the existence of the universe as distinct from the Absolute.

ACRATOPOTES In classical mythology, a name applied to the god Bacchus.
In Greek, the expression means *a drinker of sheer wine*.

ACRATUS In Greek mythology, a deity worshipped by the Athenians.

ADAD In Babylonian mythology, a god of wind and storm, known also as Ramman and, earlier in Palestine and Syria, as Hadad. The ancient storm god of the Amorites.

ADAM KADMON In the Cabala, the Archetypal Man or Humanity. It is the manifested Logos.

ADAPA In Babylonian mythology, this deity is associated with Ea, who endowed him with wisdom. Adapa was offered bread and water of life by the gods. Summoned before Anu, the sky god, he refused to accept the offer and lost the attribute of immortality.

ADDEPHAGIA In classical mythology, the goddess of gluttony. She received special worship from the Sicilians.

ADITI In Vedic Hinduism, an abstract goddess whose name signifies 'boundlessness.'

ADITYAS In Hinduism, a group of gods, all sons of Aditi. The most important of them is Varuna, and the other eleven are his personified attributes: Mitra, Aryaman, Bhaga, Daksa, Amas, Dhatar, Indra, Vivasvant, Martanda, Surya, and Vishnu.

ADONIS In Greek legend, a youth who was loved by Aphrodite but whom he repulsed. He was killed by a boar during a hunt and his death was deeply lamented by Aphrodite. Although he was required to descend into the kingdom of the dead, he was permitted to return to the upper earth in spring and summer, to live with Aphrodite. His story symbolized a vegetation myth, and his rebirth corresponds to the myth of Ishtar and her lover Tammuz, the Babylonian god of vegetation.
Adonis was annually reborn amidst great jubilation on the

part of his votaries, especially at Alexandria.

He is represented on Etruscan mirrors and vases; also on murals at Pompeii.

ADOREA A Roman goddess who was identified with Victory.

AEACUS In Greek mythology, a son of Zeus and the nymph Aegina, and the father of Telamon and Peleus. Famed for his justice and piety on earth, he was made one of the three judges in Hades.

AEGAEON In Greek religion, a marine God living under the Aegean Sea. The name given by men to 'him whom the gods called Briareus.' See Briareus.

AEGIOCHUS A descriptive epithet applied to Jupiter as having been raised by the she-goat Amalthea.

AEGIPAN In classical mythology, the god Pan, represented with goat feet.

AEGOPHAGA In classical mythology, a variant name for Aphrodite, to whom a goat was sacrificed.

AELLO One of the three Harpies, feared by the Greeks.

AELURUS In Egyptian mythology, the cat-god. He is represented as a human figure with a cat's head.

AEMOCHARES (HAEMOCHARES) This Greek expression means 'rejoicing in blood.' In classical mythology, it is a descriptive name, applied to the Roman war god Mars.

AEOLUS In Greek religion, the god who binds and looses the winds. The king of Aeolia, the inventor of sails and a great astronomer, was deified by posterity as the king of storms and winds.

AEON Among the Phoenicians, a deity that personified the passage of time.

AERUSCUTORES In the Phrygian cult of Cybele, these were her priests, the Galli, who went begging in public, ringing hand bells to invite donations.

AESCULANUS A Roman deity who presided over copper coinage.

AESCULAPIUS In Roman religion, the god of medicine. He was called the Soter (Savior) who raised the dead to life. His worship was introduced into Rome in the third century B.C. in response to an oracle promising relief from the plague.

AESIR In Norse mythology, Aesir meant the entire entourage in the Nordic pantheon, including the supreme god Odin. Their dwelling place was the city of Asgard, where the gods reveled in luxury.

AESMA In Zoroastrianism, Aesma was the evil spirit of anger that inspired vengeance.

AESYMNETES In classical mythology, a descriptive name of Bacchus, the god of wine. In Greek the word means a judge or arbiter (as, for instance, at a symposium).

AETOLIAN CULTS The deities of Aetolia included Apollo, Artemis, and Athena. The cult center of Artemis was Calydon. Apollo too was associated with Calydon, while Athena was worshipped notably at Pleuron. Other cults prevalent in Aetolia were those of Dionysus and of Atargatis (Aphrodite).

AFRICAN RELIGIONS All African religions are monotheistic in the sense that they recognize one High God as the creator of all things and the source of whatever order exists in the world. Many of the religions of Africa are polytheistic in the sense that man is separated from his maker by large numbers of gods, spirits, or ancestors. They tend to be tribal religions in the sense that the social structure is reflected in tribal beliefs. Prayer, which is likely to stress innocence of any evil intention and requests for good health and well-being, is found in all African religions. Sacrifices, usually goats or chickens, are intended not so much to cleanse as to establish communication between man and god. Throughout the continent, the sanctity of all life is primary.

Ritual plays an important role in African life. Religion is viewed as a set of goals, a frame of reference involving man and god, and a set of rituals for achieving specific goals. Religious rites mark christenings, weddings, burials, initiations, the seasons, and related factors such as planting, harvesting, rain-making, hunting, fishing, crime and punishment, war and peace. There are no idols or priests (with rare exceptions), no religious doctrines or theologies. In their attempts to cope with the crises of life, many Africans rely on witch-doctors, magic, superstition, tabus, and fetishes or charms. The universal belief in spirits or ghosts and a primitive animism is shared, despite differences in language, cultural level, and political development, by vast numbers of Negroes, Bantus, Hottentots, and Bushmen.

The supreme god is generally assumed to have created a world without regard to good or evil, then to have withdrawn from it, leaving its operation dependent on spiritual energy supplied by human effort. The degree of his withdrawal varies with tribes, but the system he created is assumed to be mechanically or organically perfect. Ancestral spirits and godlings representing different aspects of the supreme god link man to his maker. Evil enters the perfect system through human selfishness or through a trickster who perverts all the rules. Only a trickster, or fate as he is often called, can explain disaster in the absence of selfishness.

When disaster strikes, a diviner may be able to detect the device used to provoke it or to identify its author — a neglected spirit who is punishing a descendant for the faults of the group or a witch who is simply venting his envy. Divination brings to light the ritual that must be performed to correct a misfortune. All ritual involves establishing communication between the world of men and the spirit world.

Sacrifice and prayer are the two main components of most rituals, but lesser elements may include magical gesture, special implements, and distinctive items of apparel.

AFTERLIFE Among the Greeks and Romans and Egyptians in particular, there was a universal though indeterminate belief in survival after death. A primitive concept was that the dead live on in their tombs and require human sustenance. In the earliest Greek records, the Homeric epics, the belief was that the dead have their abode in a dark and grim realm. In this respect, the dead required no sustenance from the living and inspired no fear.
Another concept, also in Homer, placed certain heroes, exempted from death, in the Isles of the Blessed. In the sixth century B.C. the Eleusinian Mysteries, involving the cult of Demeter, promised their votaries a happy fate after death. In mystery cults in general, the concept of metempsychosis was maintained, and happiness would be achieved by those who in this life had led a pure existence.
The cults also of Dionysus, Sabazius, Attis, and Isis similarly offered assurance of a happy life after death. The dead were conceived as inhabiting an underground realm or being transferred to celestial regions.

AGATHOS DAEMON In Greek religion, a god to whom a libation was offered after each meal.

AGDISTIS This is an aspect of Cybele, who was called Agdistis at Pessinus. The cult of Agdistis, who was primarily androgynous, extended into many areas of Anatolia, Egypt, and Attica.

AGELASTUS A descriptive name of Pluto, god of the underworld in classical mythology. There was no joy in his grim dominion: hence his epithet, which in Greek means 'gloomy,' 'not laughing.'

AGENONA A Roman goddess of industry.

9

AGLAUROS A Greek mystery cult that was observed in Athens. It was celebrated in honor of the deity Aglauros.

AGLIBOLUS and MALACHBELUS Ancient Syrian divinities. They are represented as youths before a temple, separated from each other by a pine tree.

AGNI HOTRI In Aryan religion, the priests who served the god of fire.

AGONIUS A Roman god who presided over business affairs.

AGRAI In Greek religion, initiation into the Lesser Mysteries at Agrai had to precede initiation into the Eleusinian Mysteries.

AGRICULTURAL RITES In pagan religions, agricultural rites were performed in order to win the favor of the gods. The basic need was to secure abundant harvests. The rituals included dances around the fields, sprinkling the ground with sacrificial blood, sometimes human blood. Cattle were also offered to the deities who presided over the productivity of the earth. Phallic ceremonies were in vogue, as symbolic of fertility. Incantations, invocations to the chthonic deities were regular features of the vegetation cults. In addition, suppliants marched in procession through the fields while prayers were offered to the divinities in charge of the growing, ripening and mature crops. Rain ceremonies especially were elaborate. They included magic formulas, thunderous music, and, ultimately, joyful dancing and feasting.
All such vegetation cults, despite ethnic and geographical variations, were fundamentally identical. They sought the beneficent cooperation of the powerful, unseen forces of nature.

AGRICULTURE The discovery of agriculture and animal husbandry had a profound effect on the evolution of primitive religion. In the ancient Near East, divine triads consisting of father, mother, and son were known and worshipped with the aid of a shrine and rites as early as the sixth millennium B.C. Religion became more complex as the mythology and cultic symbolism associated with the gods of fertility evolved in the direction of the crystallized form exemplified in the Adonis-Attis-Osiris cycle of the third millennium.

AGRIPPA VON NETTESHEIM Henry Cornelius von Nettesheim (1486-1535) made religion an amalgam of Cabalistic mysticism, Neo-Platonism, and Christianity. He distinguished himself as a soldier, physician, and student of the occult. He traveled widely, lectured in Italy on Hermes Trismegistus, and wrote *The Occult Philosophy,* a defense of magic in which he tried to synthesize occult lore with the natural sciences.

AGROTES A Phoenician deity, equated with Dagon. He is represented as being borne in a chariot at his festivals.

AGRUERUS An ancient Phoenician god, equivalent to Saturn.

AHIMSA A Hindu doctrine stressing the oneness and sacredness of all life. The doctrine is held by different religious groups in India, but most strictly by the Jains.

AHONE In Algonquian religion, the great god who ruled the world but did not require sacrifice.

AHPUCH In Maya religion, the chief of the gods of darkness. His opponent was Chac, the rain god.

AHRIMAN In Zoroastrian religion, the Spirit of Evil, in perpetual conflict with the supreme deity Ahura Mazda. Ahriman is also called Angra Mainyu. Six archdemons always attend him.

AHU In Egyptian religion, the great god of the West. He is an obscure deity, later identified as an aspect of Osiris.
In Zoroastrian religion, the word designates the Spiritual Lord and Master who works with the Ratu or Prophet to protect the Creation.

11

AHURA MAZDA In the Zoroastrian religion Ahura Mazda, which means Lord of Knowledge, was the beneficent Spirit of Good, leader of the powers of light. His other name was Ormuzd. He acted in opposition to the Spirit of Evil, Ahriman, who was in control of the forces of darkness.

AIJ TAION The supreme deity of the Yakut, a Turkish tribe of northeastern Siberia.

AIJE Among the Bororos of Brazil, a mythical monster associated with the deep waters.

AIN-AIOR A Chaldean word naming the divine substance or unique 'self-existent.'

AINUS This dwindling race inhabits the Northern islands of Japan and Eastern Siberia. Their ceremonies are, as in the case of the old classical cults and the religions of the Near East, aimed at winning control over the natural phenomena. For sustenance, they need rain and sun, fire and the produce of the earth. For these purposes they use magic incantations, spells, amulets to divert the influences of evil spirits that may cause destruction, famine, disease. They also use rites, of an apotropaic nature, to ensure the safety of their swamps. The Ainus regard the bear, that is, a food-animal, fire, and crops as having an inner power, and they consider them with a kind of religious awe. Otherwise, there is no formal priesthood among the Ainus, and temple worship is unknown.

AION In the Mithraic cult, he is a deity who is represented as a human figure with a lion's head. Identified with Cronos, Aion is a time symbol.

AIR GODS These gods, in pagan religions, are associated with weather phenomena, especially winds, thunder and lightning, rain, storms.
In Egypt, the air god was Shu. In Greek and Roman myth-

12

ology, Boreas was the anthropomorphic wind god. In Greece the winds were called 'Snatchers,' because they were regarded as malefic. In the Assyro-Babylonian religion, Adad or Rammon was the storm god.

AITA The Etruscan word for Hades.

AIUS LOCUTIUS A variant name for Aius Loquens. He was the divine 'sayer and speaker' who warned the Romans of the approach of their enemies, the Gauls.

AIUS LOQUENS Latin expression, meaning 'a speaking voice.' A deity whose utterance announced that Rome would be attacked by the Gauls. When the oracle proved true, an altar was set up in his honor.

AJA A Sanskrit term meaning 'unborn' or 'uncreated' and used as an epithet of many of the primordial gods. It is used in theosophy with reference to the first Logos.

AJITAS A Sanskrit word used by the occultists to designate one of the twelve great gods incarnating in each Manvantara.

AJIVIKAS A sect of Hinduism established by Gosala Mankhaliputta in the sixth century B.C. Similar to Jainism, it differed in certain practices and in its rigorous doctrine of determinism. The sect is now extinct.

AKAR In Egyptian religion, the proper name of that division of the infernal regions corresponding to Hell.

AKASA A Sanskrit word designating one of the five elements of the Sankhaya philosophy, variously identified as space, ether, or sky. In theosophy, the primordial substance from which radiates the First Logos, or expressed thought. It is the power which lies latent at the bottom of every magical operation, the alkahest of the alchemists.

13

AKER In Egyptian religion, the dual lion-god. He presided over the course of the sun through the night sky.

AKHENATON The Egyptian pharaoh credited with the distinction of having founded the world's first monotheistic religion was born about 1370 B.C. and named for his father, Amenhotep ('Amon is satisfied'). He renounced Amon-Ra, king of gods, who was the ancient provincial god of Thebes, changed his own name to Akhenaton ('it is well with Aton'), moved the court to a site today known as Tell el Amarna, built a new city called Akhetaton, and forbade the worship of the old gods of Egypt. Aton had been associated in earlier times with the orb of the sun and had become a minor god. In the thinking of Akhenaton, he may have been worthy of worship as the spirit of animation and creation.

AKIBA In the Cabala, the only one of the four Tanaim who entered and succeeded in getting himself initiated into the Garden of Delight.

AKKADIAN-CHALDEAN INSCRIPTIONS The Royal Library of Nineveh possessed Akkadian engraving dating from the seventh century B.C. and giving directions for performing exorcisms against sickness, plague, demons, and evil of all kinds.

AKKADIANS A Semitic race that inhabited Babylonia and absorbed many of the ceremonies, rituals, and religious concepts of the Babylonians.

AKO MANA In Zoroastrian religion, Evil Mind, or the collective evil minds of men who are under the influence of the Druj.

AKUPARA In Hindu mythology, the symbolical turtle on which the earth is said to rest.

ALAGARUS The second divine king of Babylonia. He was appointed the 'Shepherd of the people' and reigned ten Sari (36,000) years). *See* Sumerian King List.

14

AL-AIT A Phoenician word naming the god of fire, an ancient and very mystic figure in Coptic occultism.

ALBIGENSES A sect which arose in Italy and southern France in the eleventh century. Also called New Manichaeans and Cathari, they were Manichaean in theology and taught the theory of transmigration of souls of the unperfected. They were almost exterminated by the Inquisition.

ALBIORIX Also called Teutates. He was a Celtic divinity, king of the universe and god of war.

ALBUNEA In Roman mythology, a Sibyl or priestess associated with a dream oracle that was near a waterfall.

ALCHEMY The forerunner of chemistry seems to have originated in Alexandria during the first century A.D. when the practical art of metallurgy developed by the Egyptians was fused with the philosophical speculations of Greek philosophy and the mysticism of the middle eastern religions. The Egyptians regarded Hermes Trismegistus as the source of all knowledge and the father of the hermetic art of alchemy. From Egypt alchemy spread to Greece, Italy, the Mohammedan world, Spain, and the rest of Europe. The earliest Chinese treatise on alchemy dates from the second century A.D. and is intimately tied to Taoism.
Although in the beginning alchemy was a practical series of chemical operations based on the accepted theory of nature and matter, the mystically minded soon developed alchemical ideas and stressed divine revelation, the search for the divine elixir, and the secret of immortality. The pseudo science reached its zenith in the Middle Ages, when learned men like Roger Bacon believed in the transmutation of base metals into gold. History records that more than one imposter was put to death for failing to produce the philosopher's stone.

ALCIS A Teutonic divinity, identified with the Roman Castor, or sometimes his twin Pollux.

15

ALCYONE In Greek mythology, the daughter of Aeolus and wife of Ceyx. In grief for her dead husband, who had drowned as he was journeying to consult the oracle, she threw herself into the sea. Out of compassion the gods changed them into kingfishers. The female is said to lay her eggs on the sea and to keep it calm during the seven days that precede and follow the winter solstice. Also, *Halcyone*.

ALEMONA A Roman goddess who presided over infants before birth.

ALETHAE In Phoenician religion, those who worship the god of fire. They are the same as the Kabiri or divine Titans. As the seven emanations of Agruerus (Saturn), the Alethae are connected with many primitive divinities of fire, sun, and storm.

ALEXANDRIA The temple of Isis at Alexandria was destroyed c. 391 A.D.

ALFHEIM In Norse mythology, this was the abode of the elves.

ALGALOA In the Hawaiian religion, he is the sky god.

ALI ILLAHIJA An Asiatic sect that practices the orgiastic rites associated with the ancient cult of Anahita.

ALKAHEST In alchemy, the universal solvent. In mysticism, the Higher Self which fuses with matter to make gold and restores all compound things such as the human body and its attributes to their primeval essence.

ALLATU In Assyro-Babylonian religion, the goddess of the Nether Regions, the abode of the dead. She was the consort of Bel and afterward of Nergal.

ALL FOOLS' DAY The first day of April, when practical jokes are perpetrated on credulous victims. It has its origin in the Celtic cult of Arianrhod.

16

ALL HALLOW'S EVE (HALLOWEEN) A festival of Druidic origin. It takes place on October 31, on the evening preceding All Saints' Day. The merrymaking and pranks which today are associated with the event are rooted in supernatural beliefs. According to Druidic traditions, Saman, the Lord of Death, was supposed at this time to summon the souls of evil men who had been condemned to inhabit animal bodies. Witches, demons, and the spirits of the dead were supposed to assemble on this night.

ALMADEL A treatise on Theurgia or White Magic by an unknown medieval writer.

ALMON A Roman river god.

ALRAUNE In Teutonic mythology, a female demon.

ALRUNES In Teutonic mythology, the gods of the household.

ALSVIDUR In Norse mythology, one of the horses yoked to the chariot of the sun.

ALTARS Among American Indians, the altar, in religious ceremonies, was of various forms. It might be the skull of a large animal, or a heap of rocks. Some altars were directed toward a particular cardinal point.
At the altars supplications were made for rain, a plentiful harvest, good hunting.

AMALTHEA In Greek mythology, the she-goat that nursed Zeus. Her horns flowed with nectar and ambrosia.

AMAN In ancient Egyptian religion, Aman was the Devourer of the Dead.

AMATERASU In Japanese religion, the principal deity of Shinto, ancestress of the imperial house; the sun goddess.

AMATHAOUNTA An Egyptian goddess of the sea.

17

AMA-USHUMGAL-ANNA In late Summerian liturgies, the name given to Tammuz. The word means 'The Mother Python of Heaven.'

AMBA RELIGION The flexible system of the Amba tribesmen of Uganda embraces many deities and rituals. The world of the Amba contains not only human beings but a host of supernatural spirits, divided into two categories: ancestors and gods. Most of a man's ritual activities are concerned with the ancestors, particularly those centering on death. The underworld is assumed to be much like the world of the living, and ancestors are seen as individuals who must be continually pacified. Shrines are erected to deified humans and to nonhuman gods. Tribesmen pay a priest to enlist the support of one of four lineage gods in ridding themselves of an enemy. Any individual who belongs to the lineage of one of these gods may make use of his services.

AMENT In Egyptian religion Ament was the land of the dead. It was conceived as a dark region, resounding with lamentation, where souls of the wicked remained everlastingly. In his diurnal course, Ra the sun god passed through Ament. The conception of Ament is remarkably similar to the Roman view of the underworld as depicted by the poet Vergil.

AMENTI In Egyptian religion, Ament was the dwelling of four presiding spirits, the Amenti. The soul entering the subterranean realm of the sun's descent is conducted by Anubis into the hall of Osiris, is judged by the 42 judges, and passes on to Aaru or is condemned to torment. The four genii, or Amenti, the children of Horus, are the man-headed Amseti (south), the dog-headed Hapi (north), the ape-headed Tuamutef (east), and the hawk-headed Kebhsenuf (west).

AMESHA SPENTAS In the Zoroastrian religion, these were Holy Immortals who were the angelic attendants on Ahura Mazda. They were also known as Amshaspands.

AMIDA (AMITABHA) In the teachings of the Japanese sect called Jodo (Pure Land), he is worshipped as the Lord of Boundless Light.

AMIDISM In China, the cult of Amitabha, which holds out to its followers the promise of rebirth in paradise. In Japan, a doctrine of Buddhism, formulated by the sect called Jodo (Pure Land), which teaches that salvation is attained through faith in Amida, the Lord of Boundless Light.

AMITAYUS In Tibetan Buddhism, he is The Boundless, The Everlasting Life. His image is venerated.

AMM In Arabian religion, the god of the moon, known also as Sin, Wadd, and Ilumquh.

AMMIT In Egyptian religion, Ammit was the Eater of the Dead. He eats men's hearts after they have been weighed in the hall of judgment and found wanting. Ammit is depicted as part crocodile, part hippopotamus, and part lion.

AMMON An Egyptian deity originally associated with the city of Thebes. Identified with the Roman Jupiter. Alexander the Great, according to tradition, on visiting his shrine, was accorded the title of Son of Ammon.
There was an oracle of Ammon in his temple situated in the Libyan desert.

AMMONIUS SACCAS An Alexandrian philosopher who lived between the second and third centuries A.D. He broke with Christianity because he was unable to find in it any superiority over the older religions.

AMM-UT Devourer of souls 'not true of voice.' See Ammit.

AMORITES A group of western Semites who worshipped Amurru. Their most prominent figure was Hammurabi, king of Babylon.

AMRITA In Hinduism, the elixir of life and food of the gods which confers immortality on men.

AMURRU In Assyro-Babylonian religion, he was the god of the Amorites, a group of western Semites.

19

AN In Egyptian religion, an aspect of Ra, the sun god.

AN The Sumerian god who, as father of all the gods, corresponds to the Greek Zeus. He is the god of the heavens. From the primal arose heaven, An. The earth was controlled by Enlil, who was also god of the winds and the air. He was the offspring of An and Ki, who was originally Earth.

ANA (ANU) In Celtic religion, the mother of the ancient Irish gods.

ANAGAMIN In Buddhism, one who is no longer to be reborn into the world of desire.

ANAHITA A Persian goddess associated with the fertilizing waters. Her cult ranged over Cappadocia, Armenia, Lydia, and Pontus. Sacred prostitution, performed by the temple attendants known as hierodouloi, was a feature of her worship. In Lydia Anahita was identified with Cybele and Artemis. Under this aspect she was known as Mater Artemis or Artemis Anahita, or the Persian Artemis. Her sacred animal was the bull and the sacrifice of bulls, the tauro-bolium, was a feature of her cult.
Anahita itself means 'the unsullied.'

ANALECTS These are the sayings of the Chinese philosopher Confucius and his followers. The Analects were written down on the basis of the traditions preserved by these followers.

ANALOGETICISTS The disciples of Ammonius Saccas, so called because they interpreted all sacred myths and mysteries by a principle of analogy and correspondence now found in the Cabalistic system and in eastern schools of esoteric philosophy.

ANANTA-SESHA In Hindu mythology, the Serpent of Eternity, couch of Vishnu, and symbol of infinite time in space.

ANATH A Canaanite goddess. She was called 'The Virgin' and was the sister of Baal. In Egypt, she was regarded as a war goddess.

20

ANATOLIAN RELIGION In ancient Anatolian religion, the principal feature was the Mother-Goddess and her young male consort. Together they symbolized productivity. The consort was identified in his various aspects with a corresponding Greek deity. In her Asian territory, the goddess was dominant. Among the native deities were Cybele, her lover Attis, Ma, Wanax.

ANCESTOR WORSHIP A form of worship found among the Romans, the Egyptians, and the Chinese, as well as among many primitive peoples in Africa and Asia and such advanced peoples as the Japanese. The importance of having sons is stressed in all societies practicing ancestor worship since it must be performed by a male descendant. The worship of a common ancestor is one of the bonds linking members of a clan.

ANDANIAN CULT A Greek mystery cult whose observances honored a number of deities.

ANDATE Also called Andraste. Among the ancient Britons, the goddess of victory. In a consecrated grove war captives were immolated in her honor.

ANDHRIMNU In Norse mythology, he daily prepared the board named Sahrimnu for the banquet of the gods in Valhalla.

ANDOUGNI A creator god among the Canadian Indians. It is said that the Indians have no form of prayer for addressing him.

ANGAKOK Among the Eskimos, a priestly class whose members have the right to cohabit with women and to enjoy other advantages by exploiting the fears of ordinary men and women.

ANGERONA An obscure Roman goddess. She is represented as holding a finger in her mouth. Possibly she is the goddess of silence.

ANGERONIA A Roman goddess who removed mental anguish.

ANGITIA An Italic goddess of serpents. She was worshipped by the Marsians of central Italy. She was also the goddess of healing.

ANGRA MAINYU In Zoroastrianism, the evil spirit or god.

ANGURBODA In Norse mythology, a giant ogress. She and her husband Loki were the parents of Fenris the wolf, Hel, the goddess of the underworld, and the serpent Ioermungandr.

ANIMAL HUSBANDRY Animal husbandry and agriculture were practiced in the Near East during the Middle Stone Age. The introduction of these practices changed profoundly the religion of the people, adding to its complexity. As early as the sixth millennium B.C., divine triads, consisting of father, mother, and son, were worshipped. Shrines and rites became a part of the religious life of the people.

ANIMAL SACRIFICES In Greek religion, particular animals were sacrificed to the gods. Poseidon was offered horses. Swine were sacrificed to Demeter. Hecate, the goddess of the Nether Regions, favored dogs. To Dionysus and Apollo goats were immolated.

ANIMAL WORSHIP In many ancient religions animals were viewed as superior beings if they manifested marked strength or intelligence or cunning. At some stage they became related to the gods themselves and acquired sanctity. They were held sacred and granted divine honors. Prayers were offered to them in specially dedicated temples. Among such divine animals were the bull, Apis, the cat, the serpent, the crocodile, and certain birds, such as the ibis and the bennu. These were held in reverence among the Egyptians. The gods, though anthropomorphic in form, manifested their animal incarnation by having animals as associates. Worship of animals is termed zoolatry.

ANIMATISM The belief that objects are alive and may be outlets of personal or impersonal power. See Mana.

ANIMISM The belief in spirits of nature; also the view that persons and objects are animated by such spirits. This belief is common in many primitive pagan religions.

ANINGAHK Among the Eskimos, the moon deity, the hunter.

ANITO Among the Bontoc Igorot, the spirit of a dead person capable of causing sickness and death.

ANKH In Egyptian religion, a symbol of a cross surmounted by a loop. It represented life triumphing over death.

ANNA PERENNA A Roman goddess of the New Year. Her feast was very popular and was celebrated joyously on March 15. Anciently, March 15 was the first day in the Roman calendar.

ANNAPURNA In Hinduism, the goddess of plenty, a popular form of Devi, especially in Bengal. Annapurna is one of the names of Kali, the female aspect of Siva.

ANNUNAKI In Babylonian religion, the judges of the dead. They lived in the underworld. See Anunnaki.

ANSHAR The mingling of Apsu and Tiamat, according to the Epic of Gilgamesh, produced first Lahmu and Lahamu, then Anshar and Kishar. Anshar was the father of the sky god, Anu.
In the Akkadian myth of creation, one of a second set of twins born to Apsu and Tiamat. From Anshar's union with Kishar, the other twin, came Anu, a son who is depicted as the yoke of the wagon star, thought to be Polaris.

ANTEROS In Greek mythology, the god of mutual love. He is the brother of Eros (Cupido).

ANTHESTERIA In ancient Greek religion, a three-day festival of flowers held in Athens in honor of Dionysus. Among the participants were slaves.

ANTHROPOMORPHISM The tendency to ascribe human characteristics to things not human. It appears as a phase of nature worship in the development of religions.

ANTHROPOPATHISM The tendency to attribute human feelings to things not human. Some writers consider it to be a factor in the evolution of notions of demons, spirits, and nature gods.

ANTUM In Sumerian mythology, she is the wife of the principal god An, and may be identified with Zeus' consort Hera.

ANU In Babylonian religion, one of the supreme triad, which also included Ea and Bel. Anu was designated as god of the heavens.

ANUBIS A very ancient Egyptian god, son of Isis and Osiris. He presided over funeral rites. He is represented with a male body and a jackal's head. Among the Greeks and Romans he was identified with the three-headed dog of Hades named Cerberus. In the judgment hall of the gods, Anubis presided over the weighing of human souls.

ANUKIT In Egyptian religion, a goddess, consort of Khnemu. A member of the triad of Elephantine, she is depicted as wearing a feather crown.

ANUM A variant name for Anu, the Assyro-Babylonian god of the heavens.

ANUNIT In Babylonian religion, a goddess of war.

ANUNNAKI In the Sumerian religion, they were the children of An, the heaven — god. They were the great gods who in the Lower Regions acted as judges of the dead.

ANURADHAPURA Founded in 437 B.C., the town was the capital of Ceylon for four centuries and one of the world's main Buddhist centers. There one may still see an ancient bo tree, said to be the oldest living historical tree. Because of the self-reproductive powers of the species, it may be the descendant of the bo tree planted there by Tissa (Devanampiyatissa), a Sinhalese king converted to Buddhism by Mahinda, the son of Emperor Asoka, a devout Indian Buddhist. To commemorate his conversion, Tissa and his followers erected many temples and shrines.

ANWYL In Celtic mythology, Anwyl was the world that was inhabited by the dead. This expression corresponds with the Homeric Greek Hades.

APAM NAPAT In the Zoroastrian sacred writings, a mysterious being corresponding to the Fohat of the occultists. It is both a Vedic and an Avestian name meaning 'the Son of the Waters.'

APAP (APOPHIS) The symbolical Serpent of Evil. In the Egyptian *Book of the Dead,* the Solar Boat carries the divine slayers of Apap. As matter left soulless and to itself, Apap is called 'Devourer of Souls.' On many monuments Horus, helped by a number of dog-headed gods, is shown killing Apap. See Apep.

APA TANIS A primitive tribe living in the Himalayas. The Apa Tanis believe that two powerful gods, Kilo and Kiru, dwell on the earth and influence the general welfare of men. They ascribe the creation of the world to Chadun and that of the sky to his female counterpart, Didun. A second myth ascribes the task of creation to three female deities, Ui-Tango, Ni-Ngurre, and Nguntre; and to their male counterparts, Ei Karte, Rup Karte, and Ain Karte. The origin of man is associated with the term Hilo, which may refer to a specific deity or a number of gods.

APE In the religion of the pre-Christian inhabitants of Hawaii, the ape had particular significance. The plucking and eating of this plant, which resembles the taro, was forbidden by Ra'i Ra'i and her divine consort, Tane. The legendary account of the behavior of the first human beings in the Garden of Sunshine in the Land of the Mu is much like the story of the Garden of Eden.

APEP In Egyptian religion, a monster serpent, the principal one among a group of such monsters that obstructed the passage of Ra, the sun god, on his way from darkness to light. Although the serpent was daily crushed and destroyed, it revived daily, having been endowed with immortality. See Apap.

APHAEA A Greek goddess who was worshipped at Aegina. The ruins of her temple are still in existence. She was worshipped with Britomartis.

APHRODITE (VENUS) In classical legend, the goddess of love, beauty, fertility.
Representations of the goddess, both robed and in the nude, were very numerous in antiquity. She appears on pottery, jars, and other artifacts, and there were sculptures of her by Praxiteles, Phidias, and Scopas.

APIA The earth, worshipped by the Lydians as a deity.

APIS The sacred bull of Egypt, the symbol of fertility. He is represented with a solar disc between his horns. In his temple of the Apeum, at Memphis, his worship attracted throngs. Apis was credited with oracular powers, and his birthday was celebrated as an important festival. On his death, a new Apis immediately succeeded him.
At Memphis, Apis was regarded as the body of the god Ptah.

APIT (APET) In Egyptian religion, she is the hippopotamus-goddess. See Thoeris.

APOCRYPHON IOHANNIS The Secret Book of John. This is a treatise, recently discovered, that belongs in the corpus of the Gnostic writings of Egypt.

APOLLO The Greek god of the sun, prophecy, medicine. He is also Phoebus, the bright. In a sinister sense, Apollo also brought pestilence and destruction. His insignia are the lyre, the bow, and the laurel. The principal festival in his honor was celebrated in Athens, in May.
Among the Romans, Apollo became principally the god of oracles and prophecies.

APOPHIS An Egyptian deity whose overthrow produced creation. He is the serpent-enemy of Ra, the sun god. He is represented as a crocodile: often, too, as a coiling serpent trying to destroy Ra. Ra defeats him daily. See Apap.

APORRHETA Secret instructions in esoteric matters given during the Egyptian and Grecian Mysteries.

APOTROPAISM A defensive or protective form of magic. By means of incantations, spells, rituals, and amulets apotropaic magic aims to ward off malefic forces or spirits that might prove harmful to human life and activities.

APPEARANCE OF YMIR In The Prose Edda, the Icelandic source of Norse mythology, the cosmic giant Ymir was created in Ginnungagap by the attraction of cold from Niflheim and heat from Muspellheim.

APPELLATION OF BACCHUS When an initiate in the Orphic mystery cult performed all the rites and ate the living raw flesh of an animal, thus absorbing Dionysus himself, the god of life, he became a Bacchus. After that, the Orphic votary abstained from meat.

APSARAS In Vedic writings, an undine or water-nymph. In popular belief the Apsarases are the wives of the gods. In occultism, they are sleep-producing aquatic plants and inferior forces of nature.

APULEIUS Roman novelist (c. 123 A.D. — date of death unknown). In his strange, exciting novel entitled the *Metamorphoses,* he describes, in Books 8 and 9, the life of Atargatis' wandering priests, the Galli.

AQHAT MYTH Texts discovered in Ras Shamra include the Canaanite myth of Aqhat. In the myth, the disappearance and return of rainfall is symbolized by dying and reviving gods of fertility.

AQUILICIA These were sacrifices performed by the Romans to secure rain in time of drought.

ARABIAN PANTHEON The Arabian pantheon contains many nameless divinities who are designated by many epithets. An astral triad, predominant in south Arabia, comprises Ashtar, the god of the morning star, the god of the moon, known variously as Wadd, Ilumouh, Amm, and Sin; and the god of the sun, called Shams in some regions and by different names in others. Not only families and tribes but also states and societies all had their tutelary divinities.

ARAHAT A Sanskrit word meaning 'the worthy one.' The name was first applied to the Jain and later to the Buddhist holy men initiated into the esoteric mysteries. Having entered the best and highest path, the Arahat is emancipated from rebirth.

ARALU In Babylonian mythology Aralu was the underworld, the home of the dead. It was conceived as a dark cavern, entered through an opening in the earth.
It was guarded by seven doors, through which passed all human beings after death, never to return. The dead, however, were believed capable of giving oracles to the living. It was ruled over by Allatu and Nergal. Here the dead were provided with food and drink.

ARAMAEAN RELIGION The supreme god of the Aramaean people was Hadad, the equivalent of the Babylonian and Assyrian Adad, the Hurrian and Hittite weather god, etc. Originally the king of the storm, he manifested himself not only in lightning and wind but also in the beneficent rain. He was worshipped in Hierapolis, Sam'al, Aleppo, and Damascus. Later he became the supreme sky god, the god of the sun, and was represented standing on the back of the sacred bull.
As god of the sun, he was later identified with Zeus and Jupiter. Atargatis in the Aramaean pantheon corresponds to the Semitic goddess of fertility. The third member of the divine triad was Simios, the son of Hadad and Atargatis. Other divinities include the Canaanite gods El and Baal, and local gods of the sun, moon, fire, etc., whose names indicate their Mesopotamian origin.

ARAMAITI In Zoroastrian religion, one of the six deities, the immortal holy ones, attendant on Ahura Mazda. These six divinities form, with Ahura Mazda, a divine heptarchy. Aramaiti symbolizes Devotion. Haurvatat is Perfection.

28

Vohu Manah represents the Good Mind. Khshthra Vairya is Absolute Power. Ameretat is Immortality. Asha Vahishta is Righteousness.

ARANI A disc-like wooden vehicle in which the Brahmins generated fire by friction with a pramantha, a stick which symbolized the male generator. The esoteric 'womb of the world' is a swastika used in a mystic ceremony replete with secret meanings.

ARANYAKA Vedic texts composed by forest-dwelling Brahmanical sages. These texts include the Upanishads.

ARASA MARAM The Hindu sacred tree of knowledge.

ARATI In Hinduism, the waving of a lighted lamp in image worship.

ARBA-IL In Sumerian religion, the Four Great Gods. *Arba* is the Aramaic word for four, and *il* is the same as *Al* or *El,* the general designation for God. Three male deities and a virginal, yet reproductive, female goddess form a common ideal of godhead.

ARCADIAN CULTS Most of the Greek deities had cults in Arcadia. Human sacrifices were traditionally associated with some of the cults.

ARCHAEOLOGICAL PERIODS The Paleolithic or Old Stone Age began at least 200,000 years ago. Cave deposits in Palestine date from the end of the Early Paleolithic Age. The Middle Paleolithic is the age of Neanderthal man, who inhabited Europe some 100,000 years ago. The first trace of religious life appears in the cult of the dead. The Late Paleolithic is marked by the appearance of Cro-Magnon man cave paintings and statuettes and figurines of nude women.
The Mesolithic or Middle Stone Age culture flourished 12,000 years ago and came to an end before 6,000 B.C. Palestinian man, small in stature but knowledgeable in agriculture and animal husbandry, probably represents the earliest appearance of a historical race. He was a firm believer in an afterlife.

The Neolitihic or Late Stone Age (7000-4500 B.C.) witnessed the spread of agriculture and the domestication of animals, the invention of pottery and polished stone implements, and the construction of megalithic burial monuments. The Chalcolithic or Copper-Stone Age (4500-3000 B.C.) is the period during which temples became centers of great influence and abstractions ('soul,' 'divine,' 'holiness') came into existence.

The Bronze Age (3000-1200 B.C.) marks the beginning of the historical period. During the Early Bronze Age (3000-2000 B.C.), great epics such as the Sumerian accounts of creation and the flood were written, and the names of deities and rulers were inscribed on objects. During the Middle and Late Bronze Ages (2000-1200 B.C.), great empires rose and fell, and monotheism first appeared. The Iron Age (1200-300 B.C.) may be studied through many written documents.

ARCHAEUS A Greek word meaning 'the ancient.' It is used in the Cabala to name the oldest manifested deity.

ARCHDRUID In ancient Gaul, the Druids had a high priest who had absolute power over religious and also secular matters.

ARCHIGALLI The high priests who administered the rituals in the mystery cult of the Phrygian goddess Cybele, the Mighty Mother of the Gods.

ARCULUS A Roman deity who presided over coffers and strong-boxes.

ARDA VIRAF NAMEH A sacred book in Zoroastrian religion. Its contents dealt with cosmology, cosmogony, and eschatology; that is, it studied the universe, its origin, and the concept of the life after death.

ARDHA-NARI The Sanskrit term used to describe Siva, who is represented as half male and half female. The literal meaning of the term is 'half-woman.'

ARDHANARISWARA A Sanskrit term meaning 'the bi-sexual lord.' Esoterically, it designates the unpolarized states of cosmic energy symbolized by the Cabalistic Sephira, Adam Kadmon, etc.

30

ARDUINE In Celtic mythology, the goddess of hunting. She was identified with the Roman goddess Diana.

ARES (MARS) In classical mythology, the god of war.

ARGOS In Argos there was a special cult dedicated to Hera (Juno). There were also temples in honor of Athena and Apollo Lykeios.

ARIANRHOD in Celtic religion, a Brythonic goddess, celebrated for her beauty.

ARIKI The high priest in Micronesian religion. He is charged with keeping the gods content in order to avoid disaster and insure an abundance of food and children.

ARMA The ancient Hittite moon god, known also as Kushah and Kashu.

AROE Among the Bororos of Brazil, a collective being into which the spirits of the dead merge.

AROUERIS In Egyptian religion, he is the husbandman. Horus is sometimes so called.

AROUSER OF THE GOD In Canaanite religion, a priest whose function was to waken the god from his sleep, at dawn.

ARRHETOPHORIA An ancient Greek festival during which pastry in the form of phalli and snakes was thrown into a pit.

ARTA In Indo-Iranian religion, a word designating the divine pattern of the universe.

ARTEMIS (DIANA) Greek goddess of hunting. Her primal function was as queen of wild beasts. Accompanied by her nymphs, she roamed the mountains and forests of Arcadia and Laconia. She was the patroness of women in child-birth but she was principally dedicated to chastity. In Sparta a barbaric mystery cult indulged in human sacrifices to Artemis. In the East, where she was worshipped as the goddess of fecundity, her most notable sanctuary was at Ephesus.

In archaic art Artemis is represented as the Queen of the Animals.

31

ARTIO A Celtic goddess who presided over the Bear clan. She was worshipped in Switzerland. The city of Berne is associated with her.

ARURU A Babylonian god.

ARUTAM SOUL The Jivaro of eastern Ecuador believe that by killing they may acquire souls to provide a supernatural power that will confer immunity from death. An arutam appears only occasionally and momentarily, but the arutam soul exists forever once it has been created. A person who acquires one arutam soul can be killed only by a contagious disease; with two arutam souls, one is assured of immortality. A man is not born with an arutam soul but must acquire it in a prescribed manner, by making a pilgrimage to a sacred waterfall and fasting beside it until the arutam appears. One who has acquired an arutam soul is likely to be seized by the desire to kill. Women rarely possess arutam souls, but all shamans possess them. Common methods of acquiring additional arutam souls are by capturing them from enemies or by coming upon them in the forest by night, in complete darkness.

ARVAKR In Norse mythology, one of the horses that draw the chariot of the sun.

ARVAL BRETHREN In ancient Rome, a brotherhood consisting of twelve priests. The Emperor was always a member of the college. At the annual May ceremony the Ambarvalia took place, when the priests walked the fields to purify them. The intention was to propitiate the agricultural deity and to induce productivity. The goddess who presided over the priesthood was a corn goddess name Dea Dia.

ARYAN RELIGION The Aryans, who settled in Iran and India some time after 2000 B.C., evolved their religion from Indo-European concepts. The supreme deity was Dyeus, god of the sky, god of rain and fertility. He is the father of gods and of men. His consort is Mother Earth.
Other gods of light worshipped by the Aryans include the sun (*svarya*), moon (*mas*), and dawn. Fire worship was

practiced, and many minor deities were worshipped locally as personifications of natural and inanimate phenomena.

The Aryan religion is a development of the Indo-European religion and marks a significant advance in that nature gods were complemented by gods regulating human society: Mitra, the defender of the sanctity of contracts and treaties; and Varuna, the defender of the sanctity of oaths. Their two classes of priests were known as the 'lighters of the fire,' and the 'callers.' The callers invoked the gods through ritual formulas and hymns. Men had to fulfill a triple requirement: good thoughts, good works, good deeds.

ARYA SAMAJ A reform movement in Hinduism initiated by Dyananda Sarasvati in 1875. The multiple Vedic gods are thought to be different names for the one true god. The movement has about a half-million members and is linked with the rise of nationalism in India.

ASALLUHE A Sumerian god of thundershowers, later identified with Marduk of Babylon.

ASANGA Founder of the Buddhist idealistic school in India. He lived about 410-500 A.D.

ASCLEPIUS (AESCULAPIUS) In classical mythology, the god of healing. His worship in Phoenicia and Egypt spread to Greece and Rome.

ASEB In Egyptian religion, he was the fire god.

ASGARD In Norse mythology, Asgard was the abode of the gods. Here Odin, the supreme god, lived with the twelve other gods and twenty-four goddesses. Asgard was the seat of Valhalla, where the slain warriors spent their time feasting. All around Asgard stretched vast forests.

ASHAVANTS In Zoroastrian religion, followers of Asha, designating Divine Law and Order, Righteousness, Truth, and Holiness.

ASHERATH In Canaanite religion, she is the consort of the supreme god El. She is the mother of all the gods. Her variant names are Baalath and Asherath of the Sea. She is identified with the planet Venus.

ASHMOG In the Avesta, a dragon or serpent with the neck of a a camel. Ancient Cabalists called it the flying camel.

ASHNAN An Assyro-Babylonian vegetation deity. Variant names for Ashnan were Dumuzi or Tammuz and Ningishzida.

ASHTAR VIDYA The most ancient of the Hindu works on magic. Only a few disfigured fragments are now extant.

ASHTORETH The Phoenician and Canaanite goddess of war, fertility, and reproduction. Equivalent to the Syrian goddess Astarte, she is also called Ashtaroth.

ASMOUG In the Mazdean religion, the chief emissary of Ahriman, the Spirit of Evil. His function was to incite discord among people and to stir up warlike feelings among the nations.

ASOKA A monk who succeeded his father as King of India about 274 B.C. and made Buddhism the state religion. He proclaimed the Law of Piety, intended to promote the growth among mankind of 'compassion, liberality, truth, purity, gentleness, and saintliness.'

ASSASSINS A secret and mystic order founded in Persia in the eleventh century by Hassan Sabbah. The Sufis who founded the order were addicted to hashish eating. They used hashish to induce celestial visions. The chief of the order was called the Old Man of the Mountains and wielded absolute power.

ASSUR (ASHUR) Among the Assyrians, Assur was the national deity, supreme over all the Babylonian gods.
His chief function was as a warrior. He was often represented as an archer.

ASSYRIAN RELIGION The Assyrian religion stemmed from Babylonia. The national god was Assur, 'king of all the gods.' His consort, Belit, was identified with Ishtar. Ninib was the Assyrian god of war, and Nergal presided over hunting. In a general sense, religious and cosmic concepts all stemmed from Babylonian origins.

ASSYRO-BABYLONIAN RELIGION Most of our knowledge of Assyro-Babylonian religion is derived from the cuneiform inscriptions that have been discovered in Mesopotamia.

Babylonia was the land of primary religious origins, while Assyria absorbed much of Babylonian concepts, rituals, and cults. Babylonia contained the Akkadians and the Sumerians, and the cults of all three races intermingled with each other. The major deities in Babylonia were taken into Sumerian and Akkadian religion. The functions of the various deities were correspondingly identical; only the names varied.

In every Babylonian city-state there was a Mother-Goddess, Ishtar, under variant appellations. Each town had its local divinity, sometimes more than one. Vegetation cults and myths were part of the religious context. Many myths associated with Babylonian religion aimed at interpretations of the cosmic origins, the beginnings of mankind, and the basic activity of agriculture.

ASTAR In the most ancient religion of the Ethiopian Semites, the chief deity, comparable to Astar among the southern Arabs. By analogy with the chief deity of the Kushite pantheon, he became the personification of the sky. Along with Meder and Mahrem, he forms the triad represented in some inscriptions.

ASTARTE Syrian goddess of fertility and love. She is variously called Ashtaroth or Ashtoreth. Her cult was highly popular and her functions were identified with those of the Babylonian goddess Ishtar. Her temple at Heliopolis was under the supervision of three hundred priests. Under the guidance of King Solomon, her worship made its way among the Israelites. Her iconographical image varies. Frequently she is represented with a cow's head and the horns formed into a lunar disc. Hence she was also regarded as a moon goddess.

ASTENNU In Egyptian religion, a form of the god Thoth.

ASTRAEA In Greek and Roman mythology, the goddess of justice. The last of the goddesses to leave the earth at the end of the golden age, she became the constellation Virgo.

ASTROLATRY The worship of the stars as a means of divination. This type of cult was predominant in the Near East and in Mesopotamia. It was also in force among the Aztecs, in the pre-Columbian period.

ASTROLOGY In many pagan religions astrology played an important role in rituals and ceremonials and in the general beliefs of the people. This was particularly the case among the Egyptians, the Romans, and the Assyro-Babylonians. The movements of the heavenly bodies, the rising and setting of the sun, eclipses were studied in order to discover the arrangement of the cosmic system and its influence on the lives of men.

The Babylonians were the pioneers in this science. Their observations, from the third millennium on, were gradually systematized into formal prognostications, based on astrological and astronomical calculations, regarding the effectiveness of any human undertaking. The interpreters were the priests attached to a particular temple, and their decisions were accepted not only by the people at large but by the rulers themselves.

The Assyro-Babylonian deities, to whom were assigned in the divine scheme special areas of the heavens, were the arbiters of human fate as manifested by astrological science.

Among the Romans, astrology was carried to even greater lengths and greater exactitude. The entire cosmic system was put under minute observation. The orderliness of the heavenly bodies suggested to the professional astrologers the possibility of mathematical precision in forecasting human events. For the gods themselves had now become identified with the heavenly bodies. During the period of the Roman Empire, astrology exerted a powerful influence in major national policies and in the imperial decisions and decrees of the ruling emperor.

From Mesopotamia and the temples where astrological practices were in force, the science spread to Egypt. Greece was not greatly affected until after the death of Alexander the Great in 323 B.C., when Oriental influences imposed themselves on Hellenistic life.

In Rome, every level of society felt the force of astrological predictions. In one particular direction, in medicine, astrology exercised a powerful influence that lasted for centuries.

ASTRONOMOS The designation attached to an Egyptian initiate in the mystery cult at Thebes.

ASURA In ancient Hindu mythology, a god or spirit; later, in a reverse sense, an evil spirit or demon.

ASURA VARUNA In Mithraism, he was the supreme being, the Father of All.

ASVINS Two Vedic deities, the twin sons of the sun and the sky. The Asvins are among the most mysterious and occult deities of all. As divine charioteers, they ride in a golden car drawn by horses or birds and are possessed of many forms. In esoteric philosophy, they are the reincarnating principles.

ASYNIUR In Norse mythology, this term was used to denote all the goddesses in the Nordic pantheon. They were the attendants of the goddess Freya.

ATAHOCAN An impersonal deity among the Algonquians.

ATAR Iranian fire god; in Zoroastrianism, symbol of the purity of Ormazd, the Creator of the good world.

ATARGATIS In Aramaic the name of this Phrygian goddess signifies 'the divine Ata.' She was also known, in Syria, as Derceto the goddess of Hierapolis-Bambyce. Like the Greek goddess Artemis, Atargatis was a huntress and shunned marriage. She would thus correspond to the Artemis depicted in the Euripidean drama of *Hippolytus,* wherein Artemis presides over chastity. Her temple, built c. 300 B.C., was still, in the second century A.D., one of the most holy and most impressive buildings in Syria. She was represented as enthroned, with lions in attendance.

At Ascalon, she appeared as half fish, half female. Fish were sacred to her, as were doves.

Mythologically, Atargatis was saved by fish, and in consequence she was symbolized by a piscine image. By the third century B.C. her religious cult had spread to Macedonia, Egypt, and Aetolia.

Atargatis, worshipped in a number of Greek cities, was originally a fertility goddess, a manifestation of Aphrodite. Usually, she was called Dea Syria, the Syrian Goddess.

The Greek satirist Lucian, in his *Dea Syria*, offers a description of her mystery cult as it prevailed in Syria.

ATASH BEHRAM The sacred fire of the Parsi, perpetuated in their temples.

ATE In ancient Greek mythology, she personified infatuation or moral blindness. She was the daughter of Strife and the sister of Lawlessness.

ATEA A Polynesian goddess, mother of the creator god Tane, she is also known as Varea and Wakea.

ATEF In Egyptian religion, the crown of Osiris, consisting of white cap with ram's horns and the sacred serpent. Its two feathers represent life and death.

ATMAN A Sanskrit word meaning 'breath,' 'individual soul,' or 'Universal Self.' In Hinduism, it is the life principle or universal essence. In the Upanishads, the ultimate reality is represented as Brahman-Atman.

ATON (ATEN) Egyptian god who personified the sun's disc.

ATTIC CULTS The most important cult in Attica was the cult of Athena. Demeter and Dionysus too had special festivals and feasts to mark their worship.

ATTIS In Asia Minor Attis was the god of fertility. His worship had also spread to Greece. His cult reflected occasions of lamentation at his death and rejoicing on his rebirth. In this respect his worship is akin to that of Adonis. Attis was loved by the goddess Cybele, who drove him into such a frenzy that he committed self-mutilation.

ATTITUDE TO ANIMALS Among Eskimos, there is a belief that animals have souls. Hence funeral customs for animals as for human beings. Hence also the avoidance of injury or affront to the food-animals. Masked dances, games, and feasts are also held to please the spirits of animals.

ATUA The gods or spirits in Eastern Polynesia.

AUCA In the mythology of the Incas of Peru, he was one of four brothers whose collective title was Ayar. The winged Auca found the site of Cuzco, which became the sun temple of the Incas. Auca afterward turned into stone.

AUDUMLA In Scandinavian mythology, the Cow of Creation, source of four streams of milk which fed the giant Ymir and his sons the Hrimthurses before the appearance of gods or men. She licked the salt of the primal ice-rocks to produce Bor, father of Odin, Wili, and We.

AUF In Egyptian religion, a name for the Lower Regions. Ra the sun god is called Auf-Ra during his nightly passage through the regions of darkness.

AUGURS In ancient Rome, the augurs, twelve in number, formed a priestly college. Their function was to interpret the flight of birds and the movements of fowl. The intention was not so much divinatory as to determine whether a proposed act was acceptable to the gods or disapproved by them. The officiant, in his performance of taking the auspices, always faced south or east.

AUSRA An ancient Baltic goddess who presided over the dawn.

AUSTRALIAN ABORIGINES The fundamental principle of the religious life of the aborigines of Australia was complete dependence on nature. Each clan consisted of human beings and of natural species and phenomena regarded as their close relations. The human members of the clan (totemites) refrained from hurting their associated

39

natural species (totems). Men who by discipline and training had learned the secret life insured, through ritual, the normal increase of essential species and phenomena. It was the study of the Australian aborigines that drew attention to totemism as a vital force and a central feature in primitive culture.

AUSTRI In Norse mythology, one of the four dwarfs who support the heavens on their shoulders. They correspond to the Greek god Atlas who similarly and alone supports the world on his shoulders.

AUTHOR OF THE BOOK OF THE DEAD In Egyptian religion, the authorship of the Book of the Dead was ascribed to the god Thoth, who was also the Creator of the Universe.

AUXESIA A Greek goddess of fertility. Her cult was often associated with Damia.

AVALOKITESWARA The first divine ancestor of the Tibetans, the complete incarnation or avatar of Avalokiteswara, 'the on-looking Lord.' In esoteric philosophy Avaloki is the Higher Self, Padmapani the Higher Ego or Manas. The mystic formula 'Om mani padme hum' is used to invoke their joint help.

AVEBURY STONE CIRCLES Neolithic cromlechs, probably more than a thousand years older than Stonehenge.

AVESTA A collection of sacred Zoroastrian texts. It consists of four main groups of texts, all fragmentary and varying in antiquity: the *Yasna,* a liturgical work which includes *Vispered,* a supplement to the *Yasna;* the *Vendidad,* a ceremonial code similar to Leviticus; and the *Yashts,* which are hymns to the good spirits.

AWE According to Robert Marett, a feeling of awe or wonder is the basis of all religious systems. The Madagascans apply the word 'god' to anything they do not understand. The Cree Indians returned to the water and sought to appease any strange-looking fish. Marett held that the generalized supernatural power attached to any object which arouses a feeling of awe was best described by the Melanesian word *mana*.

AXE In Minoan-Mycenaean times in ancient Greece, the double axe was a cult object. It had a sanctity representing the Minoan divinity itself.

AYAR Among the Incas of ancient Peru the title of Ayar was applied to four mythical brothers. The chief brother was Manco, the high priest. The three other brothers were Cachi, Uchu, Auca.

AZAZEL A powerful demon who lived in the desert and was associated with ancient Hebraic rites. The name also is found in Greek papyri and in medieval grimoires (magic handbooks).

AZILUT In the Cabala, the world of emanations. It is the great and highest prototype of the other worlds, the Great Sacred Seal by means of which all the worlds are copied.

AZOTH In alchemy, mercury, treated as the creative principle in nature. It is symbolized by a cross bearing the letters TARO. Each combination of these letters has an occult meaning. Paracelsus owned a talismanic jewel in which a powerful spirit was supposed to dwell. His jewel was called the Azoth.

AZTEC AFTERLIFE Among the Aztecs of ancient Mexico human sacrifices were regarded as a path to paradise. Hence the victims were often prepared to be immolated in the hope of future communion with divinity. Normal deaths, on the other hand, led to eternal confinement in the Nether Regions.

AZTEC CULTURE The ancient Aztecs of pre-Columbian times in Mexico had attained a high degree of culture. They were familiar with weaving, sculpture, music, metal work, and picture writing.

41

AZTEC MYTHOLOGY In Aztec mythology, the supreme gods, Tonacatecuhtli and Tonacacihuatl, created the world on the back of a crocodile monster. They also created the other gods, but they had little to do with human beings. The names of their four children vary from chronicler to chronicler: Huitzilopochtli (Tlaloc), the tribal god and chief deity of sun, war and hunting; Xipe-Totec (Tonatiuh), the god of spring planting and patron of goldsmiths; Quetzalcoatl, the god of life and fertility, originator and patron of several arts and industries; and Tezcatlipoca, the god of darkness and the most important of the priests.

AZTEC NAME Azteca stems from Aztlán, an area in Northwest Mexico. The expression means *Whiteland*.

AZTEC NATIONAL MONUMENT Pueblo ruins near Aztec, New Mexico. They represented the Anasazi people, who inhabited the area around 1100 A.D.

AZTEC PANTHEON The pantheon of the Aztecs of ancient Mexico included these divinities: Tezcatlipoca, the sky-god. Huitzilopochtli, the supreme deity, god of war and hunting, and god of the South. His symbolic color was blue.
Quetzalcoatl, the plumed serpent, the civilizing god.
Mictlantecuhtli, the god of death.
His consort, Mictlancihuatl, lady of the abode of the dead.
Black is associated with these two deities.
Xipe-Totec, god of the West. His symbolic color is red.
He is the god of vegetation.
Tlaloc, the rain-god, god of thunder.
Coatlicue, goddess of the earth.
Huehueteotl, the fire-god.
Xochiquetzal and Xochipilli, gods of flowers and beauty.

AZTEC PRIESTHOOD Both priests and priestesses officiated in the Aztec rites that required continuous sacrifices. For this purpose, neighboring tribes were the usual submissive sacrificial offerings.

42

AZTEC RELIGION The religion of the ancient inhabitants of Mexico was predominantly the Aztec religion. Until the time of the conquest of Mexico by the Spaniards under Cortez, the Aztecs were masters of the country.

The Aztec religion was a syncretism of the beliefs of the subject peoples and of earlier tribes such as the Toltecs.

The Aztec pantheon consisted of the following deities: Tezcatlipoca was god of the sky, a kind of Mexican Zeus. The supreme god was the ancient tribal deity, Huitzilopochtli. He presided over war and hunting, and in later times acquired the attributes of the sun-god. His principal temple was in Mexico. Here, at the time of the winter solstice, a great feast was celebrated, with accompanying sacrifices of prisoners. Quetzalcoatl was the civilizing spirit. He invented the calendar. He was also the god of life, crafts, and of the West. He was represented as a bearded figure, white-skinned. Mictlantecuhtli was the god of death. His consort was Mictlancihuatl, 'lady of the abode of the dead.' These two deities were associated with the North. Xipe-Totec was the god of the South. He was the god of spring and of vegetation, especially maize. At the annual festival war prisoners were sacrificed, their bodies flayed and the skins worn by the victors.

Tlaloc was in charge of rain and thunder. Children were sacrificed to him. He was depicted as an eye-ringed figure, with fangs protruding from his mouth.

Priests and priestesses officiated equally. The Aztec religion required constant sacrifices, that were secured from vanquished neighboring tribes.

The Aztec temples, pyramids, ceramic artifacts, frescoes, jewelry, hieroglyphic writing indicate a high degree of culture.

AZTEC SUN GOD Huitzilopochtli, the sun god of the Aztecs of ancient Mexico, died every evening and was reborn the following dawn. This myth is comparable to the myths involving the Demeter, the Isis-Osiris, and the Cybele-Attis cults.

B

BA In Egyptian religion, the soul, represented as a bird with the head of a human being. Immortal and eternal, it becomes divine. It is supposed to depart from the body at death but may eventually return to revivify it if the body and its *ka* or genius, together with the *khu* or transfigured soul, are preserved.

BAAL In Phoenician, Ba'al means a lord or master. In the Middle East, Baal was a generic name used by several religious cults. He is a Semitic god of fertility, whose worship was associated with gross sensuality. Among the Phoenicians, Chaldeans, and Canaanites he was the chief male divinity.
The term Baal was frequently used along with another designation: e.g., Baal-Peor, who was the Moabite god at Peor and whose worship was steeped in debauchery. In Biblical times he was at one time worshipped by the Israelites. Similarly, Baal Berith, Lord of the Covenant, was a Canaanite deity whom the Israelites worshipped at one time. There was also a Baal at Emesa, and a Baal Gad in Phoenicia. The cult of Baal was associated with sacred feasts and daily temple services. The deity was of uncertain sex, and was addressed thus: Whether you are a god or a goddess.

BAAL ADDIR The principal god of the Phoenician pantheon. The name means 'great or powerful lord.'

BABIA A Syrian deity. She was goddess of youth and infancy.

BABYLONIAN HYMNS Hymns and liturgies associated with Assyro-Babylonian religion reflect in particular the death

and rebirth of Tammuz, the vegetation god, and the corresponding lamentations and rejoicing of the people.
One such hymn runs:
The lord of vegetation no longer lives . . .
The Underworld, Aralu, is described as follows:
Unto the house of darkness, the dwelling of Irkalla
Unto the house whose enterer never comes forth
Along the way whose going has no return,
Unto the house whose enterer is deprived of light,
Where dust is their food, their sustenance clay.

BABYLONIAN RELIGION The religion of the Babylonians was directed to deities who represented, anthropomorphically, the various aspects of nature. In the major cities, there was also a local god worshipped for his special interest in the city. The local god guarded it from enemy assaults and other disasters.

The principal divinities were Anu, god of heaven; Enlil (or Bel), god of the earth; and Ea, god of the water.

Furthermore, there were the moon god Sin; Shamesh, the sun god; Adad, also called Ramman, god of the air and storms.

Anu was worshipped chiefly at Uruk, Ea at Endu, Enlil in Nippur. The god of the city of Babylon was Marduk. Nusku was the god of fire, Nergal, god of war.

The consort of Anu was Anatu. Belit was Bel's partner. Ningal was the moon god's wife. The sun-god's consort was Aja. Over them all dominated Ishtar, goddess of love.

The temples were vast and impressive. The priesthood was a powerful hierarchy. In addition to supplications, hymns, and incantations, sacrifices of animals, fruit, fish were a regular feature of worship. The priesthood also devoted itself to the study of astronomy and its applied discipline of astrology.

BABYLONIAN TEMPLES The temples of Babylonia were regularly built of brick. Every shrine had a special sanctuary for its deity, but there were also sanctuaries for lesser deities in the same temple. Attached to the temples were schools for the training of priesthood.

BACCHANALIA Roman mystic orgiastic performances celebrated in honor of Dionysus (Bacchus). This mystery cult, characterized by unbridled debauchery, was repressed by a decree of the Roman Senate in 186 B.C.

BACCHANTES Women who were dedicated to the worship of Dionysus. They dressed in skins of beasts and thus clad roamed the forests and mountains and fields, filled with the divine frenzy of the god. They were known also as Thyiades. A vivid portrayal of their ways appears in the *Bacchae*, by the Greek dramatist Euripides.

BACOTI Among the Tonkinese, a necromancer and witch.

BAETULUS (BAETYL) In antiquity, a meteorite or similar stone venerated by men and thought to be of divine origin. Among the Semites, the baetyl (literally, 'house of god') was thought to be the abode of a god and revered as the god himself.

BAIME An Australian thunder god, equivalent to the Scandinavian Thor.

BAIVA In Lapland, he is the lord of light and heat.
BALA The five powers acquired in Yoga practice, full trust or faith, energy, memory, meditation, wisdom.

BALANCE OF RA In Egyptian religion, the scales used by Osiris in the Other World to weigh the souls of the dead. Truth was used as a testing weight.

BALDER The Scandinavian god of light and beauty. He was invulnerable except with regard to the mistletoe. Hence he was killed by a mistletoe dart fashioned by Loki, who personified the principle of evil.

47

BALI Life in Bali centers on religion. The chief religion is a modified form of Hinduism called Sivaism (from *Siva*, or *Shiva*, the supreme god of many Hindu sects), fused with Malay ancestor cult as well as with animistic and magical beliefs and practices. More than nine-tenths of the Balinese belong to the Sudra or lowest caste. They live in *desas*, or self-contained communities in which the common bond is veneration of ancestors. The *desas* are further subdivided into *bondjars*, whose members assist each other in temple maintenance, festivities, and family rites. The primitive religious mythology of the Balinese is reflected in their art, dances, rites, and in almost every aspect of their daily lives. Daily they praise their benevolent gods and try to banish evil spirits. The highest gods dwell on Gunung Agung, the holy mountain. Halfway up the mountain are the *Besakih* or 'mother temples.' Each family worships at its own shrine as well as at community shrines. The practice of cremation once extended to the wife of the deceased but has recently been abolished.

BALL GAME Among the Maya of Yucatan one of the popular religious practices was a sacred ball game.

BALOMA Among the Trobriand Islanders, an invisible spirit. At death, according to the natives of Kiriwina, the deceased person's *baloma* (soul) leaves the body to lead a shadowy existence in another world. It returns to its familiar surroundings at the annual feast called *milamala*.

BALUM CULT In parts of Melanesia, initiation rites for boys.

BA-NEB-TATTU In Egyptian religion, a name descriptive of Osiris. It signifies 'Ram, Lord of Mendes.'

BAPHOMET An idol said to have been used by the Templars in their mysterious rites. The androgyne goat of Mendes was a Hermetico-cabalistic symbol.

BAPTAE In Greek mythology they were the priests of Cotytto, whose obscene rites were celebrated in Athens, at night.

For the purpose of purification, the priests at certain times dipped into water. Hence their name, which in Greek denotes 'those dipped in water.'

BAPTISM The religious ablution signifying purification or consecration appears in many non-Christian cultures. Baptism belonged to the earliest Chaldeo-Akkadian theurgy, was practiced in the Egyptian pyramids, had a place in the Eleusinian mysteries, and is preserved today among the descendants of the ancient Sabians, the Mandaeans.

BARDESANES An early Syrian writer (154-222 A.D.), called a Gnostic by some and a Christian by others. His teachings incorporate elements from Gnosticism, Christianity, astrology, Indian philosophy, and occultism. A Gnostic preacher and writer credited with winning Edessa, the center of his labors, to Christianity. Born in Persia in 154 A.D., he taught a mixture of Christianity and Chaldean mythology.

BARDESANIAN SYSTEM A system worked out by Bardesanes and called by some a Cabala within a Cabala. A very old Gnostic system, the so-called 'Codex of the Nazarenes' contains doctrines formulated before Bardesanes and the ancient names of good and evil powers.

BARD A professional poet or singer. In the early Celtic world he combined the offices of singer, genealogist, and custodian of legal knowledge. His chanted spells were supposed to give him superhuman powers.

BARESMA In Zoroastrianism, a plant used by Mobeds (priests) in their temples. Consecrated bundles of it are kept in the temples.

BARD The name given by the Druids to their poets.

BARI Among the Bororos of Brazil, the bari is a sorcerer associated with terrifying spirits that control wind and rain, sickness and death. He mediates between human beings and the evil spirits.

BARROW A tumulus covered by earth and regarded as sacred ground.

BARSOM In Zoroastrian religion, a bunch of twigs cut with certain rites and litanies. These twigs were presented in the temples by the priests, during prayer and mystic rituals.

BASILEUS The Archon or high priest who presided over the Eleusinian mysteries.

BASILIDEAN GNOSTICISM The doctrine taught by Basilides, a Gnostic of the second century A.D. The system comprises a complicated cosmology and plan of redemption. Basilides claimed to have received secret knowledge from the apostle Matthew. His writings, including a 24-volume gospel and commentary, were burned.

BASILIDES A Gnostic teacher who lived in Alexandria during the reign of Hadrian (117-138) and dealt with the problem of good and evil in terms of Persian dualism.

BAST In Egyptian religion, a lion-headed or cat-headed goddess. Her cult originated in the protohistoric cult of the lion or lioness. Termed in inscriptions 'the lady of life,' she is commonly represented as holding a shield in one hand, a sistrum in the other, and a basket over one arm. Hundreds of images of this smiling goddess, who symbolizes the life-producing power of the sun, are found in her temple at Bubastis. She was the symbol of sexual passion, and was considered an aspect of Hathor.

BATSAUM-PASHA A Turkish demon or spirit, invoked to produce good weather or rain.

BAU Also Ninisinna and Gula. In Sumerian religion the goddess who presides over medicine. She is 'the great physician of the blackheaded people,' that is, the Sumerians.

BEELZEBUB An oracle deity of the Ekronites. The name itself (also written Baalzebub and Beelzebul) means "Lord of the Flies." He was worshiped by the Philistines and by idolatrous Hebrews who, in New Testament times, called him the prince of the devils.

BEHER In the most ancient religion of the Semitic tribes of Ethiopia, a divinity assumed by some to be a sea god.

BEL The Akkadian form of the Western Semitic word *Baal,* meaning 'lord.' In Babylonian religion, he was one of the supreme triad, which also included Anu, lord of the heavens, and Ea, lord of the waters. He was originally the chief god; later his attributes were transferred to Marduk. In other settings, his name is recorded as Beli, Belus, Belenus, or Belinus.
Bel was the founder of the Babylonian Empire. In Babylon he had a magnificent temple containing numerous statues of himself, particularly a statue in massive gold. On returning from his disastrous campaign against the Greeks, Xerxes, the Persian ruler, destroyed the temple. Nebuchadnezzar set up and dedicated the golden statue of Bel in the Dura plain.

BELATUCADDRUS In Celtic mythology, a deity worshipped by the Britons. He was either a war god or a sun god: his functions were not clearly defined.

BELENUS A tutelary deity in Italy and Gaul.

BELISAMA A river goddess of the Gauls. The Romans identified her with Minerva. The Celtic goddess was the consort of Belenos, the god of light.

BELIT (BELTIS) One of the most ancient Babylonian goddesses. She was the wife of Bel, the chief god and god of the earth in the supreme triad.

BELLONA A Roman goddess of war. She was sometimes identified with Nerio, the partner of the war god Mars. In Roman Imperial times she was equated with the Cappadocian goddess Ma.

BELLONARII Priests of the Roman war goddess Bellona. They inflicted wounds on their body and offered the flowing blood to the deity.

BELPHEGOR In obscene worship, a demon with a gaping mouth and a phallic-shaped tongue.

BELTANE In Celtic religion, this was a spring festival, held on May first. A fire was kindled and a sacred tree, the oak, was burned, together with an image of the vegetation spirit. The mistletoe was cut, and human sacrifices were performed. The fire, the tree, and the victim all constituted fertility symbols.

BEMILUCIUS A Celtic deity of ancient Gaul.

BENDIS In ancient Greek religion, a Thracian goddess in whose honor the State held a special festival. A moon goddess, she was declared by Proclus to be Persephone herself.

BENJEES In the East Indies, devil worshippers.

BENNU In the Egyptian Book of the Dead, the bird known as bennu is described as 'the soul of Ra, the guide of the gods in the Tuat,' which is the Underworld. It was the emblem of immortality, and was identified with the phoenix.

BERASIT The first word of the Book of Genesis. It is a mystic word among the Cabalists of Asia Minor.

BERECYNTHIA An epithet attached to the Phrygian goddess Cybele. It is derived from Mt. Berecyntus, where her worship was centered.

BERGELMIR In Norse mythology, the giant who escaped the general slaughter of his brothers, who drowned in the blood of their raging father. He became the father of a new race of giants following the Flood.

BERGIMUS An ancient Italic deity.

BES In Egyptian religion, an ancient phallic god, represented as standing on a lotus ready to devour his own progeny. Later, his image was widely used as an amulet, throughout the Greco-Roman world down to the Middle Ages.
In Egyptian religion, he was the frolicsome god of pleasure. He was represented as human-headed, with a cheerful countenance. But he was also a god of vengeance and of battle. He was powerful too in counteracting magic practices.

BESAKIH Among the Balinese, these are 'mother temples' placed halfway up the sacred mountain of Gunung Agung.

BESTLA In Norse religion, she is the mother of the supreme deity Odin, the God of Gods, whose father was Borr. Bestla is the daughter of the giant Bolthorn.

BHAGAVADGITA A part of the *Mahabharata,* one of the two great epics of India. It records the holy dialogue between Krishna and Arjuna, an Indian king who is supposed to have lived three thousand years before Christ. It dates from the beginning of Christianity and distills the teachings of all the Vedas, which contain the first recorded religious truths.

BHAKTI-MARGA In Hinduism, one of the three recognized ways of attaining *moksha* or salvation. It is the way of devotion, love, and faith, nobly expressed in the Bhagavadgita, where salvation is promised to all.

BHRIGU One of the Great Vedic Rishis. He is called 'Son' by Manu, who confided to him his laws. He is one of the seven progenitors of mankind.

53

BHUT Among the animistic Dravidians of India, a malignant spirit which haunts cemeteries, animates dead bodies, and devours human beings.

BICHIWUNG The Makusi name of the founder of the Hallelujah religion. His English name is Eden. Bichiwung claimed to have achieved direct contact with God, from whom he received a miraculous medicine and instructions to bring the message of a heavenly abode after death to the world. Bichiwung's revelations were mingled with traditional elements from Christian and traditional sources.

BIELBOG In Slavic mythology, this expression means 'the white god.' It signifies the power of good, like Ahura Mazda in Zoroastrianism.

BIL In Norse religion, she is a child-deity associated with the waning moon.

BILLIS African sorcerers who are thought to be capable of preventing the growth of rice.

BIRTH OF THE GODS Hesiod, a Greek poet who flourished some time after Homer, is the author of *The Theogony*, the first religious writing, in verse form, in Greek. He describes the deities, their relationships, functions, genealogies, and progeny.
In Norse religion, the earth, as well as the giants, were created from the giant Ymir.

BIWIRIPITSJ One of two brothers associated with the head-hunting cult of Melanesia. See Desoipitj.

BLACK Among the Bororos of Brazil, painting oneself black is a means of eluding the evil force that brings death to a person.

BLACK MASS A mass ascribed to the reputed worshippers of Satan. A travesty of the Christian Mass, it is held in honor of Satan at the Witches' Sabbat and on other occasions.

Brocken and the church of Blokula, in Sweden, were famous as meeting places for those who participated in the medieval Black Mass. Many paintings, etchings, and sculptures have tried to capture the wild, occult nature of the rites. Worshippers met in an open area before an altar of stone adorned by a black wooden image of Satan. Sacrifices of crops and animals were common. A priestess usually embraced the phallus of the goat-formed image. Feasting and dancing followed.

BLACK SHAMAN A shaman who is associated with malignant and magic forces.

BLOOD In ancient Greece blood was poured into a grave as a means of reviving the spirits of the dead, who were conceived as thirsty for blood. In some mystery cults, as in Mithraism, blood baptism was used as an effective method of purification, both physical and spiritual.
From time immemorial, blood has been a vitalizing agent. The widespread practice of depositing bodies in pits containing ochreous powder, in Paleolithic times, may have sprung from the desire to provide the deceased with a serviceable body. Red is the color of blood, the symbol of health and life.

BOAR In Norse mythology, a sacred boar, Gullinbursti, drew the chariot of the god Freya.

BOCHICA An anthropomorphic white god worshipped by the Indians of Central America and Colombia.

BODHISATTVA In Buddhism, a 'being of enlightenment,' who has attained perfection, passed through the ten stages of spiritual development, and is qualified to enter Nirvana and become a Buddha, but prefers instead to work for the salvation of all beings. One who needs but one more incarnation to become a perfect Buddha, that is, to achieve Nirvana. The literal meaning of the Sanskrit word is 'he whose essence has become intelligence.'

BOGOMILS A Bulgarian sect originating around the tenth century A.D. and teaching that the Creator had two sons, Satan and Christ or Logos.

BOKOR A Haitian magician who exercises control over the spirits of the dead.

BON The early animistic religion of Tibet. A form of Shamanism, it is considered by some scholars to be an offshoot of Chinese Taoism. It was from the beginning a barbarous religion, abounding in sorcery and including the ritual sacrifice of human beings. It still survives but its crude elements have been modified under the influence of Buddhism.

BONA DEA A Roman goddess of fertility and chastity. Her cult was celebrated in December, women only being her votaries. Secret rites took place at the home of a Roman magistrate, the officiating priestess being his wife. While the rituals were being performed, all vestiges of masculinity were removed from the sacred area. The sanctuary was once desecrated when P. Clodius, in female disguise, broke into the gathering. In later times, men intruded into the mysteries of the goddess. Her temple was on the Palatine Hill.

BONAMPAK A cultural center of the classic Maya civilization, similar to sanctuaries established at Copan, Palenque, and Tikal. Its wall paintings dramatize the sacrificial killing of prisoners of war.

BONA-OMA (BONA-DEA) In Roman religion, an ancient goddess of fertility, patroness of female occultists, and wife (or daughter or sister) of Faunus. Also called Fauna, she was worshipped only by women.

BONDJAR Among the Balinese, a subdivision of the self-contained religious community. The members of the *bondjar* assist each other in temple maintenance, festivities, and family rites.

BONI A Japanese festival celebrating the ancestral soul return.

BONUS EVENTUS This Latin expression means 'good result' or 'success.' It applies to a Roman deity associated with harvests. His temple was in Rome.

BOOK OF SMITING DOWN APOPHIS An Egyptian papyrus containing four works on rituals, as follows:
(a) The Songs of Isis and Nephthys;
(b) The Ritual of bringing in Sokar;
(c) The Book of Smiting Down Apophis;
(d) The names of Apophis which shall not exist.

BOOK OF THE DEAD In ancient Egyptian religion, this was really a handbook for guiding the soul through the Underworld. In this manual are included exorcisms and prayers to the various deities and spirits associated with death and funerary rites. Copies were placed in the tomb along with the body of the deceased, for ready consultation.

BOR In Norse mythology, the son of Buri created out of a block of ice. He is the progenitor of the gods.

BOREAS In Greek mythology, the god of the north wind.

BOROROS Among the Bororos of Brazil, there is a belief that the human form is merely transitory, passing through a fish stage into other forms.

BORVO In Celtic mythology, the god of thermal springs, of warriors, and magic.

BOTOCUDO A primitive tribe of South America, more properly called the Kaingang. They have evolved elaborate techniques of imitative magic, closely related to animism, in their attempts to control the weather. The fundamental religious outlook of the Kaingang is animistic. Their religion is not the expression of an inner need but a naive projection of a peculiar psycho-physical orientation which focuses attention on the fundamental distinction between one's own body and all other bodies.

Death sets in motion awesome forces of destruction, causing the Kaingang to mobilize all their emotional resources. When death is momentarily actualized in the form of the *kupleng* or ghost-soul of the deceased, the most elaborate ritual forms are used to protect the living. The spouse or *thupaya* stands in greatest danger and must remove all traces of old contacts with the deceased. The thupaya must free himself from the kupleng quickly, and he performs rites designed to rid him of his personal fear as well as to protect the community. He leaves camp alone, abstains from eating cooked food, and sleeps alone at night. When he kills an animal, he opens its belly and rubs the blood on himself to 'wash off' the hunting formerly done for his wife.

BO TREE A bo tree in the Bihar province of India is said to be the tree under which Gautama received heavenly enlightenment. Also called a pipal tree, it has remarkable longevity. A shoot from the sacred bo tree, carried from India to Anuradhapura in Ceylon by Mahinda, a priest who had converted the Sinhalese monarch to the new faith, is said to have produced the oldest living historical tree.

BOULIANUS An ancient Teutonic deity.

BOUNDARIES In antiquity, boundaries between fields were often marked by stones or trees. The trees and stones later acquired a potency in themselves. Special ceremonies and rites were observed annually to confirm the boundaries and gods evolved whose function was to preside over and preserve these demarcations. Among such deities, in classical mythology, were Hermes (Mercury) and Terminus. Nebuchadnezzar, the name of two kings of Babylon, means 'O God Nebu, protect my boundary mark.'

BOVINE MYTH OF CREATION The view that primitive religions were zoomorphic rather than anthropomorphic is supported by the Berber myth which makes the original procreative couple bovine. The female, a wild cow, is called Thammuatz (Tiamat). 'The wild cow' is also the peculiar name of a net which Ninurta, a complex sky god, used as a weapon. The Milky Way, thought to have its source in the polaris center marked by a two-peaked mountain, was the source of many sacred rivers.

BRAGI In Norse mythology, the god who invented poetry. At feasts and funerals a Bragi cup was drunk. Bragi welcomed the dead warriors into Valhalla.

BRAHMA In Hinduism, one of the great Trimurti, Brahma, Vishnu, and Shiva. He is a personal god, the personification of the supreme Brahman, and the creator of the world which endures for 2,160,000,000 years before it is destroyed and recreated by him. Each such period is one day in his life. After one hundred years, he and his creation will revert to their primordial elements, to be replaced by other universes. His consort is Sarasvati, the goddess of speech.

BRAHMAN In the Rig-Veda, the term signifies prayer or the prayer spell. In the Upanishads, it stands for the ultimate, indescribable reality. All other gods may be assimilated to him as personal manifestations of the world soul.

BRAHMAN (BRAHMIN) Among the Hindus, a person of the highest or sacerdotal caste. His chief duty is the study and teaching of the Vedas, and the performance of prayer and other religious ceremonies.

BRAHMANAS Prose Vedic writings devoted mainly to matters of ritual. Produced between 800 and 600 B.C., they contain directions for ritual sacrifices and represent a transitional stage between Vedic religion and philosophic Hinduism.

BRAHMANASPATI (BRIHASPATI) In Hinduism, the apotheosis of the mysterious power that resides in Brahman. Also, an abstract Vedic deity related both to Indra and Agni.

BRAHMA SAMAJ A reform movement in Hinduism founded in 1828 by Ram Mohan Roy, one of the earliest students of comparative religions. Its chief emphasis is on monotheism, congregational worship, and moral reform. Never a numerous body (some six thousand members in 1931), it has nevertheless exercised a profound influence on Indian life.

BRAN In Celtic religion, a god of the Brythons, son of Llyr, the sea god.

BRIAREUS Son of Uranus and Gaea, or of Pontus and Gaea, he is represented in Greek mythology as a monster with a hundred hands.

BRITOMARTIS A Cretan goddess, identified with Artemis. Her worship was centered in a grove dedicated to Artemis also.

BRIZO A goddess who was worshipped by the women of the Greek island of Delos. She was the guardian of sailors. She also inspired prophetic dreams.

BROK In Norse mythology, the craftsman dwarf. He fashioned Thor's hammer and Odin's magic ring.

BRONZE AGE MENTALITY The prelogical character of primitive thought has led to the concept of 'dynamism' (replacing Maret's 'pre-animism') and to the view that belief in 'high' gods has existed since the beginnings of the Bronze Age in the Near East. The notion of an impersonal power or force (the mana of ethnologists) residing in unusual objects, persons, or phenomena, as well as in divinities and spirits, survives in Near-Eastern religion and mythology and was dominant in magic for thousands of years.

BRYNHILD In Norse mythology, chief of the Valkyries, the daughter of the supreme god Odin. Her function was to choose those warriors who would die on the battlefield and after death conduct them to Valhalla, the Norse paradise.

BUBASTIS An Egyptian goddess (Bast), the daughter of Isis and Osiris. She is identified with the Greek deity Artemis. Her cult was celebrated notably at Bubastis on the Nile.

BUBONA A Roman deity of the fields, who presided over oxen and other cattle.

BUDDHA Gautama Buddha (c. 563-483 B.C.) was the Indian founder of Buddhism. Of wealthy parentage, he renounced luxury at the age of twenty-nine and dedicated himself to the ascetic life. Religiously, he was inspired by 'the great enlightenment.'

BUDDHISM The ethical-religious system founded by the Indian Gautama Buddha. He and his disciples lived as mendicants. Gradually they formed themselves into an Order, to which women were later admitted.

Buddhism postulated four Noble Truths:

(1) To exist is to suffer (a Sophoclean concept illustrated in the Greek dramatist's tragedy *Oedipus Rex*);
(2) suffering springs from desire;
(3) when there is no desire, suffering ends;
(4) the absence of desire is achieved by means of the Eight-

Fold Noble Path. This Path involves:
right understanding;
right motive;
right speech;
right action;
right occupation;
right effort;
right mindedness;
right concentration.

Man's aim is to attain a happy state of non-existence.
In the third century B.C. Buddhism achieved great popularity in India. Then it spread to Burma, Ceylon, China, and Japan. In Tibet, Buddhism became Lamaism. In Japan, a particular sect is known as Zen Buddhism.

BULL CULT In Hittite religion, the Weather God was represented as a bull whose cult was widespread. Two bulls, Sheri and Hurri, that is, Day and Night respectively, were part of the Hittite pantheon.
In Assyria, a winged bull with a human head, symbolizing

force and domination, frequently guarded the doors of a palace.

The Akan people of Ghana sacrificed a bull once a year to symbolize the divine death and rebirth of Bosummuru, reputed ancestor of the Bono family. Melkart, the patron deity of Tyre and reputed ancestor of the royal house of Carthage founded by Dido, was incarnated as a bull.

BULL ROARER A device consisting of a slat of wood attached to a thong. When whirled, it produces a loud noise. The bull roarer, supposedly of extreme antiquity, is used in the religious rites of the Australian aborigines.

BURIAL The ceremonial interment of a corpse, suggesting belief in an afterlife and religion. The practice began during the Middle Paleolithic Age (also called the Mousterian period). Flints, ocher, and meat were often buried with the dead, inside caves under whose overhanging ledges primitive men lived.

In pre-dynastic centuries, the Egyptians buried their dead or burned them. Bodies were laid on the left side, the head facing south.

Some early European tribes offered human sacrifices at crossroads altars. Criminals and suicides often were buried at crossroads.

BURIAS A deity worshipped by the Kassites, equivalent to the Greek Boreas.

BURU BONGA A dryadic deity worshipped by the Kolarian tribes of Central India.

BURYAT RELIGION The religion of the northernmost Mongol-speaking people centers on the triple division of the spirit world and the three souls of men. The spirits include deities who are invoked for blessing and for the exorcism of sickness and evil, and to whom prayers and sacrifices are addressed. The higher spirits live in heaven and rule the world. The two subordinate orders constitute the spirits of the common people and of the slaves. Man is composed of a body, a life-principle, and a soul. The Buryat shaman knows the risks associated with the journey through life and the spirit world — and how to overcome these risks.

BUSAMA SORCERY In the New Guinean village of Busama the tribesmen recognize three types of black magic: *mwi'-sinang*, which is associated with minor illnesses; *katon*, linked to the killing of whole populations; and *balu*, used to cause the death of an individual.

BUSHMAN CULTS Many elements enter into the religious life of the Bushman tribes, nomadic hunters who once dominated most of South Africa and are now confined chiefly to the Kalahari desert. Veneration of the stars, the moon, and all living things is reflected in the ancient art of the Bushmen as well as in their daily lives. The praying mantis cult still survives, as do legends of Mantis, Dxui, and Dawn's Heart.

BUSK Among Creek Indians, a festival of first fruits, sometimes called the 'green corn dance.' It was celebrated at the beginning of the new year, when the corn was ripe enough to be eaten. It was a very solemn ceremony lasting from four to eight days. Special food and drinks were consumed, and strong emetics were taken. A new fire was made, using four logs pointed in the cardinal directions. The period of forgiveness and renewal was intended to provide everyone with a new moral and physical life.

BUTARICO Among the Bororos of Brazil, the spirits that preside over rain.

BUTO In Egyptian religion, the cobra goddess. She was the tutelary deity of Lower Egypt.

BWAGA'U Among the Trobriand Islanders, these are male sorcerers.

63

C

CABALA (CABBALA, KABALA) A system of occult theosophy used to interpret the hidden meaning of the Scriptures. It was first used by Jewish rabbis and certain Christians, handed down orally through chosen disciples, and later committed to writing. It teaches that God is the original principle of all being, that all things are created through emanation, that the triumph of morality and goodness among men can overcome the powers of evil, that the Messiah will restore the world to a perfect state once man's mind has achieved full control, that man is a microcosm, and that writing is the means through which man can penetrate into the divine mysteries.

The occult theosophy of the Cabala had a profound effect on medieval literature and is the source of much medieval and modern magic and demonology. It teaches its followers that every element of Scripture has a hidden sense. One branch of the system deals specifically with mystic operations involving anagrams, names of spirits, and other occult matters. According to the Cabala, all men are endowed with magical powers which they themselves may develop.

CABALISTIC FACES These are the three souls in man: the animal, the spiritual, and the divine (Nephesch, Ruach, Neschamah — body, soul, mind).

CABIRI (CABEIRI, KABIRI) In Greek religion, a group of gods worshipped especially in Samothrace. They were probably agricultural gods of Phrygian origin. The Cabiri mysteries of Samothrace were second in repute to the Eleusinian mysteries.

65

These Asian divinities were introduced into the Greek world in Hellenistic times. They were gods of fertility whose worship was associated chiefly with the Aegean Islands. Among the Romans they were equated with the *penates,* the gods of the household. They also protected against storms and shipwreck, and their cult was known for its obscene practices.

CABOCLO A Brazilian cult group comprising descendants of Whites, Indians, and Negroes. African and Indian gods are worshipped, generally in rural settings.

CABRUS A deity to whom fishes were sacrificed. He was associated with Pamphylia.

CACUS, CACA Probably a pair of ancient fire divinities. In later Roman mythology, Cacus was represented as the son of Vulcan. He was slain by Hercules in the Aventine cave in which he had hidden the cattle of Geryon.

CAELUS In Roman religion, the deified sky, son of Aether and Dies, associated with the cult of Mithras. He is equivalent to the Greek Uranus and the Semitic Baal.

CAGN (CAGGEN) Among the Bushmen of the Kalahari desert, the name given to the spirit of creation.

CALLIOPE One of the nine Muses in Greek and Roman mythology. She was the mother of Orpheus and Linus. Usually represented with a style and waxen tablets, she was the chief of the Muses and presided over eloquence and poetry.

CALMECAC An advanced school for priests among the Aztecs. The complex, difficult training included fasting and self-torture.

CAMAZOTZ Among the Quiché Indians, a bat-god.

CAMDEO In Hindu mythology, the god of love.

CAMENAE Nymphs of fountains or springs. Egeria was the most famous of the nymphs, whom the Roman poets often called Muses.

CANAANITE BAAL In Canaanite religion, Baal, the Energizer, presided over the sky and the rain. He was in charge of the productivity of the earth. He was variously known as Hadad or Hadd and under this appellation he was the deity of thunder. Variant designations of the Baal were 'Powerful' and 'Rider on the Clouds' and 'The Westerner.' He was depicted as a bull or a steer.

CANAANITE CREATION MYTH Philo of Byblos reported the Canaanite version of the myth of creation. Since the beginning of time, he tells us, there had been a violent wind and chaos. Their union produced a watery mass in the shape of an egg. The egg split in two, producing heaven and earth.

CANAANITE CULT At Byblos in Syria, inscriptions, recently deciphered, reveal that an Egyptianized sanctuary and cult existed there in the fifteenth century B.C.

CANAANITE DEITIES El was the personification of the power indwelling in some object or phenomenon: as, for instance, trees, or mountains, or winds.
Baal was the personification of the indwelling power in an object or phenomenon, giving it the energy to exist.

CANAANITE MYTHS Texts discovered in Ras Shamra include: the myth of Baal, the myth of Aqhat, and the myth of Dawn and Sunset. The first of these was designed for the annual festival marking the beginning of the rainy season and concerned the manner in which Baal secured dominion over the earth. The myth of Aqhat represents a literary interpretation of the seasonal cult in which the dying and reviving lord of fertility symbolizes the disappearance and return of rain. The myth of Dawn and Sunset is associated with a ritual accompanying a seasonal festival similar to the Israelitic Feast of First Fruits.

CANAANITE PANTHEON The head of the Canaanite or Phoenician pantheon was El (that is, *the* god). His consort Ashirat (Asherah) was also worshipped by the Amorites and South Arabians. El plays a somewhat passive role as 'the father of years' and is described in the Ugaritic poems as dwelling in a distant part of the cosmos known as the 'Source of the Two Deeps.' The active role is taken by Baal or Haddu, the storm god and king of all the gods, later called lord of heaven. He was the son of Dagan (Dagon), one of El's three brothers. Baal is the hero of a great mythological epic in which he is killed by monsters and carried to the land of Mot (Death), the son of El and Ashirat. The earth languishes until Baal's sister, the virgin Anath, kills Mot and performs a dynamistic ritual. In actual cult, Baal was identified with the chief deity of a particular locality.

Streams and bodies of water were under the control of Yam, who tried each year to gain possession of the earth by flooding it. A hydra-like dragon, he was called Leviathan, 'The Coiled One.'

The three-sided contest between Baal, Mot, and Yam for dominion over the earth forms the central theme of the 'Myth of Baal.' In actual cult Mot, the genius of aridity and lifelessness, was called Resheph and Horon. In Cyprus he was identified with Apollo in the Greek god's capacity of plague deity. In the mythological account of his struggle with Baal, he succeeds for a time in imprisoning the storm god in the underworld. Life on earth languishes until he is resurrected and returned to earth. He defeats Mot and banishes him to the underworld.

Besides the major powers, the Canaanite pantheon includes personifications of natural phenomena. The sun and moon were deified as Shemesh, the god of justice, and Yareah, the husband of Nikkal. Shahar and Shalem, personifications of dawn and sunset, are called 'the celestial ones.' Queen Shapash was the deified sun and Dagan the genius of the crops. The pantheon also included a divine smith known as

Koshar, Hasis, and Hayin. The male deities were supplemented by three main goddesses: Anath, Asherath, and Ashtarth (Astarte), corresponding approximately to Artemis, Hera, and Aphrodite in Greek religion. Anath, regularly styled the virgin, was the sister of Baal, the one who mourned him and searched for him when he was driven from the earth. Asherath, the consort of the storm god, was believed to be the mother of all of the gods. Astarte was the personification of sexual vigor and passion as well as the genius of warfare. In astral mythology, she was identified with the planet Venus.

CANAANITE PRIESTHOOD In Canaanite religion, the priests performed a number of functions. They were physicians and judges. They supervised levies and fines and taxes as well as ceremonial sacrifices.

CANAANITE RELIGION The Canaanites conceived the universe as embodying conflicting powers. Seeking therefore the advantage that nature could offer in the form of sun and rain and productivity, they addressed their prayers to one or another of these powers that controlled rain or sun or productivity. In other cases, the Canaanites directed the total communal efforts to the fulfilment of their needs.
Salient features of the Canaanite religion are the cruelty of some of its rites, the crudity of its emphasis on sex, and the fluid character of its pantheon, in which gods change not only their functions but even their sex. Religion reflected to some extent the lack of unity among the Canaanites and the absence of a well organized priestly class capable of framing a coherent system. Each city had its own deities and also worshipped many divinities taken over from the Babylonians or Egyptians.
Ritual prostitution, practiced as part of the fertility cult, eventually fell into disuse. The fertility goddesses, Anat and Astarte, unite the attributes of virginity and motherhood, and they are frequently represented in forms stressing sexual features. The fertility cult also included the young god who died and returned, like vegetation. Adonis, worshipped at Byblos, had the same features as the Babylonian Tammuz.

The cult of the dead points to belief in survival after death. Over the whole Canaanite area, gifts were placed in the tombs of the dead.

CANAANITE RITUAL Among the sacrifices used by the Canaanites were doves, birds of various kinds, oxen, rams, calves, kids.
The Canaanite temple was known as the 'house of god.' It gave sanctuary to refugees and aliens.
Priests, choristers, watchmen, builders were all associated with the maintenance of the temple. Rituals were also performed in the open air, in 'high places.'

CANAANITE SACRIFICES In ritual ceremonies the Canaanites sacrificed oxen, rams, fowl, calves, birds, kids. Human victims were offered as man's supreme gift to the gods on the occasion of great public disasters.

CANAANITE TEMPLES The administration of Canaanite temples was in the hands of the high priests with his attendant priests, together with a staff comprising watchmen, doorkeepers, barbers, smiths, builders, sacred prostitutes.

CANAANITE TRIAD The Canaanite divine triad consisted of Baal, Yam, and Mot.

CANIDIA A sorceress often mentioned by Horace. She used wax figures to cast her spells. She succeeded in making the moon descend from the heavens.

CANNIBALISM A customary, socially approved practice of eating human flesh. The word is derived from the name of the Carib Indians (Caribales or Canibales) who inhabited the West Indies at the time of Columbus. Since ancient times barbarous peoples have probably eaten human flesh, even though cannibalism among savages has been exaggerated by reporters. The multiple origins of the practice include hunger, human sacrifice to divinities, the disposal of the dead, and sympathetic magic.

CANOPUS In Egyptian religion, a divine being represented in the shape of a jar.

CANOPIC JAR In Egyptian religion, a jar into which the internal organs of a corpse were placed by the embalmers.

CANOPIUS HERCULES The Egyptian Hercules. He was associated with the city of Canopus.

CARDINAL POINTS In Egyptian religion, the gods of the four cardinal points are Imset, Hapi, Tuamutef. Kebehsennuf. They watched over the intestines of the dead.

CARGO CULTS These are religious movements based on the belief that valuable cargoes will be diverted into the hands of cult members. Prominent in New Guinea and the islands of Melanesia, they combine elements of Christianity and indigenous beliefs.

CARNA A Roman goddess who presided over the development of flesh and bone in infants.

CARPOCRATES In the second century A.D. he founded a Gnostic sect named after him Carpocratians. The sect was popular in Alexandria. Among his beliefs were a prior existence and metempsychosis. This sect disappeared in the sixth century.

CASTOR In Greek mythology, one of the Dioscuri. The twin brothers, Castor and Pollux, were patrons of games. Castor who alone was mortal, was slain. Pollux entreated Zeus to let him die, too. Zeus decreed that the two should live in the upper and lower worlds, on alternate days. According to another myth, Zeus placed the brothers in the sky, as the constellation Gemini. A temple was dedicated to the twins in Rome, in 484 B.C. The cult was introduced into Rome from the Dorian cities of southern Italy.

CATS The 'first pet of civilization' has long been associated with sacred rites, superstitions, and magic. The cat was held sacred in ancient India. As an Egyptian deity, it was supposed to have oracular powers. The entire city of Bubastis was dedicated to feline worship, and a festival honoring the sacred animal was attended each May by thousands of pilgrims.

The most prominent of the feline goddesses was Bast, represented in bronze as a cat-headed woman. Prayer and sacrifice were elements of the cult. Dead cats were embalmed and sent to Bubastis for burial.

The cat also had great prestige in Britain, where sacred rites were held in its honor. In Scandinavian countries, Freya was the cat-goddess, and her chariot was said to be drawn by two cats.

CATIUS A Roman deity who presided over adults.

CATOPTROMANCY Divination by a mirror. The ancient Greeks placed mirrors under water and observed the reflection.

CAULDRON OF REGENERATION A witch ceremony, also called 'Drawing down the Moon,' practiced in England on or about December 12. Spirit is poured over leaves thrown into a cauldron set in the middle of a magic circle. The spirit is lighted and Bacchus, the god of wine and fertility, is invoked by a chant led by a witch-priestess.

CAVE CULT In Greece, in the Neolithic Age, religious cults centered in caves. Excavations have unearthed female figurines. Other objects found in Crete and Candia indicate the worship of a divinity. Offerings of honey and wine were among the libations.

CELAENO In Greek and Roman mythology, one of the Harpies.

CELTIC ANIMALS Among the ancient Celts of Gaul, Ireland, the Rhine region, and the Low Countries, animals were held sacred. Among such animals were the bear, the wild-boar, and the bull, often represented with three horns.

CELTIC MYTHOLOGY In Welsh legend, the Druids, the Priests of ancient Gaul, appear as wise counselors. In Irish folklore, also, they are represented as skilled in spell-binding.

CELTIC RELIGION In Western Europe the Celtic religion was already established in Britain, Ireland, the Low Countries, in Gaul, and in the Rhine area in the seventh century B.C. The religion was primarily a fertility cult. Animal and human sacrifices were in force. Certain animals — the horse, pig, bull, bear — as well as trees and rivers, had sanctity. Worship was usually practiced in open groves. After contact with the Romans, in the first century B.C., Celtic divinities were absorbed into the Roman pantheon, or rather Celtic deities were equated with Roman divinities.

The Celtic religion slowly disappeared with the evolution of Christianity, but it survived in legends and folklore. In the sixth century Gregory of Tours refers to Celtic pagan survivals in rural districts.

In a particular sense, the Celtic religion was concentrated in Gaul and in the British Isles. The vegetation cults were predominant, as they aimed to ensure productivity of the earth. In other areas, there were gods of the natural phenomena, war, and commerce. The sky god was honored with a fire cult. The sea to the Celts was a vast expanse beneath which, in caverns, the spirits of the dead were conducted.

CENOTE Among the Mayas of Yucatan, the cenote was an underground pool. It was the shrine dedicated to the rain gods.

CENTEOCIHUATL In Aztec religion, the goddess of corn, agriculture, and fertility.

CENTEOTL In Aztec religion, the yellow-corn spirit and patron of agriculturists.

CENTZONTOTOCHTIN In Aztec religion, the four hundred gods of pulque, the harvest, and the stars, and the companions of the moon. Some of them are called Tepoztecatl, Patecatl, Totochtin, and Macuilxochitl.

73

CERAMOLITHIC A term suggested by William Albright to designate the period following the Stone Age when stone and pottery were used together (c. 3000-1600 B.C.).

CERBERUS In classical mythology, the three-headed dog that guarded the entrance to Hades.

CERES Roman corn-goddess. She and her daughter Proserpina are identified with the Greek Demeter and her daughter Persephone.

CERINTHUS The earliest Gnostic of whom there is any mention. He flourished in the second century A.D.

CERNUNNUS A Gallic god. He was depicted with a bull's head, a man's trunk, serpent's legs, and a fish tail. He presided over wild animals.

CHAC In the Mayan religion, he was the god of thunder and rain.

CHADUN The deity to whom the Apa Tanis ascribe the creation of the world.

CHALDEAN BOOK OF NUMBERS A work containing the principles taught in the Jewish Cabalistic works.

CHALDEANS An ancient Semitic tribe occupying the estuaries of the Tigris and Euphrates. They became the learned Cabalists of Babylonia. There is a resemblance between the secret doctrine of the Avesta and the religious metaphysics of the Chaldeans.

CHALCHIHUITLICUE In the religion of the Aztecs, she was the goddess of running waters. Her home was the sea, rivers, lakes. She presided over those whose duties required contact with waters.

CHALCHIUATL In the Aztec language, this was the human blood that nourished the sun god. The blood was obtained through human sacrifices of war captives.

74

CHALDAEI In antiquity, the Chaldaei, were, along with the mathematici, professional astrologers who exerted profound influence in Roman times, especially during the Empire. They cast horoscopes. They were the interpreters of astrological phenomena, and they imposed themselves to such an extent that on occasion they were banished from Rome. The Roman satirist Juvenal, who flourished in the second century A.D., attacks their baleful influence.

CHALDEAN ORACLES These prophetic announcements constituted a corpus of sacred poems. They contained Hellenic philosophical theories and matter relating to Oriental mysticism. One powerful oracle predicted success for a person who could by force of will transcend his destiny.

CHAM-ZOROASTER After the period of the Flood, he was reputed to be the first magician and father of four sons. Cush, Mizraim, Phut, and Canaan were lords of magic, respectively, over Africa, Egypt, the desert tribes, and Phoenicia.

CHANDRA In Hindu mythology, the moon god.

CHANDRAKANTA In Hindu mythology, a fabulous gem supposed to be formed of the moon's rays congealed. To it are attributed occult and magical properties.

CHANDRAVANSA In Hindu mythology, the lunar race, in contra-distinction to the solar race (Suryavansa).

CHANGING WOMAN Among Navaho Indians, she is the consort of the Sun. Their twin offspring are Monster Slayer and Child of the Water.

CHANGO A Nigerian god with a temple at Ibadan. See Shango.

CHANTICO In Aztec religion, goddess of the earth and volcanic fire, and patron of jewelers.

CHAOS In Greek religion, he was the oldest god, the father of Night and Hell.

CHARMS and AMULETS In many pagan religions verbal charms in the form of spells and incantations were employed in rituals and ceremonies associated with religious cults. Amulets or talismans, material charms, were similarly in use, for protection against disease, disaster, or evil forces. Such amulets consisted of animal teeth or claws, roots of plants, human bones or hair, arrowheads, phallic objects, tusks, feathers, written magic formulas, and inscribed objects.

CHELA A disciple, the pupil of a guru or sage.

CHEMOSH The national deity of the Moabites. On occasion, he was appeased by human sacrifice.

CHENREZI He is the patron deity of the Tibetans.

CHICHEN-ITZA A great religious center of the Mayas in the jungles of Yucatan. Settled near the beginning of the fifth century A.D., it was abandoned and resettled by the Itza, a Mexican tribe led by Kukulkan, who was later deified as a feathered serpent. It was the object of pilgrimages from other Maya centers and beyond. Archaeological findings indicate that the Mayas used rubber and aromatic resin in their sacrificial ceremonies. Here human beings were sometimes sacrificed to Chac, the rain god.

CHICOMECOHUATL In the religion of the Aztecs, she is the maize-goddess. She is depicted holding a double ear of maize. At her annual festival in September a young girl represents the goddess. At the end of the ceremonies, the girl is sacrificially immolated. The rite is associated with a vegetation cult.

CHILAN BALAM Among the Mayans, this is a collection of chronicles and records relating to the ancient traditions of the people. It includes astrological and medical information.

CHILD OF THE SUN The name assigned to the Great Inca of Peru.

CHILD SACRIFICES The Hebrew scriptures attribute the custom of child sacrifice to Tyre, the Phoenician capital. Carthaginian stelae show that children were sacrificed to Baal Hammon and to Tanit. Many people still believe that the Carthaginians systematically sacrificed their firstborn male children to one or more gods, and that the sacrifices performed at Carthage were a legacy from Tyre. Sacrifices were made to the gods to obtain favors and were conducted according to prescribed rituals. The sacrificial rite, called *molek,* was a secret one. It may have involved throat-cutting and the placing of the dead body in a sacred pit or *tophet,* where the flesh was burned.

CHINESE RELIGIONS The ordinary Chinese tends to adhere exclusively to none of the major religions of China (Confucianism, Taoism, Buddhism) but to adopt certain elements of these and other systems of belief. Ancestor worship, incorporating the traditional belief that sons must care for their parents before and after death, is the most universal system of belief in China, and this system is linked to a system rooted in the distant past. It is within the hierarchy of nonancestral gods, ranging from the Supreme Ruler of Heaven down to local gods whose temples are seen in every village, that the great religions find their place.

According to beliefs rooted in the distant past, the universe owes its origin two souls or breaths called *Yang* and *Yin.* Yang is the male, light, positive, productive, beneficent principle; yin represents darkness, cold, death. *Yang* is subdivided into many good spirits called *shen.* The evil spirits into which *Yin* is subdivided are called *kwei.* Man owes his finer qualities to his *shen,* his passions and baser qualities to to his *kwei.* By the time of Confucius (551-479 B.C.), these ancient beliefs engrafted upon the principle of the *Tao* (order of the universe), had been organized into a state religion.

The divinities of the ancient Chinese state religion included those worshipped by the Emperor — the spirits of Heaven and Earth, the Imperial Ancestors, the gods of the ground, and corn gods; those worshipped by the middle class — the sun, men credited with introducing civilization, and many rulers of the past; and those worshipped by the Mandarins

77

— ancient physicians, the gods of walls and moats, the god of fire, gods of water and rain, and many others. Confucianism, Taoism, and Buddhism in particular, have penetrated the whole of Chinese life. Most Chinese are still on friendly terms with all three, but the policy of the ruling Communists is to eradicate the ancient religions.

CHITRA GUPTA A Sanskrit word denoting the deva or god who is the recorder of Yama, the god of death, and who reads the account of a soul's life from the register when the soul appears before the seat of judgment.

CHLORIS A Greek goddess of flowers. Identified with the Roman Flora.

CHORS A Slavic deity whose functions are obscure.

CHOSEN WOMEN Among the Incas, attractive young girls were selected every year from all over the empire and trained to serve as concubines of the rulers and nobles. Their lives were consecrated to the service of the Sun and his earthly representatives, the Incas and priests. The most important convent set aside for the Chosen Women was at Cuzco near the Temple of the Sun.

CHRISTMAS The festival of the birth of Christ, celebrated on December 25, includes a number of customs of pagan origin. According to the 'plan of the ages' defined in *De Pascha Computus,* the first day of creation was March 25. This day is taken as the date of Christ's conception, making his actual birth fall on December 25, the date of the Mithraic festival honoring the end of the winter solstice. Much of the merriment associated with the Roman feast of the Saturnalia, including the giving of gifts, has been transferred to Christmas. Other important elements are of Teutonic origin. The Yule-feast marked the winter solstice and gave rise to the yule-log and Christmas cakes, a survival of the ancient practice of offering a sacrifice in the expectation of good crops in the coming year. The mistletoe is probably a Celtic element introduced to invoke the blessing of the vegetation spirit.

CHTHONIAN DEITIES Gods or spirits of the underworld. Propitiatory and magical rites are characteristic of chthonian worship among the Greeks. In classical mythology, they include Pluto, Demeter, Persephone, Hermes, Zeus. Chthonios. Much earlier, the Mesopotamians made seals and reliefs showing deities growing from mountains and plants growing from the hands of the deities. The best known of these chthonian deities is Tammuz.

CHURINGAS Among the Australian aborigines, ovoid stones or pieces of wood shaped like bullroarers. They bore sacred symbolic markings and were not supposed to be seen by women or uninitiated men. The aborigines think that their ancestors carried with them churingas identified with specific totems. They were cherished by successive generations and assumed to be invested with the spirits of ancestors. Used in all ceremonies, they were guarded by an *alatunja.*

CHYNDONAX A magician-priest of the Druids.

CHYTROI In ancient Greek religion, a festival in which offerings were brought to the dead. It corresponds to All Souls' Day.

CID A Phoenician god known at Carthage and in Sardinia, where he had a temple.

CIHUACOATL In Aztec religion, the goddess of the earth, war, and birth, spiritual patron of the Cihuateteo, and daughter of Toci.

CIHUATETEO In Aztec religion, malefic female demons. They were the spirits of women who had died in childbirth.

CIRCE In Greek mythology, a sorceress, daughter of Helios, who lived on the island of Aeaea and turned visitors into the shape of wolves and lions.

CIRCUMAMBULATION This was a ritual that involved walking around a person or an object three times in succession.

79

The procedure was common among the Romans and the Celts.

CIRCUMCISION The act of cutting the foreskin of males or the internal labia of females. The performance of the ritual operation is almost universal except among non-Semites in Europe, Asia, and America. It was observed not only among the ancient Hebrews and Mohammedans but also among the ancient Egyptians, certain African and Polynesian tribes, and some American Indians. In ancient Egypt priests and warriors were circumcised. Some African tribes exclude from society all those who have not submitted to the rite.

CLAY Creation from clay was an idea common to Babylonia, Egypt, Greece, Tahiti, New Zealand, Australia, and North America.

CLIO In Greek mythology, the Muse of history.

CLOACINA A Roman goddess who was in charge of the sewers.

COATLICUE In Aztec religion, the goddess of the earth. She is represented as wearing a robe with intertwined serpents.

COCK An occult bird much appreciated in ancient augury and symbolism. According to the Zohar, the cock crows three times before the death of a person. The bird was sacred to Aesculapius.

CODE OF MANU A Sanskrit work which predates Christianity and attributes the founding of the moral and social order to Manu, who alone was saved in the Indian account of the Flood. Manu's oblations produced a woman who gave birth to the human race. To him, the Father of Mankind, the sacred texts were revealed.

COFFIN-RITE The final rite of initiation in the ancient mysteries of Egypt, Greece, and elsewhere. The last and supreme secrets of occultism could be revealed to the adept only after he had passed through an allegorical ceremony of death and resurrection into new light.

COFFIN TEXTS Egyptian texts from the Middle Empire. They contain many incantations and hymns from the pyramid texts and reflect the fears of the common people, who hoped like the pharaohs to attain a blissful afterlife, with respect to the dangers associated with the journey to Elysium.

COHOBA A narcotic snuff prepared from the seeds of a subtropical plant, the *huilca,* and used by the Incas to induce a hypnotic state accompanied by visions.

COL In the Nuer religion, he is a spirit of the air, the spirit of lightning.

COLLINA A Roman goddess of the hills.

COLORS In certain Greek and Roman cults the colors black, white, and red had particular significance. White was associated with sacrifices to the gods. Black was used in rituals relating to the chthonic gods and to funerary rites. Red was usually related to death and the Lower Regions: also to fertility rituals.

COMMUNICATION WITH THE GODS In Egyptian religion, the usual mode of communication with the gods was through prayer. Only the prayer had a persuasive motive, which was to secure a favor.

COMMUNION WITH THE DEITY In the mystery religions communion with the deity was consummated by means of purifications, processions, fasting and other austerities. In addition there was the spectacle of a kind of passion play, a view of sacred mystery relics, accompanied by sacramental acts and liturgies.

COMUS A Roman god of revelry.

CONCEPT OF BAAL In Canaanite religion, the Baal was the personification of the indwelling force of an object or phenomenon. The Baal was usually associated with a particular locality, as Baal Hazor, Baal Hermon.

CONFUCIANISM A system of morals based on the teachings of Confucius and engrafted upon the nature religion which had existed for centuries in China. It stresses filial piety, benevolence, justice, intelligence, propriety, and fidelity, and it is the basis of much of Chinese education and religion.

Its sacred books are the five classics composed, except for the last one, by Confucius: the *Shu King* (Book of History), the *Shi King* (Book of Poetry), the *I King* (Book of Changes), *Ch'un Ts'iu* (Spring and Fall Annals), and the *Li Ki* (Book of Rites). To the five classics are added four books of a less authoritative character: the *Lun Yu* (Analects), compiled by the disciples of Confucius; the *Works of Mencius,* containing the thoughts of the ethical writer who ranks second in importance to Confucius; the *Chung Yung* (Doctrine of the Mean) and the *Ta Shiao* (Great Learning), both compiled or written by followers of the master.

Confucianism accepts the traditional *Tao* (order of the universe) and the closely connected *Jen Tao* (right human order) as the basis of an ethical system. The five classics of the master and his followers express in its entirety the Way of *jen* (humanity, love) through which an individual can establish his own character and help others to do the same. These books were studied to the neglect of all else and became the basis of Chinese education.

Foremost among the principles of Confucianism is reverence for the manifestations of *Shen,* the soul of the universe. Reverence applied not only to the chief deities (the divinities worshipped by the Emperor — the spirits of Heaven and Earth, the Imperial Ancestors, the gods of the ground and grain) but also to famous men, deities of clouds, mountains, fire, and storehouses, and to ancestors believed to be possessed of a *shen* related to that of the universe.

Confucianism retained its hold on Chinese education, govenment, and thought for two millennia. Its future was clouded in 1949 by the Communist seizure of power. Old traditions have been abolished under Communism and the family system, the central institution in Confucian civilization, has been minimized.

CONFUCIUS (551-479 B.C.) Chinese philosopher who advocated manhood as the *summum bonum,* the highest good. The superior man is the ideal being. The highest duty of man is the cultivation of life. For the individual, moral perfection is postulated: for society in general, moral and social orderliness are prescribed. To attain this status of perfection, man must follow the Golden Mean, which involves the moral essence in harmony with the universe. To attain these ends, man must increase his knowledge, cultivate a personal and domestic life, and march toward world peace.

CONGO RELIGIONS Most Congo tribes have some form of ancestor worship, identify several spirits, and believe in a supreme being. Frequently, special status is ascribed to rain makers, medicine men, diviners, and twins.

CONSUS A Roman god who presided over stored harvests. During his festival in August horses and asses rested from their labor.

COPAN A Maya ceremonial center dating from the fifth century A.D. The magnificent complex of buildings, now called the Acropolis, covered twelve acres. The religion to which the mass of pyramids, temples, terraces, and courts was dedicated probably originated in some form of nature worship. The chief god, a sky deity called Itzamná, was worshipped along with Chac, the long-nosed rain god, and a few other gods such as those of the wind and the maize. The ceremonies probably included sacrificial offering, dancing, and the burning of incense.

CORYBANTES Priests of the Asian goddess Cybele. Their functions were marked by wild ritualistic dances that degenerated into orgies and self-mutilation. The cult spread to Greece and thence to Rome, where the priests were known as Galli. In Crete the Corybantes were called Curetes.

COSMIC EGG In mystic pagan cults, particularly in Orphism, the egg symbolized the source of the world. In Egyptian religion, the goose-god, Geb, 'the Great Cackler,' laid the cosmic egg.
In Orphism, the egg of light from the upper air breaks into heaven and earth.
In Indian religion, too, the egg splits and forms heaven and earth.

COSMOGONY A theory of the origination of the universe. Among primitive tribes, a god is usually the creator. He may create the world by a magic word (Hebrews), by sacrifice (India), or be a master potter (Egypt) or weaver (Babylonia). Widely found in early cosmogonies is the notion of a union of Heaven and Earth. The Polynesians believe that the universe sprang from a cosmic egg.

COTTUS In classical mythology, one of the Hecatoncheires.

COTYS Also called *Cotytto*. A Thracian goddess whose cult involved orgiastic rites. Her worship was practiced in Athens and other Greek cities.

COVEN A band consisting of a chief and twelve members of a cult devoted to the practice of witchcraft. They celebrated religious rites, practiced as healers under the direction of their divine master, and served as consultants to those in need of witchcraft.

COW-WOMAN GODDESSES Nut, the Egyptian sky goddess, is represented as a cow with the Milky Way on her belly. She was one of a large class of cowwoman goddesses— Hathor, Isis, Ishtar, Tiamat, etc.—found in Egyptian and other ancient religions.

COYOLXAUHQUI In Aztec religion, the goddess of the moon, daughter of Coatlicue, and sister of Huitzilopochtli, who decapitated her.

CREATION In Norse religion, there is no specific Creator. Creation was spontaneous or the result of opposing forces of heat and cold.
In Egyptian religion, the papyrus of Anhai, belonging in the twenty-second Dynasty, contains a vignette representing the Creation of the World.

CRONUS (SATURN) In classical legend, an agricultural deity.

CRUX ANSATA A variant Latin designation for the Egyptian ankh, the T-shaped cross surmounted by a loop. It was the symbol of life.

CUBA A Roman goddess who presided over infants in their cradle and induced them to sleep.

CULT OF ANCESTORS An ancient religious practice. The soul or the double of the spirit of the deceased continues to live in another existence, for a fixed period of time or, in some cases, until rebirth. This spirit requires sustenance, invocations, and attention on the part of the living, for the living have a profound fear of the dead.
In modern primitive societies the skulls of the dead are preserved in special huts, as in Oceania. In China, the ancestor cult is a basic factor in the social organization.

CULT RITUALS In prehistoric Greece in Minoan-Mycenaean times, cult rituals included raising of the hands, offerings of flowers, songs, orgiastic dances.

CULTS A cult is a system of beliefs, festivals, and rituals associated with some pagan deity. In ancient Greece some divinities, among them Zeus, had a local cult in every major community.

The primary purpose of a religious cult was to ensure the fertility of the earth through the intercession of some particular deity. Symbolically, the cult reproduced dramatically and mimetically the annual decay and later the emergence of vegetation. But the cult was even more than this. It was an interpretation of the relation of the gods in terms of human needs.

CULT-TOTEMISM Australian aborigines have evolved a set of myths and rituals which is usually called cult-totemism. These myths and rituals are seen as 'dreaming,' signifying continuity of life unlimited by time and space. Only men can be initiated into cult-membership. The ritual signifies death and rebirth, or passing from ignorance to knowledge of 'dreaming' and assurance of life. The burial ritual insures the return of the spirit to its spirit home ('dreaming'), from which it will be reincarnated.

CUNIA A Roman goddess who looked after an infant's cradle.

CUPID In Roman mythology, the god of love, son of Mars and Venus, and constant companion of his mother. See Eros.

CURCHUS A Teutonic deity who presided over eating and drinking.

CURETES In Greek religion, earth-born priest-initiates in the service of Cybele, in ancient Crete. Pythagoras is said to have been initiated into their rites.

CUZCO In pre-Columbian times this was the ancient capital of the Empire of the Incas in Peru.

CYBELE This Phrygian goddess, who was called the Great Mother of the Gods, was the source of a widespread cult in antiquity. She was depicted as traveling in a chariot drawn by lions. When the forests of Ida and Berecyntus were shaken by storms, the tumult thus occasioned represented her lamentations for her lover Attis' death. Through the woods her dedicated votaries followed her, their clamorous shouts intermingling with the beating of tambourines, the shrill notes of flutes, the resounding echoes of castanets and cymbals. The adherents, roused to ecstatic frenzy by the din and the throbbing instruments, were filled with a sense of rapture, with total communion with the divinity.

The rites of this cult were characterized by wild orgies and febrile dancing. Many devotees, in a paroxysm of passion, castrated themselves, in the belief that thus they would become one with Cybele.

Cybele was an earth goddess, the mother of all nature. Her consort was the equally divine Attis. The processional features associated with her ceremonials included bands of exultantly chanting votaries, solemn priests marching in resplendent robes, all barefooted, all carrying emblems and insignia of the deity. Then, in recurrent waves of sorrow, arose the litanies over the death of the young Attis. But the mourning soon ceased. For at his resurrection there followed jubilations and hymns glorifying his rebirth.

CYNOCEPHALUS In Egyptian religion, this appellation was applied to Anubis. The term means dog-headed.

CZARNOBOG In Slavic mythology, this is an evil deity, akin to the Zoroastrian Ahriman, the Spirit of Evil.

D

DADOUCHOS A Greek expression meaning a *torch-bearer*. He was an official who performed certain sacred rites in the mystery cult of Demeter. Also *daduchus*. In the Eleusinian mysteries, the torch-bearer was one of four celebrants. The office probably symbolized Demeter's search for her daughter.

DAEVA In Zoroastrian religion, polytheists and evildoers who rejected Zoroaster's teachings.

DAGDA An agricultural God of the pagan Irish, the Jupiter of the Gaels. Called 'Lord of Great Knowledge,' 'Creator,' and 'Good God,' he also was famed as a harpist. After defeating the Tuatha De Danann, he became their king. His wife, the river goddess Boann, bore him two children, Brigit and Aengus. He had power over milk, fruit, and corn. His cauldron was inexhaustible.

DAGOBA A sacred mound or tower for holy relics. The pyramidal mounts are scattered over India, Ceylon, Burma, and other Buddhist countries. At Anuradhapura and other sites, one may still see enormous dagobas, monuments to the piety of many monarchs who built them to enshrine the sacred relics of the Buddha: a tooth, a piece of bone, a branch of the sacred bo tree, etc.

DAGON A Philistine deity whose cult was widespread. His functions, however, are obscure. He appears to have evolved from a fish-god into a god of fertility.

A magnificent temple was consecrated to him in Gaza. He had other temples at Ashdod and Ugarit. Dagon was also considered as a corn-spirit, god of crops. He was the counterpart of the Babylonian Dagan (Baal).

DAHOMEY The natives of the west African kingdom, founded early in the seventeenth century, were noted for the practice of human sacrifice, cannibalism, and 'customs.' Unlike most of the other religions of Africa, the Dahoman religion has an established priesthood and an orthodoxy, in which monasteries, secret societies, secondary gods, and divination were prominent. The grand custom, performed on the death of a king, was intended to provide the king with wives and attendants in the spirit world. In 1791, at least 500 people were said to have been sacrificed. The minor customs, held periodically to replenish the king's reserves in the spirit world, involved the slaughter of prisoners of war. Dancing, feasting, and elaborate rituals preceded the actual slaughter.

DAI-GOHONZON The original prayer scroll containing the *Daimoku* and enshrined in the temple of Taisekiji in Japan. See Soka Gakkai.

DAIMOKU A ritual prayer used by the Soka Gakkai. Its Sanskrit and Chinese words are '*Nammyoho-rengekyo.*' These words mean 'Glory to the Lotus Sutra of the Mystical Law.' The Daimoku is generally chanted in front of the *Gohonzon* until the worshipper feels satisfied.

DAMIA An obscure Greek goddess of fertility. She was worshipped at Aegina and Epidaurus.

DAMKINA In the Akkadian myth of creation, the 'Lady of the Earth,' equivalent to Ge in Greek mythology and *yin* in Chinese thinking. Her mating with Nudimmud corresponds to that of Ouranos (Uranos) and Ge, representing the great cosmically procreative couple, and of *yang* and *yin,* symbolizing heaven and earth. In Babylonian religion, she is the consort of Ea.

90

DANA In the religion of the Irish Celts, she was the Mother-Goddess. She was the symbol of fertility, and represented abundance.

DANCES In its most primitive form, the dance consists of rhythmic movements executed by a group of performers to the accompaniment of sounds. Dance is a universal form of expression and may have been a form of precultural play. Many primitive dances are performed with magical or religious intent. Dancing has been used to induce delirium or a state of ecstasy. The Bororos of South America make the attainment of such a state a criterion of priesthood.

The *abdominal dance,* based on stylized movements of the pelvic region, originated as a fertility rite. The *astronomic dance,* the most ancient form of the dance in Egypt, was performed around the altar of the sun god Ra in groups representing the signs of the Zodiac. The term is also used for a dance whose object of worship is the moon, stars, or sun. The battle astronomic dance was also performed by the ancient Greeks around the flaming altar of Zeus. The *bread dance* is an American Indian performance symbolizing sustenance, such as the Shawnee hunting dance centered around the female deity Kohkomhoena. The *calumet dance* is an Indian ceremony centered around a smoke offering to the Great Spirit. The *corn dance,* widely found in the New World, is directed to the powers that control the rain and the harvesting of maize. *Death dances* are widespread and often mimetic. They may be intended to influence the dead by sympathetic magic, to commune with or propitiate the dead, or to exorcise a malevolent spirit. Similarly, a *demon dance* is aimed at invoking or exorcising extranatural forces. The *phallic dance* is characterized by upward leaps, kicks, or stampings. The leg symbolizes the penis and its penetration of the earth is associated with fertility magic. *Snake dances,* such as those performed by the Hopi Indians, also represent fertility rites. The *sun dance,* as performed by the

91

Great Plains Indians, is directed at the sun as the symbol of life.

DANU In Celtic mythology, she was the goddess of knowledge. Her father was the god Dagda.

DAOS A Chaldean deity, whose functions are obscure.

DATANUS A Slavic deity whose functions are not known.

DATTA One of the Protohattic names of the Hittite weather god.

DAWN'S HEART The name given by African Bushmen to the morning star, the greatest of all the hunters in the sky. The Dawn's Heart is supposed to have descended to earth as a person, fallen in love, and taken as his bride a lynx.

DAY OF THE WEIGHING OF WORDS In Egyptian religion, this day corresponded to the Day of Judgment, when the souls of the dead were weighed by Osiris and his four chiefs.

DAZHBOG A Slavic deity whose functions are obscure.

DEA DIA In Roman religion, she was a corn-goddess. Her festival was observed in May by the Arval Brethren.

DEAE MATRES A Latin expression meaning Mother-Goddesses. They were Celtic and Teutonic deities who were absorbed into the Roman pantheon. But little is known of their functions.

DEA TACITA Also called Dea Muta. A Roman goddess of silence.

DEATH RITES Among the Greeks, burning the corpse and burial were both practiced. Funeral rites lasted as long as seven days. A meal concluded the ceremonies.

The Romans too practiced both burning and burial of the
the corpse. The funeral procession included hired mourn-
ers and attendants who carried the ancestral busts of the
deceased. Dancers and mimics took part in the ceremony.
Then followed a public eulogy, if the deceased had been a
notable personality.

In Egypt the deceased underwent a trial, to weigh his
virtues and his crimes. In the underworld, the soul of the
deceased was weighed against a feather, the judges being
Osiris and his divine aides.

DEATH TAXES In Sumerian religion, when a dead person was
taken to burial, the family of the deceased was required
to pay to certain officials a measure of bread, barley,
and beer.

DECREE OF ANU In Babylonian religion, the 'decree of Anu'
was fate.

DEDUN A Nubian war god, who was assimilated into the Egyptian pantheon.

DEIFICATION In Egyptian religion, animals, inanimate objects,
even concepts were deified. As examples, we find the evil
serpent Apophis, and the good serpent Wazit; Behnesa,
the oxyrhynchus-fish; the Benben stone at Heliopolis; and
the concept of magic, Heka.

DELLING In Norse mythology, he is the personification of
twilight.

DELOS A small island in the Aegean Sea where Apollo and
Artemis were born. At first a floating island, Poseidon
fixed it to the bottom of the sea to provide a resting place
for Leto, the Titaness daughter of Coeus and Phoebe.
Apollo had a famous oracle on the island.

DELPHI A Greek city in Phocis, in Central Greece. Here the
temple of Apollo offered divine oracles. In order to receive oracular guidance, suppliants flocked to Delphi from
all parts of the Mediterranean littoral.

DEMETER (CERES) In Greek legend, Demeter was a corn goddess who presided over harvests. When her daughter Persephone was carried off by Hades (Pluto) to the Underworld, Demeter went in search of her as far as Eleusis. Persephone was returned by Zeus (Jupiter) to the upper earth, but had to spend part of each year underground. Symbolically, this myth applies to the rotation of the seasons and the harvest and the death and rebirth of the produce of the earth.

A mystery cult developed from this legend, with special festivals honoring the goddess and rituals that offered immortal life to the initiated, in harmony with the annual decay and revival of the earth's produce.

The mysteries, known as the Eleusinian Mysteries, were so called on account of Demeter's arrival in Eleusis.

DEMIURGE In Greek, this expression means 'a worker for the people.' It is used in Platonic philosophy to designate the Creator of the World.

Among the Gnostics, the demiurge was the evolution of matter and the source of Evil.

DEMOGORGON In Roman mythology, he was an obscure deity of the underworld. In the late Roman Empire, in the fifth century A.D., he was invoked in magic rites.

His abode was in the center of the earth. As companions he had Chaos and Eternity. His worship was associated particularly with Arcadia.

DEMONS A word used to denote a lower order of superhuman beings generally thought to be enemies of mankind. Belief in such beings or spirits is widespread. The ancients devoted much attention to the problem of exorcising evil spirits. The ancient Mesopotamians lived in fear of demons, commonly represented in their art with human bodies and animal heads. Both the Babylonians and Assyrians thought the demons were evil spirits who came from beneath the earth or ghosts of the unburied dead. The demons were able to take any shape, enter any body, move useen to any place. Even men who led blameless lives were at their mercy, though sinfulness provided the easiest means of entering bodies.

DEO In the Eleusinian mysteries, Deo was the mystic name of Demeter.

DERCETO (DERCETIS) A Syrian goddess, mother of Semiramis, the founder of Babylon. See Atargatis.

DESA Among the Balinese, these are self-contained communities established on the basis of ancestor worship.

DESCENT INTO HELL In many pagan religions, myths and legends describe visits of both deities and mortals to the Underworld, the realm of the dead. Such descriptions appear in the mythology of the Greeks and the Romans, the Babylonians, and the Egyptians.
The purpose of the infernal visit may vary. It may be a matter of curiosity, or to secure a favor from the gods of the Lower Regions, or rescue a soul. In the Hellenistic mysteries the descent was associated with certain secret initiatory rites.

DESOIPITJ In the Melanesian myth of the two brothers, Desoipitj ('man with a wound') persuaded Biwiripitsj ('parrot man') to remove his head from his body. The severed head then taught Biwiripitsj the technique of butchering, the ritual of a triumphant return from a headhunting expedition, the roles of the participants in an initiation ceremony, and the handling of the decapitated head of a victim.

DEUCALION AND PYRRHA In Greek mythology, the only human beings that survived the great flood sent by Zeus. They became the progenitors of a new race by throwing behind them 'the bones of their mother' (stones), from which sprang men and women.

DEVA In the Zoroastrian religion, a maleficent spirit, the enemy of men and of Ormazd. In Hinduism, it is the general designation for God. In ancient Aryan religion, the Devas were the 'bright heavenly ones,' sons of Dyaus, father of the sky. *Deva* is the Sanskrit form derived from the Indo-European root seen in Latin *deus*, Greek *theos*, and English *devil.*

DEVAKI In Hindu mythology, the mother of Krishna.

DEV AZUR In the Zoroastrian religion, he was the demon of evil desires.

DEVERRA A Roman domestic deity who presided over household brooms.

DEVIL WORSHIPPERS The name applied to a small Yezidi community of the Sinjar Hills in Iraq. The name of the sect literally means 'God-worshippers.' The cult is probably a syncretism of Mazdean, Christian, and Mohammedan elements. Adherents worship both a good supreme god and subordinate gods. The chief of their subordinate gods, Melek Taus, represented as a peacock, is apparently the author of evil and therefore must be propitiated as co-creator. The Yezidis claim descent from Adam alone.

DHAMMAPADA The *Dhammapada* ('Path to Virtue') is a practical ethical handbook of Buddhism. Included in the canon of Buddhist scriptures, it is divided into twenty-six chapters. The keynote is sounded by the maxim, 'The virtuous man is happy in this world and in the next.'

DHARMA In Buddhism, a religious norm or precept. The teaching of the way of salvation is embodied in the Four Noble Truths of Buddha. See Buddhism.

DHYANA In Hinduism and Buddhism, a term meaning meditation and denoting a very important practice in both religions. The word sometimes is synonymous with yoga.

DIAKKA In occultism and theosophy, phantoms or 'spooks.' They are the communicating and materializing spirits of mediums and spiritualists.

DIASIA In Greek religion, a rite involving offering to the deities of the Nether Regions. In this infernal aspect, Zeus was entreated under the appellation of Meilichios, 'One who is Easy to be Entreated.'

DIDUN The deity to whom the Apa Tanis ascribe the creation of the sky. She is the mate of Chadun, creator of the earth.

DII ADSCRIPTICII A Latin expression that denotes the collective body of minor deities in the Roman pantheon.

DII CONSENTES A group of twelve deities, in six pairs of male and female, that were members of the Etruscan pantheon.

DII INDIGETES Early Roman deities.

DIKE In Greek mythology, she is the personification of Justice. She reports the crimes committed by mankind to Zeus.

DILMUN In the Sumerian religion, the land of immortality, where there is no sickness or death. In the epic of Gilgamesh, it is described as the garden of the gods, a sort of paradise reserved for the use of Utnapishtim and his consort.

DINGIR In Sumerian religion, the term *dingir* denotes one of the invisible anthropomorphic beings, superhuman and immortal, who control the entire cosmos.

DIONE In primitive Greek mythology, she was the consort of Zeus and the mother of Aphrodite. Originally, she may have been the female counterpart of Zeus himself. Her cult is obscure.

DIONYSIAN MYSTERIES An ancient Greek cult that originated in Phrygia and spread to other regions. The rites, honoring the god Dionysus, god of the vine and fertility, were marked by frenzied orgies. These practices were inspired by the deity himself who made his presence felt within the votaries. They were aware of the immanence of Dionysus.

DIONYSUS (BACCHUS, LIBER) In classical mythology, the god of wine and fertility. His cult was widespread in Thrace, where the Thracian women were particularly dedicated to his orgiastic rites. The women, Maenads, in their ecstatic frenzy, abandoned their homes, roamed the fields and hillsides, dancing, swinging their flaming torches. In their passion they caught and tore apart animals, sometimes even children, and devoured the flesh, thus acquiring communion with the divinity. Dionysus himself at times appeared to them in the form of some animal, usually a bull. Celebrations, of a milder type, were also held on Mount Parnassus.

In the mystic cult, Dionysus was associated with the Lower Regions. This cult became highly popular in Hellenistic and later on in Roman times. The cult of Dionysus as practiced by his devotees is presented dramatically in Euripides' tragedy *The Bacchae.*

DIS Also called Dis pater. In Roman religion, god of the Nether Regions. He is identified with the Greek god Pluto.

DISCORDIA In Roman mythology, a malevolent goddess corresponding to Eris, the goddess of discord, in Greek mythology.

DISES In Norse mythology, the principal goddesses of the Norse pantheon. They were identified with the Norns.

DITHEISM In Greek the term means *twice god.* It was a Zoroastrian tenet, postulating the existence of two supreme gods, one good and the other evil. The beneficent deity was Ahura Mazda; his opponent was Ahriman, the Spirit of Evil.

DITTANY An aromatic plant growing on Mount Dicte and Mount Ida in Crete. It posseses occult and mystical properties. The evergreen shrub was sacred to the moon goddesses and had a place in many magical performances. Occultists claim that it cures somnambulism. Pharmacy attributes to the plant strongly sedative and quieting properties.

DIVINATION In antiquity, various forms of divination were in vogue. They centered on dreams and their interpretation, augury, oracles, astrological calculations. Responses and other deductions were held to be inspired by divine guidance.

In the early Christian centuries pagan divination was viewed as being under the domination of malefic demons.

DIVINE JUDGE This title was assigned to the Babylonian god Marduk, the first of the gods, the source of all power, the layer up of treasures.

DIVINE TRIAD The divine triads of the Near East were probably known as early as six thousand years B.C. They usually consisted of father, mother, and son, all worshipped with the aid of a shrine and appropriate rites. They appear fully developed three thousand years later in the Adonis-Attis-Osiris cycle.

DIVINE VISITS In Assyro-Babylonian religion, a festival was held whenever the sacred image of a deity was transported on a visit to the temple of another deity.

DIVINE WEATHER In Hittite religion, the weather god, the supreme deity, appeared in various manifestations. He was the weather god of thunder, the weather god of lightning, the weather god of the clouds, the weather god of the meadows. He was also the weather god of the king's head and weather god of the palace.

DIVINITIES The ancient deities of pagan religions may be classified as follows:
1. Nature gods, symbolizing the sun, rain, wind, earth, heaven, dawn, storms, the moon.
2. Family deities, symbolizing the Hearth, the domestic storehouse: e.g. Vesta, the Penates among the Romans.
3. Powers or forces symbolizing abstract concepts such Love, Peace, Purity.
4. Human personalities that were deified because of their achievements: kings, warriors, great physicians. They were glorified human beings, like the Homeric deities.

5. Fertility gods, such as Dionysus and Demeter. They became the deities of the mystery cults. The principal figure in the cult was a dying deity, who was reborn. The cult was a vegetation mystery.
6. Creator gods, to whom were attributed the primal act of creation of the universe. Such was the Babylonian deity Anu and Khnum, the Egyptian creator of men and gods.
7. Impersonal gods, such as the Absolute, Fate, Zervan Akarana in Iran.

DJANGGAWUL A name given to three ancestral beings worshipped by the aborigines of Arnhem Land, in northern Australia. The Djanggawul cult is primarily of fertility significance and concerns the rhythmic sequence of the seasons, the increase of the natural species, and the welfare of man. The continuity of the tribe is the first concern of the cult. Three ancestral beings established the cult: the older sister named Bildjiwuraroiju, the younger Miralaidj, and their brother Djanggawul. These three are said to have come with a companion from Bralgu, the mythical island which today is the home of the dead, to northeastern Arnhem Land, where they instituted sacred ritual, created physiographic features, and named totems.

DJOSER The founder of the Memphite Third Dynasty. Later deified, he initiated the Pyramid Age (c. 2600-2200 B.C.) by ordering the construction of the oldest pyramid and a mortuary temple. The temple is the oldest building of stone in the world.

DODONA In Greek mythology, in a mountain retreat in Epirus, there was an ancient oracle, centered in an oak tree. Both men and women served the divine oracle. The priests were known as Selli.

DOLMEN A prehistoric monument formed by several megaliths covered by a cap-stone.

DOMESTIC SHRINES In prehistoric Greece it was the custom to have a shrine dedicated to a deity associated with the family dwelling.

DOMIDUCUS A Roman god who led the bride into the bridegroom's house.

DOMITIUS A Roman god whose function was to keep the bride at home to look after domestic affairs.

DOMOVOJ A Slavic deity who presided over domestic affairs.

DONAR In Teutonic religion, a god who was identified with the Norse Thor. Donar presided over thunder, lightning, wind, and rain.

DORIS In Greek mythology, the daughter of Oceanus and Tethys, wife of Nereus, and mother of the Nereids.

DOUBLE AXE To the Minoan the double axe was an important religious symbol. It was thought to be the aniconic image of the supreme Minoan deity. Examples of the double axe in metal have been discovered in many shrines. Small replicas were often used as votive offerings.

DOUBLE DIVINE SOUL In Egyptian religion, the double divine soul is the soul of Ra, the sun-god and the soul of Osiris. Or alternatively, the soul of Shu and the soul of Tefnut.

DOVE GODDESS A deity worshipped in ancient Greece in Minoan-Mycenaean times.

DRAUPNIR In Norse mythology, Odin's magic ring, made by the dwarfs Brok and Sindri.

DRAVIDIAN RELIGION The religion of a non-Aryan race inhabiting southern India. The Dravidians believe that many evil spirits, including those of the dead, inhabit the universe. Typically, their religion is animistic and magical, a demophobia. Animal sacrifices are performed for the

101

purpose of propitiating local gods and warding off the evil spirits which cause disease and disaster.

DREAM-TIME Among Australian Aborigines, a hero or ancestor is a human being with heightened powers. He is thought of as having totems, and is referred to by an animal name. The time during which these heroic beings traveled and created hills and valleys and rivers is called the Dream-Time, while the heroic character himself is 'dreaming.'

DREGVANTS In Zoroastrian religion, followers of the Druj. Zarathustra divided mankind into two classes, Ashavants and Dregvants.

DRESS OF DRUIDS The Druids of ancient Gaul wore long robes. Their hair was cut short but they had long beards. In their hand they carried a white rod or wand. From their neck was suspended an oval-shaped amulet.
The name Druid is derived from a Celtic or Saxon word, *dru*, meaning 'magician.'

DRUIDS The Druids were the priests of ancient Gaul whose religious traditions were incorporated in their poetry. With the coming of the Roman legions under Julius Caesar in 55 B.C. Druidism began to disappear under the impact of Roman cultural influences. The religious rites and beliefs of Druidism are described by Caesar in Book 6 of his *Gallic Wars.* The Celtic Gods, the concept of the life after death, and the Druidic priesthood are discussed in some detail. The Gauls, relates Caesar, are very superstitious. In times of danger or sickness they sacrifice human beings. As officiating priests they may also require a condemned criminal to be immolated. They believe in a future life, and for this reason tend to placate the gods. They build huge images woven from twigs, and inside they place those caught in theft or robbery, and burn them alive. If there are no criminals at the prescribed time, they sacrifice innocent people. Their principal god is a kind of Gallic Mercury, who presides over the arts. Their Gallic Apollo dispels disease. Their Jupiter is the supreme divinity, while a Gallic Mars is the god of war. After a victory, they offer sacrifices of animals. Whatever booty is taken in battle is considered inviolate. They reckon time beginning with the night, because they believe themselves descended from Pluto, god of the dark underworld. Their funerals are lavish and together with the deceased they consign to the funeral pyre friends of the deceased, as well as animals and slaves. The mistletoe is sacred to the Druids. Among the names of their gods are Teutates, Taranis, Esus, and Ogmios.

The Druids were exempt from taxes and military service. They were skilled in divination. A high priest was elected by the rest of the priesthood. In addition to their priestly functions the Druids were judges and also teachers of the young. They taught astronomy, law, and medicine. In the first century A.D. the Druidic religion was forbidden by Claudius the Roman Emperor.

There are traditional accounts of the Druids fleeing from the Roman advance beyond Gaul, and crossing over into the remote Hebridean Islands of Western Scotland. Certain stone slabs are reputed to have been altar stones for sacrificial purposes, but there is no definitive proof of such practices in the Islands.

The poets among the Druids were known as Bardi. Their augurs were called Eubages. The Saronidae were the judges. The priests themselves were the Vacerri. The religion of the Druids had such a hold on the ancient Gauls that no activity or business could be performed without the consent of the Druids.

DRUJ In Zoroastrian religion, a word designating Lie, Falsehood, Untruth, originating in the wrong moral choice made by the individual between the Twin Spirits (Twin Mainyu). The Druj was personified in later Avestan writings as a foul hag or demon.

DRUJO DEMANA In Zoroastrian sacred literature, the House of the Lie where the wicked dead reside.

DRUSES A sect living on Mount Lebanon in Syria. They resent being called Druses and refer to themselves as the disciples of Hakim, their Messiah. Their religion is an outgrowth of Mohammedanism and dates from the eleventh century. They regard Hakim as the tenth and last incarnation of God, conceived as a mystical supreme being who holds intercourse only with the Universal Intelligence. The religion was introduced in Syria by a follower of Hakim, Darasi, from whom the name Druse is derived. The cult mingles Christian, Moslem, and Sufi elements. Adherents believe in one God, transmigration of souls, and final perfection.

DRYADS In Greek and Roman mythology, these were nymphs who presided over the woods and whose lives were bound up with those of the trees.

DUGPAS A Tibetan sect (literally, 'Red Caps') whose members, since the fourteenth century, have given themselves over to sorcery, drunkenness, and immorality.

DUKHOBORS A Russian sect which professes to follow the inner light in interpreting the Scriptures. Adherents follow the leadership of inspired prophets and believe in several divine incarnations. The sect was founded in 1785. In 1898, because of persecution, thousands of the Dukhobors migrated to Canada.

DUMAH In the Cabala, the angel of silence or death.

DUMUZI In Sumerian religion, the shepherd-god who was in charge of stables and sheepfolds. He is the god of vegetation, whose death is lamented by Ishtar. This myth coincides with the Greek cult of Demeter and her daughter Persephone. Dumuzi is the Babylonian Tammuz.

DUSTCHARITA A Sanskrit word denoting the 'ten evil acts', three acts of the body (taking life, theft, adultery); four evil acts of the mouth (lying, exaggeration in accusations, slander, foolish talk); and three evil acts of mind (envy, malice, unbelief).

DXUI Among the African Bushmen, the first spirit of creation. When the sun rose, he was a flower upon which the birds fed until sunset, when he lay down and slept. When the sun rose again, he was another, larger kind of flower. Subsequently he underwent various transformations, becoming a man, a palm, many different species of plants, water, a bird, and finally a lizard. The process of unending change and renewal in recorded accounts of Dxui stresses the fact that the first spirit of creation is forever committed to life on earth.

DYAUS The sky god of the primitive Indo-European peoples. The term also denotes the father of Dawn, Fire, and other luminous gods, an image which appears in various branches of the Aryan religions.

DYNAMISM A word coined by A. Bertholet to replace Marett's 'preanimism,' denoting a primitive power of abstraction leading to the idea of an impersonal force which resides in persons, objects, gods, etc. The notion of such an impersonal power (*mana, orenda,* or *wakonda*) survives in early religions of the Near East and remained dominant in magic until the Renaissance.

DYNAMISTIC SACRIFICIAL RITUAL The practice of extolling in hyperbolic terms the qualities and symbolic meaning of an animal to be sacrificed. In ancient Babylonia, for example, a black bull was sacrificed in the ritual of the temple musician. The bull was symbolically designated as the great cosmic bull, companion of Ningizzida and decider of fate. Similarly, all the parts of the body of Ninurta, the Babylonian war god, were associated with the lesser deities of the pantheon: Enlil and Ninlil were his two eyes, Ishtar his chin, etc.

DZEWANA An ancient Polish goddess whose functions and attributes are not known. Identified with Diana.

DZYDZILELYA An ancient Polish goddess whose functions are not known. Identified with Venus.

E

EA The chief deity of ancient Eridu, he later was incorporated in the supreme triad with Anu and Enlil in the Babylonian system. He was the god of the underground waters, giver of arts and sciences, healer of the sick, creator of the earth and man, champion of the good powers in the struggle against Tiamat, the ocean. He told Utnapishtim of the impending flood and urged him to save his family in a ship.

EARTH In Norse religion, the earth was made from the body of the giant Ymir.

EARTH-GODS In polytheistic religions Earth is commonly reverenced as the source of all good things, a conception which leads easily to the cult of Earth-gods. Sometimes the Earth-deities are thought to animate physical substance, sometimes to assume anthropomorphic features. Among them are the Greek Demeter, the Teutonic Nerthus, the Babylonian En-lil, and the Mexican Centeotl, a god of corn. The great goddess of the old Cretan religion and the three great mother-goddesses of the Semitic lands, Astarte (Ashtarte), Istar (Ishtar) and Anath (Anat), are supposed to have been Earth deities.

ECHO In Greek mythology, an oread who pined away for love of Narcissus, until at last only her voice remained.

EDDAS Knowledge of Norse religion is derived mainly from two sources: The Prose Edda, also called The Younger Edda; and The Poetic or The Elder Edda. The former Edda belongs in the thirteenth century, while the latter is assigned traditionally to the twelfth century.

107

EGALMAH The 'Great Palace' of Uruk, a city-state of Sumer lying between Babylon and Ur. Called Erech in the Bible, it contained large temples for the worship of Ishtar and Anu. It was also the seat of kings, of whom Gilgamesh was the fifth.

EGERIA A nymph from whom Pompilius was said to have received instructions concerning the establishment of public worship in Rome.

EGYPTIAN AFTERLIFE Ancient Egyptian religion believed that at death the *ba* or soul and the *ka,* the double of the deceased, could live on if the body was preserved. Hence arose the practice of mummification of the corpse, sheltering it in a tomb, and providing food for its sustenance.

EGYPTIAN ART In Egypt, art and literature were closely linked with religion. Every work of art, in line or word, had a purpose in the overall scheme of things, which was pre-eminently religious. From the simplest tale to the tallest pyramid, art tended to stress the centrality of Egypt within the universe and the supremacy of the divine king who ruled Egypt.

EGYPTIAN BELIEFS Many beliefs incorporated in the Egyptian *Book of the Dead* were anciently taken from other nations. They may also have been introduced from Asian territories. It is not known, however, who these immigrants into Egypt may have been.

EGYPTIAN COSMOGONIES In the Memphite ennead, Ptah is the creator of eight deities. The second and third of the lesser gods united to create Atum, the chief god of Heliopolis, through whose creative word everything came into being. The Memphite system dates from about three thousand years B.C. and incorporates primitive dynamism in the form of the creative word. In the cosmogony of Heliopolis, the sun god Atum arose from Nun, the ocean, before heaven and earth had been created. After climbing a hill and discovering that he was alone, he masturbated in order to create a companion. He conceived and vomited forth the air god Shu and the goddess Tefnet, whose union produced Geb and Nut, parents of Osiris and Isis as well as of Seth and Nephthys.

EGYPTIAN CREATION In Egyptian religion, the concept of creation is identified with the manifestation of the heart and tongue of the god Ptah.

EGYPTIAN DANCES In Egyptian religious ceremonials, kings performed sacred dances before their gods. For instance, Seti I danced before Sekhet. Usertsen danced before Min. Pepi I danced before Osiris.
These performances correspond to King David dancing before the Holy Ark of the Lord.

EGYPTIAN EMBALMING The Egyptians embalmed the dead in order to preserve the physical body of the deceased on earth. Or they considered that the future life of the deceased depended on the preservation of the body.

EGYPTIAN ILLUSTRATIONS In the vignettes heading the chapters of the Egyptian Book of the Dead and on other papyri, the Egyptian artist has drawn scenes relating to the text. Vignettes depict the Judgment scene in the Other World, the Elysian Fields, Sunrise and Sunset and other features associated with the journey of the dead through the Nether Regions.

EGYPTIAN INFLUENCE ON ROME Between the time of the Roman emperors Theodosius, who died in 395 A.D., and Justinian, who died in 565 A.D., pagan religion died out in Egypt. But elsewhere the cults of Isis and of Sarapis persisted for more than 500 years.
The Roman emperor Domitian, who belongs in the first century A.D., restored the Iseum, the temple of Isis and brought from the Nilotic Valley sphinxes, cynocephali, and obelisks. Hadrian too, who died in 138 A.D., celebrated his feasts with reproductions of the luxuries of Canopus. He commissioned statues of black basalt, in Egyptian style.

EGYPTIAN PRIESTS Besides their priestly functions, Egyptian priests also participated in education and training of young priests, in medicine, finance, political affairs, and in recording historical matter.

EGYPTIAN RELIGION Egyptian religion goes back to proto-historical times. The Nile and the fertility of the Nile basin became a fundamental concept in the religious system of Upper and Lower Egypt. Animals were aspects and manifestations of deities. Magic and mystery cults played a dominant role among the people. The sun, the source of light and fecundity, and the notion of rebirth as illustrated in the annual vegetation cycle, acquired a divine character. The sun had a variety of appellations, while the the Nile inundations were deified in Osiris. Myths evolved as interpretations of the phenomena of the sun and the Nile floods.

Rulers, on their death, were identified with Osiris himself, while the ruling king was equated with the deity Horus. The ennead or group of nine deities of Heliopolis was the best known. The supreme god of this group was the sun-god.

Egyptian myths, like the myths of other pagan cults, concern the origin of the deities and of the universe. The myth of Isis-Osiris is the most important of such myths.

Magic was an integral element in Egyptian religion. It was practiced regularly by the priesthood attached to each deity.

The life after death was a matter of deep concern to the Egyptians. *The Book of the Dead* — which is virtually a guide for the spirits entering the Nether Regions — contained the essence of the Egyptian concept of the afterlife. There were temples dedicated to the national gods, besides sanctuaries of local deities.

In the fifth century B.C. Egyptian religion tended largely to animal worship. Many species were endowed with sanctity, while the deities assumed the attributes of certain animals or were actually identified with them.

110

EGYPTIAN TEMPLES In Egyptian religion, the temple was the 'god's dwelling' or the 'house.' Temples were erected and maintained by decree of the ruler. Often the Egyptian temple, richly endowed, became a powerful factor in national affairs.

EGYPTIAN THEOLOGY When the official priesthood of a community tried to systematize theological thinking, the greatest god of the system became the creator. Thus at Heliopolis, the creator was Ra (Re); at Memphis, it was Ptah; at Thebes, it was Amon (Amun).

EIBE In Celtic mythology, a tree that had sanctity.

EILEITHYIA A Greek goddess of birth. She is identified by Romans with Juno.

EINHERJAR In Norse mythology, this is the collective name for all the heroes in Valhalla. On the final day of the world they will support the gods against the giants.

EIR In Norse mythology, the goddess who presided over healing. This young goddess also acted as physician to the other gods. Her variant name was Eira.

EK CHUAH In Maya religion, a god of war and of merchants.

EKISHNUGAL A temple complex in the city of Ur, dedicated to the tutelary deity of the city, the moon god Nanna.

EKUR In the Sumerian religion, the Ekur was a temple in the city of Nippur dedicated to Enlil, god of the air.

ELDER EDDA The Elder Edda is a collection of poems known as The Poetic Edda. The subjects of these poems are the myths of the gods and the legends of heroes. They were composed between 800 and 1200 A.D., in Icelandic and Norwegian.

111

ELEGBA An erotic deity to whom the Yorubas believed that they were performing a sacrifice when they were circumcised.

ELEUSINIA A Greek festival held in honor of Demeter (Ceres). The festival was celebrated at Eleusis, in Attica: then it was transferred to Rome, where it was observed until the reign of the Emperor Theodosius in the fourth century A.D. The festival was part of a mystery cult, wrapped in secrecy and scrupulously guarded against profane eyes. The mystery cult revolved around the vegetation myth of Demeter and her daughter Persephone.
Both sexes were initiated into the rites. The cult promised happiness after death. Various mystic and dramatic performances took place at appointed times. The hierophants were required to observe chastity and celibacy during the period of the festival and also to perform certain prescribed rituals. They tended the altar, offered sacrifices. In Greece the festival continued for nine days.

ELEUSINIAN INITIATES In the Eleusinian mysteries men, women and children were eligible for initiation into this mystery cult.

ELEUSINIAN MYSTERIES In ancient Greek religion, the cult of Demeter was associated with the city of Eleusis. The members of the cult comprised a triad: Demeter, Kore the Maid, that is, Persephone, the daughter of Demeter, and Triptolemus, an agricultural deity.

ELISSA A Tyrian princess, reputed founder of Carthage. She is better known as Dido.

ELIVAGAR In the cosmogony of the Norsemen, the icy, poisonous streams flowing from Nifelheim into Ginnungagap (Chaos).

ELYSIUM In Homer's *Odyssey* and in Hesiod Elysium is a Greek paradise. 'No snow is there, nor yet great great storm, nor any rain; but always ocean sends forth the breeze of the shrill West to blow cool on men.' In later times, the Greek poets set Elysium in the Underworld. Vergil, the Roman epic poet, followed this concept.

EMESH AND ENTEN A Sumerian myth which resembles the biblical account of Cain and Abel. Enil, the leader of the Sumerian pantheon, wishes to establish prosperity in the land. He assigns specific duties to the two cultural beings he has created for this purpose. They quarrel and take their case to Enlil, who decides in favor of Enten.

EMPANDA A Roman goddess who presided over villages and towns.

ENBILULU In Sumerian religion, the god who was in charge of the waters.

EN-GAI The supreme being of the Masai.

ENGASTRIMUTHI The priestesses of Apollo who uttered the oracles of the god without moving the lips.

ENKI The Sumerian god of wisdom and of the sweet waters. He was the benefactor of humanity and a patron of the arts.

ENKI AND NINHURSAG A Sumerian myth containing elements which reappear in the biblical account of the Garden of Eden. The Sumerian Paradise is called Dilmun. Trouble occurs after Enki, the water god, brings fruits to Uttu, his great-granddaughter, then commits the sinful act of eating eight plants plucked for him by his messenger, the two-faced god Isimud. Ninhursag utters a curse against Enki, saying that until he dies she will not look upon him with the 'eye of life.'

ENKINDU In Sumerian religion, the god who presided over the ploughing of the fields.
In Mesopotamian mythology, the friend and faithful companion of Gilgamesh. His death caused the hero of the famous epic of Gilgamesh, which contains the story of the

113

Flood, to set out on his quest for the secret of life and death.

ENLIL A storm god of Sumerian origin. In the supreme triad of the Babylonian system he had authority over the earth and upper air, Ea the waters under the earth, and An the heavens above the earth. He replaced Ninib, the sun god, at Nippur. He was later identified by the Babylonians and with Assur by the Assyrians. His name became synonymous with that of the Canaanite Baal.

ENLIL AND NINLIL A Sumerian myth which tells the story of Enlil, the air god, and Ninlil, the air goddess, who unite to produce the moon god Nanna. Afterwards, Enlil is banished to the underworld. Ninlil follows him, is impregnated by him under three different guises, and gives birth to three underworld deities, Nergal, Ninazu, and a third deity whose name is destroyed in the text.

ENNEAD In Egyptian religion, the nine gods who composed the Egyptian pantheon. They were Ra the sun god, Tefnut and Shu, Geb and Nut, Isis and Osiris, Set and Nephthys.

ENUMA ELISH The Mesopotamian myth of creation, set forth in a long Akkadian poem known from its two opening words ('When above'). It dates from the first dynasty of Babylon and seeks to glorify Marduk, supreme god and creator of the universe. In the beginning, according to the poem, there was only the primeval sweet-water ocean, personified by Apsu, and the primeval salt-water ocean, personified by Tiamat. These two divine principles, representing living, uncreated matter, became the father (Apsu) and mother (Tiamat) of a vast number of troublesome gods. Apsu was slain, but Tiamat continued the struggle, giving birth to a host of hideous monsters. The gods elected Marduk as their champion. He killed the mother goddess, split her body in two with his sword, and divided the waters, forming heaven and earth. He fashioned the stars, perhaps plant and animal life (portions of the text are missing), and finally mixed earth with the blood of the slain god Kingu to produce man, the servant of the gods.

114

ENYALIOS Among the Greeks of Sparta, a war-god; a variant name for Ares (Mars).

ENYO She was a Greek war goddess.

EOSTRE A Teutonic goddess. The festival of Easter is derived from her name. Her own festival took place annually, in April.

EPICTETUS A Stoic philosopher who was born in Phrygia and lived in Rome as a slave of Nero. He taught the common brotherhood of mankind and freedom from slavery of circumstance. 'Man's end,' he wrote in his *Discourses*, 'is to follow the gods.'

EPITHALAMITES In Roman mythology, the god of marriage. Mercury was invoked under this name.

EPONA A Gallic goddess who was the protectress of horses. Her cult was also known in Italy and in the Danube region. She was particularly popular among the Roman legionary soldiers.

EPOPTEIA In the Eleusinian mystery cult, this was the culmination of the sacred rites, when initiates were introduced to mystic *things said, things done, things shown.*

EQUINE GODS In ancient Greece, many deities were associated with horses and with riding the horses. In sculptural art a divinity often appears on horseback or standing beside the animal. This is the case with Castor and Pollux. Sometimes the deities are depicted astride a horse, in the air.

ERAM ESE In the headhunting cult of the inhabitants of New Guinea, the word names the special magic objects which each ancestor has left to his tribe.

ERAM OKOP In the headhunting cult of the Asmat the *eram okop,* or magic mat, is the receptacle of the inedible parts of the body, the leaves in which the mixture of brains and sago are wrapped, etc.

ERECH The site of a remarkable temple of the god Anu. Erech, like Eridu in the south and Tepe Gawra in the north, contains ruins dating from the protoliterate period of Mesopotamian civilization. The temple of the god of the heavens stood upon a forty-foot mound covering an area of more than four hundred thousand feet, dominating the plains for miles around. Near its base was a great shrine dedicated to the goddess of love and fecundity, Inanna.

ERESHKIGAL In Sumerian mythology, she performed the same functions as Persephone, Queen of the Underworld. Just as Persephone was carried off by Pluto to the Nether Regions, Ereshkigal was carried off when heaven and earth were separated.

ERI ERI (ELI ELI) In Tahunaism, the holy name of Tane, who was the son of Teave, the Primordial God of the Sun.

ERINNYES (FURIES) Avenging deities credited by the Greeks with bringing retribution upon those who violated certain laws or customs.

ERIS In Greek mythology, the goddess who provoked discord and rivalry. She is the daughter of Night, and her offspring are Disputes, Lawlessness, and Slaughter.

EROS (CUPID) In classical legend, the son of Aphrodite (Venus). God of love.

ERPET In Egyptian religion, a term applied to the god Geb as the primal ancestor of the gods.

ESKIMO RELIGION Present-day Eskimos are Christianized, but they have a common heritage based on shamanism coupled with animism. Shamans used amulets and charms to ward off evil spirits, and fear of the spirit world to rule the people. The old religion was free of excessive ritual but interwoven with folklore. The old semireligious ceremonies persist as pastimes and express in original form historical events and tales of prowess which make up a cultural heritage uniting all areas of the Eskimo country.

ESSENCE OF MYSTERY CULTS The principal purpose of all mystery cults was to produce symbols of death and of resurrection.

ESSENES A small sect of some four thousand pre-Christian Gnostics scattered throughout the villages of Palestine. Their ascetic views set them apart from other Jews. Initiation into the sect involved a long period of isolation after the novice had received his hatchet, girdle, and white garment. They abjured marriage, practiced the fullest community of goods, lived by manual labor, forbade conversation on nonspiritual matters before sunrise, and introduced a fantastic method of interpreting sacred writings which was revived by the Cabalists of the Middle Ages.

ESUS A god worshipped by the ancient Druids.

ETANA In Babylonian mythology, a heroic figure who attempted to reach heaven in an eagle's claws. Together with the eagle, he fell into the sea. The myth corresponds to the Greek tale of Icarus, the son of Daedalus, who sought to reach the Sun God.

ETEMENANKI The temple-tower of Babylon was one of the wonders of the ancient world. The name means 'the House of the Foundation Platform of Heaven and Earth.' In an Ugaritic saga of the fifteenth century B.C., King Pabel (for *Babel*) is represented as a legendary figure. In Hebrew tradition, the Tower of Babel is the center from which men had dispersed throughout the world. It was destroyed by Mursilis, a Hittite king, about 1530 B.C.

ETERNAL DREAMING An Australian aboriginal term for the view of life as a continuum in which past, present, and future are essentially one.

ETHIOPIAN PANTHEON In the most ancient religion of the Semitic population of Ethiopia, the chief diety was Astar, who gradually came to represent the sky, under the influence of the Kushite cult of the sky. Alongside him were

117

Meder, mother earth, and Mahrem, the national god of war. To the divine triad was added Beher, thought by some to be the god of the sea and by others to be one aspect of Mahrem. The Ethiopian pantheon also included a number of minor local deities and spirits.

ETRUSCAN AFTERLIFE The Etruscans conceived that the dead continued their life in their tombs. In Etruscan art the dead are depicted as proceeding to the Nether Regions accompanied by monstrous demons.

Some Romans also thought that the Etruscans believed in the deification of souls.

The Etruscans themselves envisaged the Underworld under the dominion of Hades and Persephone. This was a Greek concept which, together with Italic religious beliefs, was absorbed by the Etruscans. Again, Hermes Psychopompos, Hermes the Conductor of Souls, led the dead into the Underworld.

ETRUSCAN CULT OF THE DEAD The chief of the deities of the underworld seems to have been a colossal goddess. The satanic figure of Charun (Charon) appears in many representations. The Etruscans communicated with the underworld deities by deep wells lined with stone. On sacred days the covers of the wells were lifted. The Etruscans took pains to provide the departed with the comforts and necessities of daily life.

ETRUSCAN DIVINATION As a factor in Etruscan religion, divination was highly organized. Portents and omens occurring in natural phenomena, as well as observations of animal entrails, constituted a precise priestly science that was later taken over by the Romans.

ETRUSCAN RELIGION Knowledge of this religion is still obscure and in the process of continued investigation. Information has come from inscriptions. The chief god was Tinia. The priests praticed hepatoscopy; that is, predictions were made by an examnation of the liver of sacrificed animals.

The Etruscan religion involved many forms of divination, processions, a cult of the dead, funeral games. There was a belief in the life after death. Greek and Italic deities were absorbed by the Etruscans, among them Juno, Minerva, Neptune, Apollo, Artemis. Among the Etruscan divinities were Tuchulcha, Vanth, Mantus, Voltumna (Veltna), Sethlans, Fufluns, and Tarchon. Heavenly bodies were also deified: Usil, the sun; Tiv (Tiuv), the moon.

ETRUSCAN TRIAD A group of three deities — Tinia, Uni, and Menvra. They correspond to the Roman Jupiter, Juno, and Minerva. Three temples were dedicated to this triad.

EUBAGES Among the Druids of ancient Gaul, the Eubages were the augurs or soothsayers.

EUBULEUS (EUBOULEUS) A mane of Dionysus, meaning 'of good counsel,' identified by the Orphics with the Syrian Adonis and the Infernal Zeus.

EUMENIDES This euphemistic name was given by the Greeks to the Erinnyes.

EUMOLPUS In Greek mythology, son of Poseidon, god of the sea. In Eleusis, Eumolpus was regarded as having founded the mystery cult of Demeter.

EUPHROSYNE One of the three Graces.

EURYNOMUS In Greek mythology, a deity associated with the Lower Regions.

EXORCISM The act or process of expelling evil spirits by means of magical or religious ceremonies, regularly practiced by the ancient Egyptians, Assyrians, and Babylonians. Methods used to drive out evil spirits include words or incantations, flagellation, and sacrificial acts.

EYE-IDOLS Small, thin, biscuit-like bodies surmounted by eyes in human form. Fashioned from black and white alabaster or stone, they vary in size and shape. Many of these idols have been found in Mesopotamia, at sites such as Brak, Ur, Mari, and Lagash. They probably represent the dedication of the people to an all-seeing god. One idol bears the engraving of a stag, the symbol of Ninhursag, the Sumerian goddess of childbirth. This idol, like all the others, is of uncertain interpretation.

EYE OF HORUS In Egyptian religion, a name for an aspect of Ra, the sun god. A charm worn around the neck as a protection against evil forces was called by this name.

EYE OF TEM In Egyptian religion, a name for an aspect of Ra, the sun god.

EZRA A famous Cabalist whose full name was Rabbi Azariel ben Manahem. Also known as Azareel and Azriel, he is the author of a work on the Ten Sephiroth. He lived in Spain in the twelfth century.

F

FABULINUS A Roman tutelary deity of children.

FALCON-GOD The god Horus, the falcon-god of Upper Egypt, became the major Egyptian deity.

FASTING In some pagan religions and ancient mystery rites fasting was practiced as a means of purification and achieving spiritual visions. Shamans, the priests and medicine-men of the Tunguese people, thus communicated with spirits. Consultation of the Greek oracles involved a period of fasting. But Zoroastrianism forbade the practice.

FATE In Norse mythology, three deities controlled the destiny of man. They were Urda, the Past: Verdandi, the Present: Skuld, the Future.
According to the Greek concept, Fate, *Moira,* assigns to all living things, including the gods, an individual sphere that must not be transgressed. Among the Greeks three sisters controlled destiny. Clotho spun the threads of life, Lachesis twisted the threads, and Atropos cut off the threads of life 'with her abhorred shears.'

FATHER SKY The Indo-European prototype, *Dyeus-Pater,* from which later peoples derived *Jupiter, Zeus pater,* and *Dyaus pita,* each the embodiment of goodness and power.

FAUNUS In Roman religion, a rural deity, partly human in form. He was the patron of husbandry, hunting, herding, and guardian of the secrets of nature. His priests were

121

the Luperci, who celebrated the feast of Lupercalia. Under Greek influence, Faunus was identified with Pan, the god of flocks and pastures.

FAUSTITAS A Roman goddess of fertility.

FAVISSA In Roman antiquity, the underground storage chamber of a temple. In it were stored sacred objects which were not displayed in the temple itself.

FEAR OF SLAUGHTER In the Egyptian Book of the Dead the fear of being slaughtered in the Underworld obsessed the spirits of the dead. They therefore identified each part of the body with the corresponding member belonging to a god. For instance, the head belonged to Horus, the face to Ap-uatu, the mouth to Khens-ur, the heart to Bastet, the nose to Thoth, the shoulders to Set.

FEDAHIL The lower creator in the cosmogony of the Mandaeans.

FEINN CYCLE A body of Celtic mythological lore. It depicted the supernatural exploits of the Feinn. This cycle includes Norse religious motifs and mythology.

FELLENIUS A Roman deity associated with Aquileia.

FEMALE SOCIETIES Among the Hopi Indians secret societies that admit women only are the Lakon, the Oaqol and the Marau.

FENRIR In Norse mythology, Fenrir or Fenrisulf is a wolf-like creature who is the offspring of the evil god Loki. Fenrir too is hostile to the gods. On the last day he will swallow Odin himself. But Odin's son Vidar will tear his jaws apart. Fenrir is also destined to swallow the sun.

FERENTINA A Roman goddess presiding over the town of Ferentium.

FERHO The highest creative power among the Mandaeans.

FERONIA A Roman goddess of the woods; perhaps of Etruscan origin. She had the care of trees. Her temple stood in a grove. At her shrine slaves were set free.

FESTIVALS In Egyptian religion festivals played a significant role among the people. The most impressive festival was associated with the procession of the solar boat.
In Greece, festivals were associated with the divine protectors of the city and with vegetation deities.
In Rome, such festivals were dedicated to the domestic deities, and later to the deified emperors.
In Polynesian festivals tribal dances and feasts are special features. In Asiatic countries the New Year holds a special significance: so with domestic events such as the birth of a child, initiation ceremonies, marriage.
In Greek religion, worship of the gods possessed special features, rituals, ceremonials. Demeter had her Thesmophoria, a festival that only women observed. The principal celebration of Apollo was the Targelia. Hera had her Herrera, held at Argos.

FETISHISM Any form of belief in fetishes, which are material substances or objects assumed to be the abode of supernatural spirits or powers. The essential idea of fetishism, that spiritual powers reside in material objects, finds expression in the reverence of primitive and advanced peoples for sacred places, trees, relics, etc. The mistletoe of the Druids, the Cross, and great numbers of amulets and charms attest to the tendency to adopt fetishistic beliefs. The word *fetishism* is derived from Portuguese *feitico,* which first meant a charm and was applied to relics, rosaries, and images thought to possess magic qualities. Portuguese explorers applied the word to objects worshipped by the natives of West Africa. Fetishism was used by Auguste Comte to explain his theory of early religion. He believed that primitive men could reach the stage of star worship without a priesthood. Fetishism, according to him, allowed free exercise to man's innate tendency to attribute to all external bodies 'a life analogous to his own with a difference of mere intensity.'

123

FEVER DEMON The demon most feared by the Mesopotamians had the head of a lion, the teeth of an ass, and the limbs of a panther. His hands held terrible serpents, and a black pig and a dog nibbled at his breasts.

FIALAR In Norse mythology, one of the two dwarfs who killed the wise Quaser.

FIELDS OF AARU In Egyptian religion, the reference is to the Sekhet-hetepet, the Elysian Fields. Here the spirits of the dead dwell in everlasting happiness.

FIG-TREE In ancient primitive religion, the fig-tree has a phallic significance. In Greek mythology Dionysus planted a fig-tree at the entrance of Hades.

FINRI In Norse mythology, one of Loki's daughters.

FIRE In pagan religions fire was regarded as a sacred element. It related to the household and also the fires from heaven, particularly lightning.
Among the principal pagan deities was the god who presided over fire: Hestia in Greece, Vesta among the Romans. So with the Celts, the Incas of Peru.
One of the functions of the pagan priesthoods was the perpetual maintenance of the temple fires.

FIRE-PHILOSOPHERS The name given to Hermetists and alchemists of the Middle Ages. The name was also applied to the Rosicrucians, who regarded fire as the symbol of Deity.

FIRSTFRUITS The earliest gathered fruits of agriculture; also, the firstborn of animals and human beings. They may be offered to ancestral spirits or eaten during a religious feast. Primitive people in New Guinea, China, India, Peru, and Africa sacrifice firstborn children or eat them in solemn feast.

FISH In the Near East and in Egypt, in antiquity, fish were sacred. In Egypt priests were forbidden to eat fish. In Syria, fish were held in reverence. The goddess Atargatis had in her temples pools where fish were tended. But in Thrace the mystery cults ate fish as a sacred ritual.

FLATHINNIS Among the Druids of ancient Gaul, this was the Celtic name for Heaven.

FLAYING The act signifies transformation from a worse to a better state and is therefore a symbol of renewal and rebirth. Among the Aztecs, for examples, a young woman was decapitated and skinned, then her skin was put around a youth to represent the risen goddess. The snake casting off its skin every year is the prototype of this renewal. In classical mythology, Apollo tied to a tree and flayed Marsyas, the famous piper of Celaenae in Phrygia. Since the earliest times head-shaving (tonsure) has been associated with consecration or spiritual transformation. The priests of Isis were shaven bald.

FLOOD The Biblical narrative of the universal Flood appears, with some local variations, in many pagan religions, especially among the Babylonians, Greeks, and Romans.

FLUDD, ROBERT The chief of the fire-philosophers was generally known by his Latin name, Robertus de Fluctibus. A celebrated English philosopher and Hermetist (1574-1637), he was a voluminous writer on mystic and occult subjects.

FOHAT A term used in Tibetan Buddhism to represent the active (male) potency of the Shakti (female reproductive power) in nature.

FOLKVANG In Norse mythology, this was the palace of the goddess Freyja. The chambers perpetually resounded with love songs.

FORCULUS A Roman minor deity who was in charge of doors.

FORNAX In Roman mythology, she is the goddess who presides over ovens.

FORSETI In Norse mythology, he was the son of Balder and Nanna. He was the god of justice and reconciliation. His palace was Glitner.

FORTY-TWO GODS In Egyptian religion, a deceased person, on his passage through the Other World, addressed forty-two different gods. Their function was to punish the sins associated with their names.

FOUR GODS In Egyptian religion, these were the four sons of Horus, the four glorious gods.

FRAVASHI In Zoroastrian religion, the guardian spirit of a Zoroastrian.

FREKI In Norse mythology, one of the two wolves that accompanied the god Odin.

FREY (FREYRA) In Norse religion, god of fertility, son of Njord, and consort of Gerda. His cult, which had its main seat at Uppsala, is related to that of the Ingaevonic Nerthus. His wife is Gerda. He is also the god of fertility, rain, and sunshine. Associated with his cult were phallic rites. His worship centered in Uppsala, in Sweden. He required human sacrifices. His chariot was drawn by the boar Gullinbursti.

FREYJA The Norse goddess of fertility and love. In her functions, she corresponds to Venus. She was the daughter of Njord and the sister of Freyr. Her abode was in the palace of Folkvang, at Uppsala. Friday is derived from her name and this day was dedicated to her. Also known as Freja and Freya.

FRIGGA In Norse mythology, Frigga was the wife of the supreme god Odin. She was the mother of Thor. One of her functions was to preside over conjugal love. She was also regarded as goddess of the earth and the air.

FROGS In Egyptian religion, frogs symbolize the resurrection of the body. Representations of frogs were used frequently as amulets.

FROST GIANTS In Norse mythology, the Frost Giants (Hrim-thurses) are the great builders, the Cyclopes and Titans of the Edda. They build a strong wall around Asgard to protect it from the Jotuns, the wicked giants.

FUFLUNS In Etruscan religion, a local deity worshipped at Populonia. He was later associated with Dionysus and Bacchus.

FUJIYAMA Mount Fujiyama is the most venerated sacred mountain of Japan. It is described in *Manyo-shiu* as 'a wondrous deity and guardian of the land of Japan.'

FUNCTIONS OF DEITIES Marcus Terentius Varro (116-27 B.C.), the Roman encyclopedist, calculated that the number of deities had reached some 30,000. In the course of time other deities were added to each national pantheon, each with individualized attributes.
Among the various categories of divinities may be listed the following:
heavenly gods (Jupiter, Venus, Apollo, Mercury);
gods of the Lower Regions (Pluto, Proserpina, Hecate);
gods of the woodlands (Pan, Priapus, Satyrs, Flora);
gods of the sea (Neptune, Thetis, Proteus, Triton).

FUNCTIONS OF SHAMAN Among Eskimos, the shaman provides food, animals and fish, and he also cures sickness. He can change the weather, prophecy the future, and resist sorcerers.

FUNERARY RECITAL In the Egyptian Book of the Dead, sixty-four gods are invoked in behalf of the deceased as he passes through various stages in the Underworld. The god Osiris is addressed by fifty names identifying him with every place where he decides to be.

FUNERARY RITUALS In ancient Egypt, burial rites were accompanied by formulaic prayers to the gods of the dead and by apotropaic petitions and recitals for protection of the deceased against reptiles, wild beasts and other hostile creatures.

FURIES In Roman mythology, the three goddesses of vengeance. They were named Alecto, Megaera, and Tisiphone. See Erinyes.

FYLGJA In Norse mythology, the *alter ego* of a man. Similar to the Egyptian *ka*.

G

GAEA In Greek religion, an earth goddess who was the object of many local cults. She was the daughter of Chaos and mother of Uranus and the Titans.

GALAR In Norse mythology, one of the two dwarfs who killed the wise Quaser.

GALLI The name given to the priests of the Phrygian goddess Cybele, *Magna Mater Deorum*, the Mighty Mother of the Gods. The Galli smeared the statue of the goddess with blood when they castrated themselves in dedication to the divinity. They also sprinkled the blood on their fellow priests, and even drank it as a symbol of their total immersion in the identity of the goddess.

The Galli performed services as temple attendants. Some, too, became wandering mendicants.

The same type of eunuch-acolytes were attached to the worship of the goddess Atargatis, who was associated, like Cybele, with a Phrygian mystery cult.

The Roman poet Gaius Valerius Catullus (c. 84 B.C. - c. 54 B.C.) describes, in his poem *Attis,* how in a delirium of passion a youth castrated himself to become a Gallus, a eunuch-acolyte of Cybele:

Across the roaring ocean with heart and with eye of flame,
To the Phrygian forest Attis in an eager frenzy came:
And he leapt from his lofty vessel, and he stood in the
    groves of pine
That circled round with shadows Cybele's mystic shrine:
And there in a frantic fury, as one whose sense has flown,
He robbed himself of his manhood with an edge of
    sharpened stone.

But as soon as he felt his body bereft of its manly worth,
And saw the red blood trickle on the virgin soil of earth,
With his blanched and womanish fingers a timbrel he gan
   to smite
(A timbrel, a shawn, Cybele, thine, mother, O thine the
   rite!),
And he beat the hollow ox-hide with a furious feminine
   hand,
As he cried in trembling accents to the listening Gallic
   band:

"Arise, away, ye Gallae! to Cybele's lofty grove!
Together away, ye straylings of our Lady of Dindyma's
   drove!
Who have sought with me, like exiles, a far and a foreign
   home:
Who have borne with me the buffets of the sea and the
   fleeting foam:
Who have followed me, your leader, through the savage
   storms of night:
Who have robbed your frames of manhood in dainty love's
   despite.
Make glad the soul of our Lady with the rapid mazy dance.
Away with slothful loitering. Together arise, advance
To Cybele's Phrygian forest, to the Goddess's Phrygian
   home,
Where ring the clanging cymbals, where echoes the
   bellowing drum,
Where slow the Phrygian minstrel on his reed drones deep
   and dread,
Where the Maenad tosses wildly her ivy-encinctured head,
Where the mystic rites of the Goddess with piercing shrieks
   they greet,
Where our Lady's vagrant votaries together are wont to
   meet —
Thither must we betake us with triply-twinkling feet."
And thus to his eager comrades the unsexed Attis cries,
In a sudden shriek the chorus with quivering tongue replies:
The hollow timbrel bellows, the tinkling cymbals ring.
Up Ida's slopes the Gallae with feverish footsteps spring.

At their head goes frantic, panting, as one whose senses
    rove,
With his timbrel, fragile Attis, their guide through the
    glimmering grove,
Like a heifer that shuns, unbroken, the yoke's unaccus-
    tomed weight;
And with hurrying feet impetuous the Gallae follow
    straight.

So, when Cybele's precinct they reached in the inmost
    wood,
With over-travail wearied they slept without taste of food.
On their eyelids easy Slumber with gliding languor crept,
And their spirit's fanatic ecstasy went from them as they
    slept.
But when golden-visaged Phoebus with radiant eyes again
Surveyed the fleecy aether, solid land, and roaring main,
And with mettlesome chargers scattered the murky shades
    of night,
Then Attis swift awakened, and Sleep fled fast from his
    sight.
(In her bossom divine Pasithea received the trembling
    sprite).
So, roused from gentle slumber and of feverish frenzy freed,
As soon as Attis pondered in heart on his passionate deed,
And with mind undimmed bethought him where he stood
    and how unmanned,
Seething in soul he hurried back to the seaward strand;
And he gazed on the waste of waste of waters, and the
    tears brimmed full in his eye;
And he thus bespake his fatherland with a plaintive,
    womanish cry:
"O fatherland that bore me. O fatherland, my home!
In an evil hour I left thee on the boundless deep to roam.
As a slave who flees his master I fled from thy nursing
    breast,
To dwell in the desolate forest upon Ida's rugged crest:
To lurk in the snows of Ida, by the wild beast's frozen lair:
To haunt the lonely thickets in the icy upper air.

O where dost thou lie, my fatherland, in the ocean's broad expanse?
For my very eyeball hungers upon thee to turn its glance.
While my soul for a little moment is free from its frenzied trance,
Shall I from my home be hurried to this grove so far away?
So far from my goods and my country, from my kith and my kin shall stray?
From the games and the crowded market, from the course and the wrestling-plain?
Ah, hapless, hapless Attis, thou must mourn it again and again.
For what form or fashion is there, what sex that I have not known?
I was a child and a stripling, a youth, and a man full grown:
I was the flower of the athletes, the pride of the wrestlers' zone.
My gates were thronged with comrades, my threshold warm with feet;
My home was fair encircled with flowery garlands sweet,
When I rose from my couch at sunrise the smiling day to greet.
Shall I be our Lady's bondmaid? a slave at Cybele's hand?
Shall I be a sexless Maenad, a minion, a thing unmanned?
Shall I dwell on the icy ridges under Ida's chilly blast?
Shall I pass my days in the shadows that the Phrygian summits cast,
With the stag that haunts the forest, with the boar that roams the glade?
Even now my soul repents me: even now is my fury stayed."

From the rosy lips of Attis such plaint forth issuing flowed,
And straight the rebellious message rose up to the Gods' abode.
From the brawny neck of her lion Cybele loosed the yoke,
And, goading on his fury, to the savage beast she spoke:
"Up, up!" she cried; "dash onward! Drive back with a panic fear,
Drive back to the lonely wilderness, the wretch who lingers here!

Who dares to flee so lightly from the doom that I impose!
Lash, lash thy side in anger with thine own impetuous
    blows!
Let the din of thy savage bellowing roar loud on the
    startled plain,
And thick on thy tawny shoulders shake fierce thy shaggy
    mane!"

So threatening spoke Cybele and loosed from his neck
    the yoke;
And the brute, himself inciting, with a roar through the
    thicket broke:
And lashed his side in anger, and he rushed to the hoary
    main
Till he found the fragile Attis by the shore of the watery
    plain:
Then he gave one bound. But Attis fled back to the grove
    aghast.
There all the days of his lifetime as Cybele's thrall he
    passed.
Goddess! Mighty Goddess! Cybele! who rulest Dindyma's
    height,
Far from my home, Lady, let thy maddening wrath alight!
Upon others rain thy frenzy! Upon others wreak thy might!

(Grant Allen)

GAMADEVAS In Hindu mythology, a class of celestial beings who rule our Kalpa (Cycle), equivalent to one Day of Brahma.

GAMEWAY CEREMONIALS Among the Navaho Indians, these were magic hunting rites.

GANDHARVAS In Hindu mythology, the celestial choristers and musicians who revealed the secrets of heaven and earth to mortals. They had charge of the sacred soma plant and its juice, the ambrosia used in the temple to confer 'omniscience.'

133

In the Vedas, a very old figure, said to be the measurer of space and a relative of the sun. In the Avesta, he is a dragon-like monster. In later times the Gandharvas are represented as divine musicians in Indra's heaven.

GANESA In Hinduism, the elephant-headed god of wisdom, the son of Siva.

GARM In Teutonic mythology, a creature with four eyes and blood-dripping jaws. He is the Hell Hound, similar to the classical Cerberus.

GARMIR In Norse mythology, the hell hound of the Underworld. His abode is Helheim, the home of the dead. On the last day of the world, he fights against the principal deities. He will be killed by the god Tir, who at the same time is destined to lose his own life.

GATA The place reserved for divination by the African *nganga*. Here the witch doctor casts his *hakata* on the ground and studies the patterns formed by the individual pieces of the set.

GATHAS In Zoroastrian religion, the gathas are the oldest part of the Avesta, the sacred writings. There are seventeen hymns arranged into five groups or gathas. They preserve the most authentic form of Zoroastrian teaching.

GAYATRI The most popular of the mantras used by orthodox Hindus. The famous prayer, taken from the Rig-Veda, is repeated daily: 'Let us meditate on the adorable splendor of Savitar; may he enlighten our minds.'

GAYOMART In Mazdean religion, Gayomart died and then produced creation, like Attis.

GEB The Egyptian god of the earth. Husband of his sister Nut, the sky-goddess. His parents were Isis and Osiris. Geb is represented as a bearded figure with a goose perched on his head.

134

GEBURAH A Cabalistic term denoting the fifth Sephira, a passive, female potency.

GEDA Among the ancient Britons, a deity whose functions are not known.

GEFION A Teutonic virgin goddess. She was the patroness of all virgins. At their death, she took them into her service.

GELUG The form of Tibetan Buddhism which followed Kagyud and preceded Langdarma.

GELUKPA The highest and most orthodox Buddhist sect in Tibet. The literal meaning of the word is 'Yellow Caps.'

GEMATRIA A division of the practical Cabala. It shows the numerical value of Hebrew words by adding the values of their letters, and it uses the same principle to show analogies between words and phrases.

GEPHEN In Canaanite religion, a personification of the vine; messenger of the god Baal.

GERDA In Norse mythology, a goddess who symbolized the frozen earth. She was the consort of Frey.

GERI In Norse mythology, one of the two wolves that accompanied the god Odin. Their food was given to them by Odin, who drank wine only.

GEROVIT A Slavic war god.

GHARMA A title of Kartikeya, the war god of Hindu mythology.

GHOST DANCE Among American Indians the ghost dance was a ceremony in which the dancers regarded themselves as being in touch with the dead.
The cult of the Ghost Dance, or 'Messiah religion,' originated in 1889 in the doctrine of Wovoka, the Indian Mes-

siah, who taught that a millennium was at hand in which all Indians would be 'reunited upon a regenerated earth, to live a life of aboriginal happiness, forever free from death, disease and misery.' The chief rite of the new religion was the Ghost Dance, which relied on trance and vision to establish communication between the dancer and the spirits of the departed.

GHOST LAND Royal wives, relatives, and servants were expected to accompany a deceased ruler into *Obio Ekpu,* or Ghost Land, according to Nigerian custom. Human sacrifice was finally corrupted into an instrument for consolidating political power.

GHOSTS In ancient Greek religion, the Greeks acknowledged ghostly and evil spirits that harassed human beings. Among such monstrous creatures were Kurko, Sybaris, Empousa, Gello, and Mormo.

GHOSTWAY CEREMONIALS Among the Navaho Indians, these were magic rites.

GIALLAR In Norse mythology, the trumpet that Heimdal, god of light, blows to announce the arrival of the gods in Valhalla.

GIBIL In Assyro-Babylonia religion, a god of fire.

GILGAMESH A famous Sumerian epic which recounts the life of a legendary king of Urak. Gilgamesh undertook a hazardous pilgrimage to find Utnapishtim, the immortal, and learn the answer to the eternal question. His mission was doomed to failure, for even though he talked with Utnapishtim and obtained the plant of life, it was stolen from him by a serpent. Utnapishtim explained his own immortality by relating the story of the Flood which, purified of its polytheistic elements, was incorporated into the story related in the Book of Genesis. The poem itself probably predates the invention of writing.

GINNUNGA GAP In Norse mythology, the primal chaos from which all things sprang.

GISHKHUR A Sumerian word designating the divine plan of the universe.

GIZZIDA In Babylonian religion, the father of Tammuz, who died with the plants in winter and revived with them with the arrival of spring. Like his son, Gizzida was a vegetation god.

GJOLL In Teutonic religion, the river of Hell. It is guarded by the dog Garm.

GLADSHEIM In Norse mythology, this was the abode of joy. Here the gods indulged in wrestling and banqueting.

GLITNIR In Norse mythology, the palace of the god Forseti.

GNA In Norse mythology, the swift messenger of the goddess Frigg.

GNOMES The Rosicrucian name for the spirits of the elements.

GNOSTICISM A religious system that postulated the concept of absolute and complete knowledge. The name stems from the Greek term *gnosis, knowledge.*
Gnosticism attempted to expound man and the universe by emanations, whose source was the One Supreme Being. An esoteric cult, it was confined to initiates who were distributed among some seventy sects in the early centuries of the Christian era. To the gnostic, matter was evil. Hence some gnostics practiced asceticism and other austerities, while others considered themselves superior to the normal moral code. Gnosticism was compounded of several religious and moral elements, including Neoplatonic concepts and Judaic beliefs. In a later age it turned to magic practices. The Gnostics were largely associated with Alexandria, in Egypt. Among the most notable adherents were Marcion, Bardesanes, Valentinus, and Carpocrates.

GO A Greek mystery cult that was observed at Phlya. It celebrated the deity Go.

137

GOD AT THE TOP OF THE STAIRCASE In Egyptian religion, this was a descriptive title of the god Osiris.

GODDESS OF HEALING A deity who was worshipped in prehistoric Greece in Minoan-Mycenaean times.

GODDESS OF THE MOUNTAINS A goddess who was worshipped in prehistoric Greece in Minoan-Mycenaean times.

GODDESS OF THE SEAS A goddess who was worshipped in prehistoric Greece in Minoan-Mycenaean times.

GODS AND ANIMALS Among the Greeks and Romans, certain animals and birds were associated with individual deities. The eagle was the bird of Jupiter. The peacock and the cow were associated with Juno; the wolf and the woodpecker with Mars; the swan with Apollo; the dove and the sparrow with Venus.

GOHEI In Shinto, the *gohei* is a small pole or wood or bamboo fitted with a paper or cloth. It is a substitute for an offering of fibre cloth, offered to the gods of old on the branch of a tree. It is a symbol of sanctity and is found in every temple.

GOGARD In the Avesta, the Tree of Life.

GOHONZON A small wooden altar containing a replica of the *Dai-Gohonzon,* the original prayer scroll enshrined in the main temple of the Soka Gakkai, the Taisekiji Temple in Japan. Adherents of the Soka Gakkai sect place themselves before the altar and chant the *Daimoku.*

GOLDEN BOUGH In Graeco-Roman tradition, the Golden Bough was plucked by Aeneas before he descended to the underworld. It was supposed to be a certain bough in a grove near Aricia, on the shores of Lake Nemi, where the most famous shrine of Diana stood. The officiating priest at the shrine was the 'King of the Wood.' Before succeeding to the office he had to slay the reigning king in a duel, a feat which he could accomplish only after plucking the golden bough. Sir James George Frazer started from the mysterious ritual of the wood divinities at Nemi and elaborated a series of studies in primitive religion, his monumental *The Golden Bough*. The book contains detailed accounts of an amazing variety of religious cults devised by man to control celestial bodies and terrestrial elements, leading to the development of what has been termed the vitalistic view of religion.

GONPA In Tibet, a temple or monastery; a lamasery.

GOSPEL OF TRUTH A mystical treatise that belongs in the corpus of Gnostic writings.

GRACES In Greek mythology, three maidens who attended Eros, Aprhodite, and Dionysus. They were named Aglaia (Brilliance), Euphrosyne (Joy), and Thalia (Bloom).

GREAL In the ancient mythology of Britain, this was a magic drink that gave inspiration. It was prepared by Ceridwen, a fertility-goddess, from the juices of six plants.

GREAT GODDESS The Minoans are considered to have worshipped a Great Goddess who ruled over the universe, including the Nether Regions. Most other nature cults included the mother goddess, or Great Goddess, as a central figure. In the Mediterranean area, the traditional mother goddesses were Astarte in Phoenicia, Isis in Egypt, Cybele in Phrygia, Dana in the Celtic lands, and Demeter in Greece. Though Cybele was the only one to be given the official sanction of the state, every mystery religion except Mithraism (which was for men only) had a mother goddess.

GREAT HOUSE In Egyptian religion, The Great House was a variant name for the Hall of Judgment in the Underworld.

GREAT WITCH OF BALWERY The name popularly given to Margaret Aiken, a sixteenth-century Scotswoman who, in order to save her own life, went about the country detecting other so-called emissaries of the Devil.

GREEK RELIGION Greek religion is a syncretism of many local rites and cults, along with Minoan-Mycenaean cults. Deities were also absorbed into Greek religion from Cyprus, Anatolia, and other areas of Asia Minor. The Homeric epics consolidate religious beliefs into a common religion, with the Olympian gods headed by Zeus as the central factor. In addition, the mystery cults of Dionysus, Demeter, and Orpheus furnished an assurance of salvation to the individual votary and eternal happiness in the life after death.

GREEK TEMPLES The earliest Greek temple is believed to date somewhere in the ninth century B.C. It is a one-room structure, the abode of the god and his image. The temples usually faced east.

GUD In Babylonian religion, the name of a deity. He was known as the bull-god.

GUDATRIGAKWITL The supreme deity of the Wishosk Indians of California. By the power of his mind, he brought people into existence.

GUGNER In Norse mythology, the sword that Odin uses against the wolf Fenrir.

GULA In Assyrian religion, the consort of Ninurta, the war god.

GULLVEIG In Norse mythology, a goddess whose burning by the Aesir brought about war with the Vanir. It is said in the Edda that during the Golden Age, before man developed his lust for gold, the whole earth was happy. But when the bewitching enchantress came, she arose more beautiful each time from the fire into which she was cast three times, and she filled the souls of gods and men with unappeasable longing.

GUNUNG AGUNG The holy mountain of the Balinese. The high gods are supposed to dwell at the top of the mountain.

140

GURU In India, a religious teacher; a master in metaphysical and ethical doctrines.

GUYA VIDYA The secret knowledge of mystic Mantras.

GYAN-BEN-GIAN The king of the Peris, the Sylphs, in the old mythology of Iran.

GYLFAGINNING A Norse compendium of mythology that deals with the old Nordic religion. It is composed in the form of questions and answers.

GYMIR In Norse mythology, a giant. He is father of Gerd, the consort of Freyr.

GYNAECIA A Greek goddess who corresponds to the Roman Bona Dea.

H

HAAR THE HIGH In Norse mythology, one of the members of the Norse triad.

HABAL DE GARMIN According to the Cabala, this is the Resurrection Body, an inner fundamental spiritual type remaining after death.

HACHIMAN In Shinto, the war god, identified by tradition with the Emperor Ojin. His cult has been strongly influenced by Buddhism.

HACHOSER A name for the minor powers in the Cabala. The literal meaning of the word is 'reflected lights.'

HADAD In Syrian religion, a god whose name denotes *one*. He was identified with the sun. He was also called Hadar.
As Adad or Ramman he was the Babylonian deity who presided over the winds, storms, rain, thunder and lightning. He was a beneficent divinity but he was also a war god.

HADES In Greek mythology, the god of the dead. Hades also came to mean the actual kingdom of the dead. Hades possessed all the treasures hidden in the earth. Hence he was also called by the Romans Pluto, *ploutos* in Greek meaning wealth.

HAIR In occult philosophy, hair is considered to be the natural receptacle of the vital essence which often escapes with other emanations from the body. With various sects, cutting of the hair and beard has been regarded as a sign of defilement.

In many religions, hair is given deep significance. Shaving the head signifies humiliation, punishment, or penance. The tonsure dates from the beginning of Christianity and signifies renunciation of the world. In Greece, youths offered hair to the gods at the initiation rites.

HAJASCHAR In the Cabala, the powers of light, which are creative but inferior forces.

HAKATA Bits of bone, ivory, or wood used by African witch doctors in divination and prognostication. Each piece of the set is carved with a symbol resembling a sign of the zodiac. The pieces are cast on the ground and studied by the witch doctor, who is seldom seen without his treasured hakata.

HALLELUJAH The Hallelujah religion of the Akawaio flourishes today among the Carib-speaking inhabitants of the borderlands of Brazil, Venezuela, and British Guiana. It incorporates elements of Christianity and indigenous features. A supreme, omnipotent God, prayer, and worship had no part in the traditional ritual. The essentials of the primitive Akawaio system of beliefs are expressed in three words: *akwa,* an abstract force which manifests itself as light as is symbolized by the sun; *akwalu,* the light that is within a person; and *akwalupo,* the ghost spirit, as opposed to the living spirit.

HALMASUIT In Hittite religion, a goddess representing the deified throne.

HALOA In Greek religion, a festival that was held at the beginning of January. It was associated with the cult of Demeter. Sexual symbols were displayed during the celebration.

HAMADEVA In the Hindu pantheon, the god of love.

144

HAMMEMET In Egyptian religion, heavenly beings, once human beings or not yet created human beings.

HAMMURABI The Babylonian political and military genius Hammurabi (1792-1750 B.C.) is supposed to have received his famous code from the god Shamash. The Mesopotamian god of the sun is supposed to have dictated the code to him, upon a mountain-top.

HAMSA The Universal Intelligence as personified in the vizier of Hakim, the founder of the mystic sect of the Druses of Mount Lebanon.

HANSA In Hindu mythology, the white goose (or swan), the vehicle of the Asvins and, later, of Brahma. The mystical bird is analogous in occultism to the pelican of the Rosicrucians.

HANUMAN The monkey god of the *Ramayana,* the son of Vayu, the wind god, and a she-demon. He helped Rama, the Avatar of Vishnu, to conquer Ravana, who had abducted Rama's wife Situ, bringing about the celebrated war described in the Hindu epic poem.

HAOMA In Mazdaism, a drink prepared from the juice of the haoma plant with milk and sugar. It was used in the rites of the cult, and symbolized the drink of immortality.

HAPANTALIYA In Hittite religion, he was a tutelary deity.

HAPI In Egyptian religion, one of seven deities linked with funerary rites. One of the gods of the four cardinal points, he watched over the lungs of the dead.

HAPY The Nile was personified and worshipped as Hapy.

HAR In Norse mythology, one of the variant names for Odin. It means the striker. It is also written Haar.

HARAKHTE Flying like a falcon across the heavens, the Egyptian solar deity was known as Harakhte, the 'Horus of the Horizon.' With three other Horuses he formed the four deities of the eastern sky. In the morning he was Khepera, a winged beetle rising from the east. At the end of his daily course he was Atum.

HARES In Egyptian religion, hares are symbols of eternity.

HARMACHIS In Egyptian religion, the god of the morning sun. The Great Sphinx of Giza is associated with his worship.

HARPIES Winged monsters of loathsome appearance who polluted everything they touched. Originally, they were regarded as personifications of devastating winds. In later Greek and Roman mythology, they were assigned the role of snatching up the souls of the dead and executing divine vengeance. They were names Aëllo, Ocypete, and Celaeno.

HARPOCRATES The Greek name of the Egyptian sun god, the offspring of Isis and Osiris.

HARSHANA A Hindu god who presides over offerings to the dead.

HARUSPICES Among the Etruscans, they were soothsayers who interpreted weather conditions, the entrails, especially the liver, of sacrificed animals, the flight of birds, unusual phenomena. The purpose was to discover the will of the gods regarding any proposed action by human beings. These Etruscan soothsayers were later on imported into Rome, where they acquired powerful influence.

HARVEST FESTIVALS In pagan religions, grain is an embodiment of the vegetation spirit. The festival was a symbol of gratitude to the beneficent deities who protected the harvests that were vital for the sustenance of life.

HAS-BEEN, BEING, WILL-BE In Norse mythology, three maidens who shape the lives of men.

HASINA Among the Malagasy, the equivalent of mana.

146

HASIS In Canaanite religion, a variant name for Koshar, the sun-god. He built the homes of the gods and fashioned their weapons. In the latter aspect he corresponds to the Greek god Hephaestus (Vulcan).

HATEPINU In Hittite religion, the mother of Telepinu and consort of Taru.

HATHOR Egyptian goddess of many names and attributes. She is represented sometimes as a cow, at other times as a woman. Conceived as a cow-goddess, she stood embracing all four corners of the earth. She was likewise the goddess of love.

HATI and SKOLL In Norse mythology, they are the two wolf-dogs that continuously pursue the sun and the moon. Whenever they are on the point of devouring them, there is an eclipse.

HATTATAL Books of directions for poets. They form part of the Younger Edda, one of the two sources on Norse religion.

HAUMEA In Tahunaism, the reigning princess of the celestial spheres, also known as Papa.

HAVATNAAL A poem that inculcates precepts of wisdom. The traditional authorship is assigned to the Norse god Odin.

HAWAIIAN RELIGION The pre-Christian religion of the Polynesian inhabitants of Hawaii is known as Tahunaism. It is known mainly through the *Tumuripo*, a body of sacred knowledge transmitted orally and recorded only recently. Shrines, called heiau, were used in common by several cults. The priesthood served only the upper level of the community. For the people in general, there were shamans and magicians. See Tahunaism.

HAWAIKI In the central and marginal islands of Polynesia, except for Easter Island, Hawaiki is usually regarded as an ancestral homeland. Unlike Pulotu, it is not peopled with the dead.

HAYIN Another name of Koshar, a divine smith in Canaanite religion.

HEART OF RA In Egyptian religion, the heart of Ra, the sun god, was the bennu bird. The bennu bird is identified with the phoenix.

HEBAT A Hittite goddess. Her sacred animal was the lion.

HEBE In Greek religion, the goddess of youth, daughter of Zeus and Hera, and cup-bearer of the gods.

HEBON An ancient Italic deity who was identified with Bacchus.

HECATE Greek goddess of the infernal regions. She was a triple divinity: in heaven she was Luna; on earth, Diana; and Hecate in the Underworld. She was identified with the Egyptian god Anubis. At first she was represented with one face and a single body. But the Greek traveler Pausanias says that Alcamenes, in the fifth century B.C., made a triple-faced, triform statue of Hecate. At Rome dogs were sacrificed to her. One of her functions was to preside over the magic arts.
A mystery cult in her honor was observed at Aegina.
In the Orphic cult, she was revered at Eleusis. She remained the patron saint of sorcerers through the Middle Ages and Renaissance.

HECATESIA A Greek festival in honor of the goddess Hecate. In Athens it was celebrated with a public banquet during the New Moon.

HECATONCHEIRES In Greek mythology, three hundred-handed giants, Briareus, Cottus, and Gyges, sons of Uranus.

HEIDHRUN In Norse mythology, the goat that grazes on the top of the tree of the world. She nourishes the chief gods on her milk.

148

HEIMDAL In Norse mythology, he is the god of light. He is the son of Odin. At the entrance to Valhalla he guards the gods. With his trumpet he warns them of any threatening dangers. He is also the guardian of Bifrost, the bridge that stretches between heaven and earth.

HEKA In Egyptian religion, this expression denotes *words of power* or magic formulas that can achieve the wishes of the spirit of the deceased.

HEKET In Egyptian religion, she was the goddess who presided over childbirth. See Hiquet.

HELA In Norse mythology, the daughter of the evil god Loki. He was the goddess of death and presided over the Lower Regions in Nifleheim.
She was regarded as mistress of nine worlds. She had two attendants, a male called Ganglate and a maid-servant named Gangloat.

HELBLINDI In Norse religion, this is a variant name for the supreme god Odin.

HELHEIM In Norse mythology, the realm of Hel, who is goddess of the Underworld. It is a dark misty region, encircled by the river Gjoll.

HELIOPOLIS THEOLOGY Egyptian religious concepts at Heliopolis are illustrated in the Pyramid Texts and in the Book of Smiting down Apophis.

HELIOS In Greek religion, the sun god, later identified with Apollo or Phoebus. The famous colossus of Rhodes was a statue erected in his honor.

HELL The concept of Hell, the abode of the dead, varies in detail with each religion, but they all have certain significant features in common. The most detailed imaginative description appeas in Book 6 of the Roman poet Vergil's *Aeneid.*

It deals with punishments of the wicked, the Elysian Fields for the spirits of the righteous, and the transmigration of souls until perfection is attained.

HENNU In Egyptian religion, the sacred boat in which the shrine of Seker, god of the dead, was placed.

HEPATOSCOPY Divination by inspecting the liver of a sacrificial animal. It had an important part in the state religions of Babylonia and Assyria.

HEPHAESTUS (VULCAN) In classical mythology, god of fire and workman of the gods.

HERA (JUNO) Greek goddess, sisters and wife of the supreme god Zeus. She presided over marriage.

HERCULES (HERACLES) In classical mythology, the son of Zeus (Jupiter) and Alcmene. The most famous hero of antiquity, he was credited not only with the performance of the twelve labors imposed on upon him by Eurystheus but also with the liberation of Prometheus and Theseus. According to some accounts, Hercules was put on a pyre on top of Mt. Oeta. His mortal part was burned in an act reminiscent of an ancient ceremony involving both human victims and puppets in human shape. Here, as in his last two labors — bringing the golden apples of the Hesperides and bringing Cerberus up from the underworld — his acts represent the forcible seizure of immortality. In cult, Hercules is sometimes a hero, sometimes a god. Among the foreign gods with whom he was equated is the Phoenician Melqart. Athens was the first city to give him divine honors. In Italy, he was worshipped as a god of merchants and traders. His most famous cult was in the Forum Boarium of Rome.

HERMAEA In ancient Greece, this was a festival observed in honor of Hermes (Mercury).

HERMANUBIS In Egyptian religion, this was a variant name for Anubis.

HERMES (MERCURY) In classical mythology, the messenger of the gods.

HERMES TRISMEGISTUS A late name of Hermes (literally, 'Hermes thrice greatest'), as identified with the Egyptian god Thoth. He was the reputed author of many works embodying Neo-Platonic, Judaic, and Cabalistic ideas. It was applied by the Neoplatonic philosophers to the Egyptian god Thoth. Thoth was putatively considered the author of a body of treatises, religious and philosophical in content, known as *Hermetica*. These Hermetical Books were current in the third and fourth centuries A.D.
Hermes Trismegistus was also reputed to have written on magic, astrology, and alchemy. These works were actually written by Greeks who resided in Egypt. Their attribution to the Egyptian god Thoth resulted from a widespread desire to acquire the ancient secret knowledge associated with Egypt.

HERMETIC WRITINGS A body of writings, known as the Corpus Hermeticum, attributed to Hermes Trismegistus, who is identified with the Egyptian god Thoth. The writings are dialogues between Hermes and his son Tat or between Hermes and Asclepius. The first treatise in this corpus is called Poimandres. Together, these writings represent Hellenistic mysticism.

HERMETISM Hermetic speculation. Doctrines derived from the teachings of Hermes Trismegistus.

HERMETISTS They were mystics, devoted to the writings of Hermes Trismegistus. They constituted an esoteric sodality, whose purpose was to achieve mystical experience.

HERMOD Also called Hermodur. In Norse mythology, he is the son of Odin and the messenger of the gods. He has the same function as the Roman god Mercury. At the

151

death of Balder, Hermod rode on Odin's horse Sleipnir to Hell, to request Balder's resurrection.
The story is akin to the classical myth of Orpheus and Eurydice.

HERTHA In Teutonic religion, a personification of the earth. She was worshipped by the ancient Germans, Anglo-Saxons, and Norsemen. See Nerthus.

HERUKHENTIAN-MAATI In Egyptian religion, one of seven funerary divinities.

HESPERUS A personification of the evening star, worshipped with divine honors in ancient Greece. According to Hesiod, he was the son of Astraeus and Eos.

HESTIA (VESTA) Greek goddess of the hearth and domestic life.

HESUS. Also called Esus. In Celtic religion, he was the supreme god.

HIEROCORACES In Mithraism, they were the Sacred Crows, ministers of Mithra himself.

HIEROPHANT In ancient Greece, a priest, often the chief priest of the Eleusinian mysteries. He represented the Demiurge and explained to the postulants for initiation the esoteric doctrines and secrets relating to the various phenomena of creation.

HIGH GODS Cosmic deities of primitive religions. Found among many primitive peoples in all parts of the world, including Africa and South America, they may reside in heaven and be credited with the creation of the universe. They may be all-powerful and coexist with spirits.

HIGH PLACES Canaanite worshippers established sanctuaries at high points. Divinity is associated with high places in many parts of the world.

HILARIA A Roman festival, borrowed from the Greeks. It was observed on the first of April in honor of the goddess Cybele.

HILDUR In Norse mythology, she is one of the Valkyries.

HILL In Canaanite religion, the term *hill* or *high rock* was a common appellation for deity.

HILO A deity of a class of deities to whom the Apa Tanis ascribe the creation of man.

HIMINBORG In Norse mythology, a celestial city.

HINA In the Hawaiian pantheon, one of the members of the third heavenly trinity, wife of Tu, and goddess of agriculture.

HINAYANA The earliest tradition of Buddhism, based on scriptures written in Pali. Conservative, nontheistic, and dominantly monastic, it survives in Burma, Ceylon, and Thailand.

HINDU In English and Indian usage, the word designates an adherent of Hinduism.

HINDUISM The native religious and social system of India. In the broad sense in which the word is used by modern historians of religion, Hinduism reflects the entire life, past and present, of the whole people called Hindus. The religious creeds and practices of the Hindus vary immensely, and their variety has been a salient feature of Hinduism for more than three thousand years.
The kernel of Hinduism consists of two groups of ideas, the first dealing with the social system and the second with the concepts of *karma* (works or causality), *samsara* (transmigration), and *nirvana* or *moksha* (salvation).
The social system is grounded on the idea of *dharma* (duty) and caste. The only universally recognized feature of Hinduism traditionally has been the acceptance of caste

153

and everything implied by the term. Birth and conduct are more important than any single belief which has been incorporated into the religious system.

The system recognizes no creed or founder and is best described as a polymorphic theism with a philosophical background. The expression of personal religious feeling is wholly voluntary and optional. Characteristic features include — in addition to belief in karma, samsara, and nirvana — worship of images, pilgrimages, and respect for yoga, asceticism, and a personal guru.

Hinduism probably is older than the Vedas and has evolved without interruption from the Stone Age to the present. Among the many sects, all infused with Vedantic philosophy, mysticism, and pantheism, are the Shakta, Saiva, and Vaishnava. As an organized system embracing both Aryan Vedic and indigenous Dravidian features, Hinduism took shape mainly during the first century B.C.

As a faith, in the words of Jawaharlal Nehru, it has long been 'vague, amorphous, many-sided, all things to all men.' The various stages of its development are as follows: (1) Vedic Hinduism, (2) Brahmanic Hinduism, (3) Philosophic Hinduism, (4) Sectarian Hinduism, and (5) Reformed Hinduism.

HIPPONA A Roman goddess in charge of horses and stables.

HIQUET In Egyptian religion, the frog-goddess. She was one of the symbols of immortality and of the water principle. The early Christians are said to have had their lamps made in the form of a frog to denote that baptism conferred immortality. Also called Heket.

HISI The principle of evil in the *Kalevala,* Finland's epic poem.

HITTITE Fragmentary knowledge of the religion of the Hittites, who anciently occupied the highlands of Asia Minor, is derived from literary and archaeological sources. Many Hittite religious concepts and deities were borrowed from Babylonia and Egypt. The god of vegetation and of the sky, Teshub, was identified with Attis, the lover of the Mother-Goddess Ma, who was herself identified with Astarte.

HITTITE CULTS Among the Hittites, mountains were regarded as divinities. Rivers and springs were equally divine. Mountains were gods, while rivers and streams were held to be goddesses. Religious cults were associated with these natural features.

HITTITE DEITIES In Hittite religion, many deities associated with certain places bear the same name. For example, there was the weather god of the city of Nerik and the city of Samuha. In some cases, the Hittites combined a number of deities into divine families. Deities worshipped by the Hittites were associated with the different ethnic communities of ancient Anatolia. When the Hittites addressed their gods they did so in their native tongue. These native languages were: Hattili, spoken in Hatti, in Central Anatolia. Palaumnili, spoken in Pala, in Paphlagonia.
Luwili, spoken in Luwiya, in southwest Anatolia.
Hurlili, spoken by the Hurla, in southeast Anatolia.

HITTITE FEASTS Some religious feasts were associated with the seasons of the year. The king or the king and his consort usually celebrated the festival.
The sequence of a festival was as follows. First of all there was a purification, when new robes were put on in a special building used for that purpose. The king entered the temple courtyard, where religious rituals were performed. Libations were then offered in various parts of the temple chamber. When the king was seated, his insignia were placed at his side. A banquet followed, at which the god was toasted, while there was a musical accompaniment. A crowded audience watched the ceremony. Later on, the audience received a share of the food.

HITTITE MAGIC The law prohibited the practice of black magic. Infringements resulted in the death penalty. White magic so called, however, was used in purificatory rites.

155

Magical texts prove that incantations were in vogue, to banish evil spirits, the result of uncleanliness.

HITTITE MOON GOD The god of the moon was called Kasku in Protohattic, Kushah or Kushuh in Hurrian, and Arma in Hittite. His sacred animal was the lion.

HITTITE OMENS In Hittite religion, astrological and birth omens were recognized. Hepatoscopy was practiced, or predictions by the examination of the liver of a sacrificed animal. Oracles too were consulted and responses were given from observation of animal entrails, the flight of birds, and the casting of dice.

HITTITE PANTHEON The main gods of the Hittites are Protohattic: the weather god Taru, his consort Wurusemu, their daughter Mezzulla, and their granddaughter Zintuhi; the sun god Istanu and the moon god Kasku; the warriors Sulinkatte and Wurunkatte; and the tutelary gods Karzi, Hapantali, and Zithari. In addition, the pantheon included: the goddess Inar; the disappearing god Telepinu, son of the weather god, and his consort Hatepinu; Halmasuit, a goddess representing the deified throne; the queen goddess Kattaha; Kait, a goddess of grain; and Katahzipuri (Kamrusepa in Hittite), a goddess skilled in witchcraft.

HITTITE TUTELARY DEITIES In Hittite religion, tutelary deities protected cities, animals. One deity was called Lama the Shield. In the Akkadian language, Lama was a generic term for a goddess.

HLER In Norse mythology, one of the cosmic trinity. The three sons of Ymir, the Frost Giant, were Kari, god of the air and storms; Hler god of the sea; and Logi, god of the fire.

HOBOMOCO An evil spirit in the mythology of certain Algonquian tribes.

HODER In Norse mythology, Odin's blind son. A mistletoe arrow, given him by Loki, killed his brother Balder. The mistletoe arrow was the only weapon that could destroy

156

the otherwise invulnerable Balder. He is also called Hod. He is the god of night. Comparable myths appear in many mythologies.

HOHODEMI In Japanese mythology, Ninigi is said to have descended to earth and married the daughter of a mountain god. Hohodemi, their second son, is supposed to be the father of Jimmu Tenno, the first emperor.

HOLLER In Norse mythology, he was the god of death. He caused sickness and disaster. He dragged men into his cave, where he inflicted tortures on them. Also Uller.

HOLY DAYS In the ancient Roman calendar, *dies fasti* were days that permitted legal business. On the *dies nefasti* no legal business was permissible. Or, if such a transaction were negotiated, it would require an expiatory sacrifice.

HOLY MOUNTAINS In Hurrian religion, mountains were regarded as deities. The most famous was Mt. Hazzi. Another such mountain god was Mt. Namni.

HOLY PEOPLE Among the Navaho Indians, the Holy People are beings similar to humans or capable of assuming human form. They are powerful and dangerous. Each has charge of some special activity. Together they constitute the Navaho pantheon.

HOPI AFTERLIFE The Hopi Indians believe in the continuity of life after death. They conceive man as having emerged in the beginning from an underground home to the upper earth. Life in the Lower Regions is a shadowy counterpart of life on earth. The dead perform their normal functions. They till the fields, partake of food, and perform the same ceremonies as they did when alive.

HOPI CULTS Among the Hopi Indians, there are secret societies called the Flute Society, the Snake Society, the Antelope Society.

157

HOPI RITUALS Among the Hopi Indians major rituals last for nine days. They involve the erection of altars, prayer offerings dedicated to the patron gods, preparation of a medicinal liquid, smoking, dancing, singing, and, occasionally, dramatic performances.

HOPI SOCIETIES Among the Hopi Indians, every village has several secret societies, each associated with a particular ceremony. Prayers, dances, songs constitute the rituals.

HOPI VIEW OF DEATH Among Hopi Indians a dead person is regarded as one who will attain supernatural power by undergoing a change of status into a cloud or a katcina, a supernatural being.
Every Hopi ceremony involves the cult of the dead.

HORAE In Greek religion, goddesses of the seasons. According to Hesiod, they were named Dike (justice), Eirene (peace), and Eunomia (wise legislation). They represented orderliness in nature and society.

HORON In Canaanite cult, a name given to Mot, the deity who presided over death.

HORSCHIA An ancient Etruscan goddess whose functions are unknown.

HORTO A Roman goddess who exhorted men to noble enterprises.

HORUS Also called, by the Greeks, Harpocrates. Egyptian sun god. His parents were Isis and Osiris. He had a temple dedicated to his worship at Edfu. He is represented as a human form, falcon-headed, bearing a solar disc.

HOSTILINA In Roman mythology, a rustic goddess who presided over the regular growth of ears of corn.

HOTTENTOT'S GOD A name given by the early European colonists of South Africa to the praying mantis, revered by some of the aborigines of the Cape. The Europeans confused the Hottentots, who actually had a first spirit of creation of their own, with the Bushmen, who credited Mantis with the giving birth to man.

HRIMTHURSES In Norse mythology, the Frost Giants who built the strong wall around Asgard.

HRUNGNIR In Norse mythology, one of the most powerful giants who dwelt in Jotunheim. He was crushed by Thor's hammer.

HSUAN-WU The Taoist Dipper god, often symbolized by the tortoise and the snake. Most Chinese villages have erected a shrine in honor of the Lord on High in the Dark Heaven. He was immensely popular during the Han dynasty (206 B.C. - 220 A.D.).

HUACA Among the Indians of Peru, this designated an oracle.

HUANG LAO A religious movement which involved divination and alchemy, and which provided Taoism with some of its essential features.

HUEHUETEOTL In the Aztec religion, the god of fire; akin in function to the Roman god Vulcan.

HUGIN In Norse mythology, the crow that belongs to Odin. The name Hugin means 'knowledge.' At dawn Hugin traverses the world. In the evening it returns and, perched on Odin's shoulders, relates what happens on earth.

HUITZILOPOCHTLI In Aztec religion, the supreme deity. He was the sun-god and the war-god. He was depicted wearing a cloak of humming-bird feathers. At the winter solstice his festival included the sacrifice of captives.

HULDA In Teutonic mythology, she was the goddess of marriage.

HUMAN SACRIFICE The ceremonial killing of human beings is generally associated with peoples who have advanced beyond the stage of savagery. The practice of sacrificing one individual to atone for the wrongs of the group is widespread.

HUNA A Hawaiian word meaning depths or profundities and referring to the wisdom contained in the sacred chants and prayers preserved by the *tahunas.*

HUN In Chinese religion, the active, positive, or divine part of the soul.

HUNAB-KU In Maya religion, the creator god, supreme and invisible. He is the father of Itzamma. From corn he fashioned the world and the first men.

HURRIAN PANTHEON Religious texts dealing with Hurrian deities are numerous. The main gods in the Hurrian pantheon include: the weather god Teshub, his consort Hebat, and their son Sharrumma; the sun god Shimegi and the moon god Kushuh; Shaushka (Ishtar) and her attendants, Ninatta and Kulitta; the bulls Sheri and Hurri; the mountains Namni and Hazzi; and the warriors Shuwaliyatta and Ashtabi; gods of Babylonian origin, such as Nikkal (Ningal), consort of the moon god, and Aya, the wife of the sun god; and Aryan gods, such as Indra, Mitra, Varuna, the Nasatyas, and Agni, mentioned only incidentally in Hurrian writings.

HURRIANS (HORITES) An ancient tribe whose homeland was probably the region south of the Caucasus. They first appear in history about 2400 B.C., chiefly in connection with Urkish, their religious center. They exerted a strong influence on the religious life of the Hittites and passed on to them the cuneiform writing of the Babylonians as well as the epic of Gilgamesh. The Hurrians (called Horites in the Bible) adopted the principal gods of the Sumerians and Akkadians, combining them with their own to produce an extraordinary syncretism.

HUWASI In Hittite religion, Huwasi were stones that were regarded as divine symbols.

160

HUTSAB A Mesopotamian deity whose functions are not known.

HYBRISTICA A Greek festival involving sacrifices and ceremonials at which there was transvestism. The festival honored Aphrodite in a dual capacity as both god and goddess.

HYGEIA The personification of health, recognized as a goddess
by the ancient Greeks and ultimately regarded as the
daughter of Asclepius, the god of medicine and healing.

HYMEN In Greek religion, god of marriage, son of Apollo and
Urania (or, according to some, of Bacchus and Venus),
and bearer of the bridal torch.

HYPERBOREAN A mythical people associated with the cult
of Apollo. They were thought to dwell in a region of
eternal sunshine, beyond the north wind (Boreas), and to
be the favorites of Apollo, who allowed them to enjoy
everlasting youth and health.

HYPNOS (SOMNUS) Greek personification of Sleep. He was
regarded as the brother of Death. Both dwelt in the Nether
Regions.

I

IACCHAGOGI Crowned with myrtle leaves, they carried the statue of Iacchus or Bacchus at the Eleusinian Mysteries.

IALDABAOTH In alchemy, the demiurge who lies captive in the darkness of matter. He is that part of the deity that has been swallowed up in his own creation, the dark god who reverts to his original state of luminosity in the mystery of the alchemical transmutation. In Hebrew legend, he is the arch supreme archon. The Hebrew word means 'child of chaos' and suggests a parallel between Ialdabaoth and Baal, Kronos, and Saturn.
In the writings of the Gnostics, he is the evil spirit who created the Lower World.

IAMBLICHUS A Syrian Neoplatonic philosopher who was born c. 250 and died c. 325 A.D. In Rome, he studied under Porphyry, also a Syrian, who was a pupil of the Neoplatonist Plotinus. Iamblichus founded a school of his own in his native Syria. Among his other works is a noted defense of magic, entitled *De Mysteriis Aegyptiis*, The Egyptian Mystery Cults.
He initiated the attempt to construct on the basis of Neo-Platonism a complete theology encompassing every myth, rite, and divinity associated with paganism.

IANUS Among the Romans, the two-faced god of beginnings. In ceremonial prayers, he is mentioned first, before all the other gods. The month of January is derived from his name. In rituals, a ram was sacrificed to him. See Janus.

163

IAPETUS Probably a deity of pre-Hellenic origin, he seems to have been worshipped as a god by the Semites (as Japhet). In later Greek mythology he was identified as the father of Atlas, Prometheus, and Epimetheus, and as the ancestor of the human race.

IASO A Greek goddess of medicine.

IBIS The ibis was a bird that was held sacred among the Egyptians. It was considered to be the abode of the god Thoth. On its death, the ibis was often mummified as an object of worship.

IBMEL Among the Laplanders, the name for their deity.

IBN GABIROL An eleventh-century Jewish poet, philosopher, and Cabalist, Solomon Ben Judah Ibn Gabirol, also known as Avicebron, was born in Malaga and died in Valencia. His chief philosophical work *Fons Vitae* (*Fountain of Life*) introduced Neo-Platonism into Europe. In his system, universal matter emanates from the essence of God and universal form from His will. All beings are composed of matter and form. *Fons Vitae* is supposed to reveal some of the secrets of the speculative Cabala.

ICHTHUS In Greek, this term means 'fish.' It was the name given to the son of Atargatis, who is identified with Cybele. The cult of Cybele worshipped fish, and the consumption of fish was hence forbidden to her priests.

IDEA OF GOD A significant development in the recent study of the history of primitive religion has been the recognition of the worship of 'high' gods as well as of lesser divinities or spirits. High gods are found among primitive peoples in all parts of the world. They are generally considered to be all-powerful, cosmic deities who reside in

IDENTIFICATION OF HORUS The Egyptian god Horus, called by the Greeks Harpocrates, was often identified with Hercules, Eros, and Apollo.

164

heaven and may have created the world. W. Schmidt has collected much anthropological data to support the view that primitive monotheism evolved into the different theological patterns found in existing primitive cultures.

IDISI In Teutonic mythology, demoniac female spirits. Their worship was associated with seaports.

IDOLS In the eleventh century A.D., in Uppsala, Sweden, there were three idols on display: Thor, Odin, and Freyr.

IDUNA In Norse mythology, she was the young goddess who was the consort of Bragi. In Asgard she was the guardian of the apples that rejuvenated the gods.

IDWATSARA One of the five periods that form the Yuga.

IFING In Norse mythology, the broad river that divides Asgard, the home of the gods, from Jotunheim, the home of the giants.

IFURIM The island of the cold climate. In Celtic religion, this was Hell, infested with venomous and dangerous creatures. Those who had led a criminal life were confined to dark dungeons. The least guilty dwelt among heavy steaming vapors.

IGIGI In Babylonian religion, cruel heavenly spirits associated with Anu.

IKHIR BONGA Among the Kolarian tribes, a spirit of the deep.

IKSHWAKU The progenitor of the solar tribe (the Suryavansas) in India and son of Vaivaswata Manu, the progenitor of the human race.

ILA In Hindu mythology, the daughter of Vaivaswata Manu and wife of Buddha, the son of Soma. By the decree of Saraswati, Ila was a woman one month and a man the next.

165

ILAVRITI In Hindu mythology, a region in the center of which is placed Mount Neru, the habitat of the gods.

ILDA BAOTH A Gnostic term designating the creator of the earth. The literal meaning of the expression is 'the child from the egg.'

ILLAPA Also called Katoylla. The god of the underworld among the Incas.

ILLUYANKAS A Hittite myth that has come down to us in two versions associated with the festival of the Weather God of Heaven. It concerns the dragon (or snake) called Illuyankas and the Weather God. In one version Illuyankas first overcomes the Weather God but is tricked by the Protohattic goddess Inar, who invites him to a feast, and encourages him to drink too much. Illuyankas is then killed by the Weather God. In the second version, much more elaborate than the first, the Weather God kills both his own son and Illuyankas.

ILMARINEN In ancient Finland, a deity who was identified with the Roman Vulcan.

ILMATAR In the epic poem of Finland, the Virgin who falls from heaven into the sea before creation. She is the mother of the seven forces in nature.

ILUMQUH In Arabian religion, the god of the moon, known also as Sin, Wadd, and Amm.

ILITHYIA A goddess who presided over women at childbirth. An early Greek divinity.

IMAGES Pagan religions made images to represent their divinities. These images were fashioned in a variety of materials. They were made of stone, or wood, or metal. Among the oldest images are those of Cybele, the Mother-Goddess. Among the Egyptians, images of deities were a composite of human and animal features. The Babylonians fashioned

166

deities in bas-relief. The Greeks made their divinities dimensional, rounded.

IMUTHES (IMHOTEP) The chief minister of King Djoser, founder of the Memphite Third Dynasty at the beginning of the Pyramid Age (c. 2600-2200). He built the step-pyramid of Djoser, the oldest of the pyramids, and the mortuary temple at its foot. He became a culture-hero of the Egyptians and was deified.
As the Egyptian god of knowledge, later, of medicine, invoked by magicians to help in exorcisms. He is represented as a priest, seated, holding a papyrus roll. His worship was centered at Memphis.

INADA-HIME In Japanese mythology, the spouse of Susa-no-wo, who rescued her from a huge serpent.

INANNA The Sumerian goddess of love and fecundity. She was also the goddess of war, and was known as the Queen of Heaven. She was equated with Ishtar.

INAR A Hittite goddess.

INARI In Shintoism, the name given to a pantheon of food and fertility gods. The nine deities included in the pantheon are worshipped at the so-called Inari shrines.

INCA In pre-Columbian times the term Inca, in the singular form, denoted the ruler of the Incas in Peru. In its plural form, the term also refers to his subjects in general.
The empire was founded approximately in the thirteenth century and reached its cultural height in the sixteenth century.
The first Inca was a war-like chief of the Quechua tribe who ruled over the region of Cuzco about 1200 A.D. According to a descendant of a long line of Incas, Manco Capac settled with his brothers in Cuzco, married one of his own sisters, made good laws, conquered many lands,

and came to be regarded as the founder of the Inca dynasty. He may have established his court at Vilcapampa (Machu Picchu) following an earthquake that ruined many buildings in the region of Cuzco.

INCA CULTS The pre-Columbian Incas of Peru had a vegetation cult dedicated to a Mother-Earth goddess. Another of their cults was associated with the dead. Still another involved the huacas, the spirits that protected the villages, crops, and herds.

INCA FESTIVALS The pre-Columbian Incas of Peru observed festivals every month, but particularly at the solstices and the New Year.

INCA FETISH The fetish of the sun god of the Incas of Peru was a bird-shaped figure. It was enclosed in a basket and was regarded as endowed with oracular powers.

INCA MYTHOLOGY Among the Incas of Peru the tribal progenitors issued from caverns.

INCA RELIGION The pre-Columbian Inca empire embraced a body of people speaking different languages but welded together. The State was in control. In matters of religion, there was an official cult of the Sun, with a religious head as administrator. There were also other cults related to the Moon, the Earth, Thunder. A priesthood, composed of both men and women, formed the religious hierarchy. Animal and human sacrifices, divination, and monthly lunar feasts characterized the religious practices. The progenitor of the Incas was Viracocha the creator.
The head of the Incas was the Inca himself. The religion flourished in Peru, particularly in the thirteenth century. Among the ancient peoples, religious practices were influenced by the climate of the region. In oppressively hot regions there was a strong tendency to worship the stars and the moon. In the high Andes, more attention was paid to the sun. Other natural phenomena — high mountains,

168

waterfalls, thunder and lightning — also had a place in the religious life of the Incas.

Huge sundials, called *intihuatana* ('the place to which the sun is tied'), enabled the priests of the Sun to chart the seasons and to exercise to power by appearing to control the action of the sun.

INCA RITUALS The mythical progenitor of the Incas of ancient Peru was Viracocha, to whom offerings were made consisting of feathers, shells, animal sacrifices, and, during important festivals, human sacrifices.

INCARNATION The process by which a deity or spirit inhabits a human or animal body. The idea of the union of the human and the divine is present in all religions. For example, the Pharaohs of Egypt were divine because the sun god Ra inhabited their bodies in impregnating their queens. Accounts of divine incarnation served to elevate men, to unify religions, or to bring a divine power closer to mankind by presenting it in human form.

INCUBATION This was a practice among the Greeks and Romans of sleeping for a night in a temple. The purpose was to receive dreams and visions or to secure relief from sickness. There was a ceremony during which an animal was sacrificed and the suppliant slept on the animal's hide. The most popular center of incubation was at Epidaurus, in the temple of Aesculapius, the god of healing. There were records of many cures of nervous and mental conditions. Official interpreters expounded dreams, and other attendants called aretalogists chanted the praises of the god.

INDRA In the religion of the ancient Aryans, a young, heroic god of storms and lightning who gradually displaced Dyaus, the father of gods and men. About one-fourth of the hymns in the Rig-Veda are addressed to him.

INITIALIA This was a variant name for the mystery cult of Demeter.

169

INITIATION Among Australian aborigines, initiation into religious mysteries is associated with a ritual death and a rebirth. All males are subject to this practice.

INITIATION CEREMONIES Among many primitive peoples, initiation ceremonies are a ritual and forceful expression of the power of tradition. They also serve to impress on successive generations the power and worth of this tradition. Often cruel, they are nevertheless an efficient means of transmitting tribal knowledge and achieving tribal cohesion.

INTERCIDONA A Roman goddess who first taught the art of cutting wood to make a fire.

INTI The sun god worshipped by the Incas.

INTICHIUMA In Australia, this was a rite performed by the natives of Central Australia. It consisted of a series of ceremonies directed toward the maintenance of the annual supply of food and drink. At the rain-making ceremony the flesh of the kangaroo was eaten ceremonially.

INUATS Among Eskimos, they are spirits in human form, or they are capable of assuming human form. Among some Eskimo communities, inuats are also the human soul.

IO In Greek mythology, the daughter of the river god Inachus, beloved by Zeus, who turned her into a heifer because he feared Hera's jealousy. Io wandered about until she came to Egypt, where she regained her own form, married Osiris, and was worshipped by the Egyptians under the name of Isis.

IRANIAN RELIGION The early Iranian religion was a naturalistic polytheism resembling Homeric Greek religion. Ahura Mazda, lord of wisdom, stood at the head of the pantheon. Other important deities included Mithra, the god of light, and Ardvisura Anahita, the goddess of fertility. Ahura Mazda created minor deities, called 'the Beneficent Immortals.' His enemy, Angra Mainyu (Ahriman), the representative of evil and the dark forces of nature, created opposing evil deities. Zoroaster simplified the native cult by stressing the sacredness of fire, the cow, and a plant used to make a fermented drink, the haoma.

IRENE The Greek goddess of peace.

IRIS In Greek religion, the goddess of the rainbow. Originally the personification of the rainbow, she became the fleet golden-winged messenger of the Olympian gods.

IRKALLA A god of the underworld, called by the Babylonians 'the country unseen.' This is a variant name for Ereshkigal, the Sumerian Queen of the Lower Regions.

IRMINSUL In ancient Saxon religion, this was a tree or a pillar that had sanctity and was worshipped as the support that upheld the universe.

ISHKUR In Sumerian religion, god of the winds. He may be identified with the Greek god Aeolus, whose functions were identical.

ISHTAR A Sumerian-Akkadian goddess, identified with Astarte. She was called by Hammurabi, King of Babylon, 'the lady of battles.' In Babylonia and Assyria she was depicted as a lion, holding a weapon in her hand. Ishtar was the goddess of carnal love and in Uruk, in Mesopotamia, she had her temple of Eanna. In one myth, she is the sister of Ereshkigal, Queen of the Underworld in Sumerian legend. Ishtar was the most widely celebrated deity in the entire Middle East, and temples dedicated to her were to be found in every principal city.

A temple erected in her honor at Mari was filled with precious offerings left by pilgrims who may have crossed the desert to prostrate themselves at her feet. In her role as morning goddess, she marked the hour of battle, but as goddess of the evening, she presided over love. To 'virile Ishtar' of Mari, men and women of every degree dedicated statuettes of alabaster or gypsum which have survived through the centuries.

ISIA A festival that was observed in honor of Isis. The votaries, in commemoration of Isis as a corn-goddess, carried offerings of wheat and barley. The celebration itself was marked by orgiastic rites, and continued for nine days. The obscenities were so flagrant that the festival was abolished by the Romans. But the Emperor Commodus re-established it.

ISIASI Priests of the goddess Isis. In their hands they carried a branch of sea-wormwood, and chanted the praises of the goddess at dawn and in the evening. They dressed in linen robes. Their heads were shaven. They practiced continence and abstained from the use of sheep, pigs, and salt.

ISIMUD In Sumerian religion, the two-faced god who is the messenger of the god Enki.

ISIS In Egyptian religion, Isis is the supreme, the most widely worshipped goddess. Sister and consort of Osiris, mother of Horus, all three form the triad that was most dominant in Egyptian religious life.
The cult in time spread to Asia Minor and the entire Mediterranean world as well.
Isis is the daughter of Seb and Nut. She gave burial to the mutilated body of her consort Osiris. Her cult involved his death and his rebirth, accompanied with lamentation and jubilation respectively.
Identified with Demeter, who too represents a vegetation cult, Isis has many aspects, attributes, and functions.
She watches over sailors. She presides over magic arts, and she is the moon-goddess.
Isis was eagerly adopted into the Greek cities, and in Rome her temples were constantly filled with votaries. During the last four centuries B.C. and far into the fourth century A.D. her worship prevailed in the ancient world.

172

She had temples in Egypt, Greece, Rome, and Asia Minor. Isis had her official priests and her special festivals. Among the practices of her cult were the interpretation of dreams, lavish banquets, resplendent processions, and dances to the accompaniment of tambourines, cymbals, the sistrum, and other musical instruments.

Isis is identified with Aphrodite too, with Hathor, and with numerous other divinities, so that, to avoid offense, she was often addressed as 'O Thou, of countless names.' She was Ceres and Juno, Diana the huntress and Bellona the ear-goddess, Hecate of the Lower Regions, Cybele the Phrygian Mighty Mother of the Gods. In this polyform aspect she was known as Myrionyma, the deity of one thousand names. One inscription in Latin reads: To you, goddess Isis, who are one and all things. Isis is the eternal divinity, without beginning, without end.

The Roman philosopher and novelist Apuleius, who flourished in the second century A.D., describes the rites of the cult of Isis in his amazing novel the *Metamorphoses*.

Isis is sometimes represented as a woman with cow's horns, and holding a sistrum. She is also depicted veiled, her head topped with towers, with the earth at her feet. Again, she is winged, with a quiver over her shoulder, or holding a flaming torch or a cornucopia.

ISTANU In Hittite religion, a god called the Sun God of Heaven.

ISTHMIAN GAMES Greek games held every two years in the Isthmus of Corinth in honor of Poseidon (Neptune).

ITALIC RELIGION The old Italic religion from about the fifth century B.C. to the first century B.C. was a synthesis of various religious beliefs brought from Mediterranean regions, from Illyria, Greek colonists, and the Near East. Hence the deities of these immigrant peoples were absorbed into the Italic religion.

There were also cults associated with certain families; also functional deities, as among the Romans, with their respective votaries, sacrifices, and purificatory rites.

173

ITZAMNA In Maya religion, he was the sky god. He is represented as an old toothless figure.

ITZPAPALOTL In Aztec religion, goddess of the stars, associated with fire and lightning, and sometimes identified with Itzcueye, a two-headed deer captured by Mixcoatl.

IUNONES In Etruscan religion, these were female deities who were later on absorbed into the Roman pantheon.

IUVENTAS In Roman religion, the goddess of young men. Contributions were made to the temple funds by youths entering on manhood, that is, when they assumed the *toga virilis*.

IWALDI In Norse mythology, the dwarf whose sons made Odin's magic spear.

IXCHEL In Maya religion, the goddess of childbirth, the moon, rainbow, medicine, and weaving, personification of water as a destructive force, and wife of Itzamna.

IXTAB In Maya religion, the goddess of suicides. She is represented as an evil spirit that seduces and kills men at crossroads.

IXTLILTON In Aztec religion, the deity who presided over songs and health.

IZANAGI AND IZANAMI In ancient Japanese religion, the last pair of the celestial deities, supposed to have created the Japanese archipelago and lesser objects of nature. Izanagi alone produced Amaterasu, the sun goddess and ancestress of the imperial house, and Susanowo, the storm god.

IZDUBAR Gilgamesh, the legendary master of ancient Urku. He sought out Utnapishtim, who told him the story of the Deluge.

174

J

JAINA CROSS Swastika-like symbol of the Jains of India.

JAINHAAR The equal to the High. In Norse mythology, one of the members of the Norse triad.

JAINISM The religion of a heterodox Hindu branch founded by Mahavira Jnatiputra about the sixth century B.C. Like Buddhism, Jainism rejected the Brahman ritual and sacred books. Unlike Buddhism, it stressed asceticism as a means of salvation. The *Digambara* sect allow ascetics to go naked, while the *Svetambara* sect clothe them. Later sects, the *Lunka* and *Dhundia* reject image worship.

JALARUPA One of the most occult and mysterious signs of the Zodiac. The literal meaning of the Sanskrit word is 'water-body, form.' This is one of the names of the Makara. It figures on the banner of Kama, god of love.

JANUS A very ancient Italian divinity who presided over gates, doors, and passages, he was originally worshipped as the sun god. As god of the beginning of time and of the world, he was invoked as 'father' at solemn sacrifices. See Ianus.

JAPANESE BUDDHISM The Great Vehicle (Mahayana) school of Buddhism, established in Japan in 594 A.D. by the regent Shotoku Taishi, embraces several sects. During the Nara period (709-784), six philosophical sects were introduced from China: (1) the Sanron, which taught the

175

doctrine of the Void; (2) the Hosso, which taught that everything is mere consciousness; (3) the Kegon, which stressed the interrelatedness of all things in the Total Universe; (4) the Ritsu, which stressed the rules of discipline; (5) the Jojitsu, which emphasized the unreality of the self; and (6) the Kusha, which concentrated on the seventy-five real elements of the universe.

In the Heian period (794-1184), new sects were founded by two priests who had studied Buddhism in China. The Tendai sect, founded by Saicho, is based on the doctrine that all varieties of Buddhism were present in the historical Buddha's mind from the time of his Enlightenment. The Shingon doctrine teaches that truth is somehow inherent in all living beings.

During the Kamakura era (1185-1336), four new sects arose. The Jodo (Pure Land) sect, founded by Honen, promised its adherents rebirth into Amida's Pure Land. The Shin sect, founded by Shinran, held that faith alone matters. The Zen sect originated in the twelfth century. The Rinzai branch stressed meditation on paradoxes, the Soto branch meditation on whatever enlightenment arises as the thinker sits silently. The Nichiren sect is named for its founder, who taught that the salvation of Japan itself depended on absolute faith in the eternal Buddha and the attainment of a Buddha-like nature.

JAPANESE CREATION MYTH Izanagi and Izanami were commanded by the heavenly deities to descend to earth in order to create the world. They stood on the Floating Bridge of Heaven, pushed down their jewelled spear, stirred the brine beneath, and retracted the spear, which dripped until the drippings formed an island. They descended to the island, married, and gave birth to the islands plains, and elements. Then they created the deities, wh' are physical objects and forces of nature. Izanami died in giving birth to fire. Izanagi followed her to the underworld, then was pursued by her until he blocked her exit with a great rock. She became the goddess of the underworld.

JAPANESE RELIGIONS Today Shinto, Buddhism, Confucianism, and Christianity are the major religious movements of Japan. The earliest religion of the Japanese was primarily a naïve nature worship in which any object that gave rise to fear or awe was regarded as a *kami*. There were two groups of deities: seven generations of celestial gods and a number of terrestrial gods. The celestial gods represented creative or productive powers. The last pair of these celestial deities, Izanagi and Izanami, were supposed to have produced the Japanese Archipelago.

JARNSAXA In Teutonic mythology, she was the consort of Thor.

JETZIRAH The *Sepher Jetzirah* ('Book of the Creation') is the most occult of all the extant Cabalistic works. It explains the evolution of the universe in terms of a system of correspondences and numbers. God is said to have created the universe by thirty-two paths of secret wisdom, corresponding with the twenty-two letters of the Hebrew alphabet and the ten fundamental numbers. These ten primordial numbers, from which the whole Universe evolved, are followed by the twenty-two letters divided into three Mothers, seven double consonants, and twelve simple consonants.

JIMMU TENNO Usually reckoned as the first emperor of Japan, he is supposed to be the son of Hohodemi and the daughter of the sea god. Hohodemi is said to be the second son of Ninigi and the daughter of a mountain god.

JINGU A Shinto shrine (literally, 'God's palace') of special dignity.

JINNI In the ancient belief of pagan Arabs, a spirit or demon. In Mohammedan tradition, one of a class of intangible beings similar to the guardian angels of the Christian faith.

JIVANMUKTA An adept or yogi who has separated himself from matter and reached the ultimate state of holiness.

177

JNANA MARGA In Hinduism, one of the three major ways of attaining salvation.

JORD In Norse mythology, she is the goddess who personifies the earth. She is one of Odin's consorts and is the mother of Thor.

JOTUNNS In Norse mythology, giants or earth monsters whose abode was Jötunnheim.

JUDGES In classical mythology, the judges in the Nether Regions were Minos, Rhadamanthus, and Aeacus.
In Egyptian religion, there were forty-two judges in the Hall of Osiris in the underworld.

JUDGMENT HALL In Egyptian religion, the Judgment Hall of Osiris was the hall in the Underworld where the divine ministers of the god Osiris assisted him in the nightly weighing of souls. There were forty-two such attendant judges, among them Bast, Hu, Kenemti, Serkhi, Anaf, Qerti, Neba, and Khemi.

JUGATINUS A Roman god who joined man and woman in matrimony.

JULA A Slavic deity whose worship centered in Julin or Wollin.

JULIAN THE APOSTATE This Roman Emperor ruled from 360 to 363 A.D. He attempted to reinstate the religion of Mithraism in the West. But after his death it gradually disappeared from Roman territories.

JUMALA An ancient deity of Lapland and Finland. He was regarded as the supreme divinity, god of life and death. He was depicted as holding on his knees a cup of gold filled with gold coins. His worship was associated with forests.

JUNO In Roman religion, an Italian goddess, consort of Jupiter, and guardian of women. See Hera.

178

JUOK Among the Shilluk, who inhabit the Nilotic region, Juok is the Creator of the World.

JUPITER CAPITOLINUS When Egypt became a Roman province in 30 B.C., one of the new deities introduced from Rome was Jupiter Capitolinus, mainly for the benefit of Romans living in Egypt.

JUPITER DOLICHENUS Jupiter, the supreme god of the Romans, was so called when identified with a Weather-god worshipped at the town of Doliche, in Anatolia. His weapon was a double-edged axe. Previously, he had been assimilated with the Semitic Baal-Shamen. When the Persians under Cyrus conquered this region, he had been absorbed into Ahura Mazda.

K

KA In ancient Egypt, the Ka was held to be a person's double, the astral body. It was conceived as a companion of the soul in the physical body and in the life after death.

KABTA In Sumerian religion, the god who was in charge of brickmaking.

KACHINAS In Zuñi religion, the word means 'masked gods.' They are impersonated in dances and worshipped in ritual. See Katcinas.

KADAKLAN The deity recognized by the Tinguians as the supreme being.

KAIGA'U Among the Trobriand Islanders, a powerful magic designed to bewilder and ward off the *mulukuausi,* or evil sorceresses.

KAIT In Hittite religion, a goddess of grain.

KAKARMA The power gained by a Jivaro tribesman when he acquires an *arutam* soul. A person may possess only two arutam souls at one time, but the power of an indefinite number of previous souls may be accummulated.

KALEVA Finnish mythic land of happiness and abundance.

KALEVALA A Finnish epic poem containing matter on myths, legends, and magic practices.

KALI In Hinduism, a goddess, the wife of Shiva, represented with a necklace of human heads and a bloody dripping sword in one of her many hands. She is the personification of cosmic force, the creator of all things, even the gods.

KALKI AVATAR The 'White Horse Avatar' which will be the last incarnation of Vishnu, according to the Brahmins; of Maitreya Buddha, according to certain Buddhists; of Sosiosh, according to the followers of Zoroaster. In his tenth avatar, Vishnu will appear seated on a milk-white steed and with his drawn sword will destroy the wicked and restore purity.

KALLOFALLING In Eskimo religion, he was a terrible creature who dragged brave hunters down beneath the water.

KALPA In Hinduism, a world period. It is the time between the creation of the world and its destruction, a cycle of time representing a day and night of Brahma, a period of 4,320,000,000 years.

KALU A Fijian term denoting anything marvelous or divine.

KAMARUPA In theosophy, the subjective form created after death by the principle of desire.

KAMI The Japanese word for god. The word simply means 'superior' and is applied in the earliest legends to any object considered to have superior qualities.

KAMRUSEPAS (KATAHZIPURI) In Hittite religion, a goddess who was skilled in witchcraft.

KARAPS In Zoroastrian sacred literature, the sacrificial priests of the Daevas, who rejected the teachings of Zarathustra.

KARMA A Sanskrit word meaning act, action, action-influence, deed. Every act sets in motion certain forces. Karma in its rigorous religious application in Hinduism and Buddhism came to mean the result of these forces, the sum total of the acts determining a man's life.

182

KARTIKEYA In Hindu mythology, Skanda, the war god, son of Siva, whose seed had fallen into the Ganges.

KARZI In Hittite religion, he was a tutelary god.

KASABWAYRETA In the Trobriands, the mythical hero who was marooned by his companions but escaped by climbing a tree to the sky.

KASINA A mystic Yoga rite used to free the mind from agitation.

KASKU In Hittite religion, the moon god. He was also known as Kushah and Arma. His sacred animal was the lion.

KASSITES The Kassites invaded Babylonia in the sixteenth century B.C., bringing with them their divine symbol, the horse, which became common in the land only after their entry. The names of their deities suggest that the Kassites were of Indo-European origin. Another innovation was the boundary stone, which served as a charter of a gift of land. Such stones bear engravings of symbols of the gods who protect boundary rights and indicate the curse to be placed on violators. The tribal god was called Kassu. The Kassites also worshipped Burias (Buriash) and Shuriyas (Suriyas), equivalent to the Greek Boreas and Indian Shuriyan (Surya).

KASSU (KASHSHU) The tribal god of the Kassites.

KATAHZIPURI (KAMRUSEPAS) In Hittite religion, a goddess skilled in witchcraft.

KATCINA CULT Among the Hopi Indians, a secret society. Boys of six or eight years of age start their religious life by initiation into the cult.

KATCINAS Among Hopi Indians, these are supernatural beings identified with clouds and the spirits of the dead. The katcina cult involves impersonation of the gods. Masks

183

are worn. These masks impart sanctity to the wearer. At the principal katcina ceremony, held in February, beans and corn, grown secretly, are distributed to the people, to impose the belief in the cult's supernatural power to grow food in winter.

KATTAHHA In Hittite religion, the queen goddess.

KEBAR-ZIVO In Gnosticism, one of the chief creators.

KEDESH A West Asiatic goddess of love and beauty and divine harlot of the gods. She was introduced into Egypt when the nation became a world power.

KERIDWEN An ancient Celtic deity. To drink from her cauldron, which was called Amen, was to be inspired with divinatory powers. Also *Ceridwen*.

KESTA In Egyptian religion, one of the gods of the four cardinal points. He watched over the intestines of the dead.

KESTHA In Egyptian religion, one of seven deities associated with funerary rites.

KETHER In the Cabala, the Crown or highest of the ten Sephiroth; the first of the supernal triad.

KHA The Laotian name for the primitive hill people of Indo-China. They have retained pagan cults and are reputed to have practiced cannibalism, including the ritual eating of human livers.

KHADO In popular folklore in Tibet, evil female demons.

KHAIBIT The third member of the Egyptian triad, the shadow. The other members are Ka, the astral body, and Ba, the soul.

KHEM In Egyptian religion, he symbolizes the generative force. He is represented as a figure displaying the ithyphallus, or erect penis. He corresponds to the Roman god **Priapus.**

KHENSU See *Khonsu.*

KHEPERA In Egyptian religion, he is the rising sun. He is also the god of inert matter that passes into life. In addition, he presides over the dead body from which the spiritual body will arise. His symbol is a beetle.

KHEPRI Equivalent of Khepera.

KHERIBEQF In Egyptian religion, one of seven funerary divinities.

KHERIHEB In Egyptian religion, a body of priests who recited the sacred texts.

KHNEMU (KHNUM, KNEPH, CHNOUMIS) In Egyptian religion, a symbol of creative force. According to Plutarch, he is the 'unmade and eternal deity.' He is represented as blue (ether) and with an asp between the horns of his ram's head.
In Egyptian religion, he is the god who assists Ptah in executing Thoth's commands to create man. His name denotes *The Fashioner*. He is represented as producing a man's head on a potter's wheel. An extremely ancient god, he was credited with fashioning the sun-egg from the mud of the Nile.
He was also the guardian of the inundations of the Nile. He is represented frequently with a ram's head.

KHNUM See *Khnemu.*

KHONS Equivalent of Khonsu.

KHONSU In Egyptian religion, the moon god of Thebes, represented as a young man, crowned with lunar disc and crescent upon his head.
Son of Ammon and Mut, when identified with Horns, he is represented with a falcon's head. At Thebes and Karnak temples were consecrated to him.

KHORS A Slavic deity who presided over the art of healing.

KHU In Egyptian religion, the transfigured soul. With the *ba* and the *ka,* it could enable the individual to achieve immortality.

KHUS In Egyptian religion, a group a seven deities associated with funerary rites. They were: Imset, Hapi, Tuamutef, Qebhsennuf, Maat-atef, Kheribeqf, Herukhentian-maati.

KI Among the ancient Sumerians, the earth goddess. Her union with Anu, god of the sky, produced Enlil, the war leader and storm god. Her union with Enlil produced vegetable and animal life on the earth. She may be identical with Ninhursag.

KIKUYU A Bantu-speaking agricultural Negro tribe living near Mount Kenya in eastern Africa. The Kikuyu religion, unlike most of the other religions of Africa, practices sacrifice mainly for the purpose of cleansing.

KIKYMORA In Slavic mythology, he was the god of night.

KILO One of the most powerful gods recognized by the Apa Tanis, a primitive tribe living in the Himalayas. The great annual festival of the tribe is devoted to the worship of Kilo and his mate, Kiru.

KINGU In Babylonian religion, god of the forces of darkness and the black arts. In the Mesopotamian epic of creation (*Enuma Elish*), Marduk mixes his blood with earth to produce man.

KINICH AHAU He is the sun god of the Mayas.

KISHAR In the Akkadian myth of creation, the twin of Ashar. The union of the twins, children of Apsu and Tiamat, produced Anu. Kishar was one of the seven guardians of the house of Ereshkigal, represented by the constellation Hydra, thought to be the land of the dead.

KIRU Among the Apa Tanis, the female counterpart of Kilo. These two deities influence the general welfare of the tribe.

Mloko, the great annual festival of the Apa Tanis, is devoted to their worship.

KIVAS Among the Hopi Indians, these were underground chambers, where rites were held in the main house of the clan.

KOJIKI Written in mingled archaic Japanese and Chinese the *Kojiki* ('Records of Ancient Matters) was compiled in 712 A.D. and is sometimes called the Bible of the Japanese. It was written mainly to prove the divine origin of the ruling family. It is a prime source for our knowledge of the earliest forms of Shinto.

KOLASKIN CULT A prophetic religious cult of the Indians in the Plateau region of the United States.

KONY-OM-PAX Mystic words used in the Eleusinian mysteries.

KORLANG A word used by the Apa Tanis to designate three deities worshipped annually at a rite performed by a village priest: Niri Korlang, who protects the people against hailstorms; Tagung Korlang, who wards off excessive rain; and Anguro Korlang, who protects the Apa Tanis against disease.

KORLANG-UI A rite performed by the Apa Tanis in honor of the Korlang deities.

KOSHAR A Canaanite god. His name means 'skillful.' He was also known as Hayin, 'dexterous,' and Hasis, 'intelligent.' He was the counterpart of the Greek Hephaestus (Vulcan), the craftsman-god. He had a forge in Crete or on the island of Carpathos. Among the Egyptians he was equated with the potter-god Ptah. Koshar was also credited with the invention of magic incantations.

KOSI Among the Trobriand Islanders, the part of the soul or spirit that leads a short existence after the death of a person. The *kosi* remains near its familiar surroundings and may be seen or heard for a few days before it disappears forever.

187

KOTAN A deified culture hero of the Tzentales of Mexico, similar to Quetzalcoatl.

KRIKOIN In Eskimo religion, an evil demon who pursues dogs caught outside when winter storms rage. Dogs die in convulsions when they see his face.

KRISHNA In Hinduism, one of the most widely worshipped deities. He is the greatest of the incarnations of Vishnu, the supreme god. In legend he is represented as a warrior hero, cowherd, prankster, lover, and slayer of dragons. In the Bhagavadgita, he is the supreme object of *bhakti-marga*.

KRITA-YUGA In Hindu mythology, the first of the four Yugas or Ages of the Brahmans. It lasts 1,728,000 years.

KRODO An ancient Saxon deity, whose functions were similar to those of Saturn.

KRUTSANAM An ancient Teutonic deity whose functions are unknown.

KUBABA In Hittite religion, she was the Queen of Carchemish.

KUBERA The king of the evil demons in the Hindu pantheon. The god of wealth.

KUKSU CULT A cult in north central California in which young male initiates are taught to disguise themselves as Kuksu, ghosts, or other gods.

KUKULCAN The Maya word for 'plumed serpent,' a name given to the deity equivalent to the Quetzalcoatl of the Aztecs.

KUKWANEBU In the Trobriand Islands, these are folk tales of a special type, ordinarily recited in the villages when wet weather sets in and thought to have a beneficial influence on recently planted crops.

KULLAB In Sumerian religion, a city presided over by the shepherd god Dumuzi.

KUMARBI In Hittite religion, he was the father of the gods.

KUNDALINI SAKTI The power of life, known only to those who practice concentration and Yoga.

KUPALO In Slavic mythology, he was the god who presided over fruit.

KUPAPA A name of a goddess often mentioned in ancient Hittite sources. See Kubaba.

KUR In the Sumerian religion, this expression means 'the foreign land.' It is the space between the earth and the sea. It is the abode of the spirits of the dead. The Sumerian account of the entrance into Kur, with its river and its ferryman, corresponds to the classical myth of the Styx and Charon the ferryman.

KURDAITCHA Shoes worn by the Australian aborigines for ceremonial killing by black magic. They are made of emu feathers glued together with human blood.

KURDAITJA A sorcerer and executioner among the Arunta of Australia.

KURUNA The Australian aborigines believe that the Kuruna is the sacred spirit part of man.

KUSA A sacred grass used by Indian ascetics.

KUSHAH (KUSHUH) The Hurrian name of the Hittite moon god.

KUSHITE DIVINITIES A Temple of the Sun constructed by the inhabitants of the ancient city of Meroë was known to Herodotus. The Temples of Naga, the best preserved of all the ruins of the Kushite civilization, contain engravings

189

of a lion god. The Kushite Pharaohs of the twenty-fifth dynasty took both rams and lions to their temples at Barkal. Afterwards the ram, symbol of Amon, became one of the great divine symbols of Kush. Common elements of the Kushite culture, which flourished more than three thousand years ago, are the cult of the sky god, *Zar* or *Waq*, and the attribution of divinity to kings and queens.

KUYENFUCHA The god of the moon to whom the Mapuche Indians offer sacrifices during the elaborate fertility rite known as the *nillatun*.

KWOTH Among the Nuer in Nilotic East Africa, a god who is like the air or wind. Pure in spirit, he is far away in the sky, yet present on the earth.

L

LACANDONES The name for the present descendants of the Maya of pre-Columbian Yucatan.

LACTUCINA A Roman minor goddess. She presided over the budding ears of corn.

LACTURA Also called Lactucina. In Roman mythology, a rustic goddess who was in charge of the ears of grain filled with milk.

LADA A Slavic goddess of love and marriage. Her functions would correspond to those of the Roman goddess Juno.

LADY OF LIFE In Egyptian religion, a name for the goddess Isis.

LAGA In Norse mythology, she is the goddess who presides over springs and streams and history.

LAHAMU AND LAHMU In the Akkadian myth of creation, twins born to Apsu and Tiamat.

LAKSHMI The Indian Venus, born of the churning of the oceans by the gods. She was the goddess of beauty and wife of Vishnu.

LAMAISM A popular term, not used by the Buddhists themselves, for Tibetan Buddhism. It is based on Vairocana as the embodiment of the law of the Buddha, Amitabha as the Supreme Being, and Avalokitesvara as the chief being of enlightenment. It stresses the fourfold teachings of confession, worship of images, recitation of the magic formula containing the 'true words,' and discipline.

LAO TZU A mysterious figure who became a popular object of worship in the Ch'in and Han dynasties (249 B.C. - 200 A.D.) and was considered the founder of Taoism.

LAPANG A sacrificial rite preceding a raid to be carried out by Apa Tani tribesmen.

LARES In Roman religion, the lares were primarily deities associated with the farm: then with the household. They also guarded crossroads, and special festivals were celebrated to honor this function. The symbol of the lares was a dog, implying trust and faithfulness.

LARTHY-TYTIRAL An Etruscan deity who was identified with Pluto, the ruler of the Other World.

LARUNDA A Sabine goddess who presided over houses.

LARVAE In Roman religion, they were the spirits of the dead.

LASAE In Etruscan religion, these were minor demons.

LATARAX In Sumerian religion, a deity who presided over the cities of Bad-tibira and Umma.

LATERANUS A Roman god who took care of the hearth.

LATOBIUS Corinthian god of health.

LAVERNA A Roman goddess who protected thieves. Hence they were known as Laverniones. The thieves hid their plunder in a grove consecrated to the deity. She was represented as headless.

LEDA In Greek mythology, a queen of Sparta who was seduced by Zeus in the form of a swan. Helen of Troy and Castor and Pollux were born from her eggs.

LEGBA In Dahoman religion, the name given to the 'joker' who perverts all the rules and hence allows evil to manifest itself in the form of sickness, disaster, etc. His ineptitudes, malice, and carelessness pose a constant threat to society. He may also on occasion propitiate other gods on behalf of men and carry messages to human diviners.

LEMURES In Roman mythology, they were the spirits of the dead. They were conceived as hungry ghosts prowling around a house in search of food.

LEONES The Latin term for *lions*. This name was given to one class of the devotees of Mithra.

LEOPARD SOCIETY A native secret organization of West Africa. Among its functions was that of carrying out human sacrifice following the death of a tribal leader. The departed leader's wives and servants were sacrificed in order that they might accompany the leader into Ghost Land.

LETHE In classical mythology, a river in the Underworld whose waters brought forgetfulness.

LETO In Greek religion, the mother of Apollo and Artemis by Zeus. The Romans called her Latona.

LEVANA A Roman goddess who presided over new-born infants.

LEZA Among the Bantu of Africa, he is the High God who presides over the rainfall.

LIADA An ancient Polish deity whose functions are obscure. Sometimes identified with Mars.

LIBITINA In Roman mythology, the goddess who presided over funerals. Burials were registered in her temple.

193

LIF and LIFTHRASIR In Norse mythology, they were the only couple spared in the Twilight of the Gods. They became the progenitors of a new race. The story of Deucalion and Pyrrha in classical mythology is a comparable myth.

LIGHT AND DARKNESS Primitive men associated darkness with evil forces. Religion helped them to overcome their fears. In early religious symbolism, light stands for good, darkness for evil. Most religions assert that darkness prevailed before life began.

LING CHOS The collective myths of the ancient Tibetans who practiced the Bon cult.

LIR In Celtic mythology, a god who presided over the sea.

LOBO Annual rites performed by the Heiban grain priest in the Nuba Mountains. The first rite precedes planting, the second occurs when grain must be 'made to grow,' the third coincides with the last weeding of crops, the fourth with reaping, and the fifth with storage of the harvest.

LOFN In Norse mythology, she was a goddess whose function was to reconcile separated lovers.

LOKI In Norse mythology, the spirit of evil, that creates discord among the other deities.

LOPT In Norse mythology, Lopt was a variant name for the evil god Loki.

LOTUS SUTRA Buddhist scriptures containing the tenets of the Mahayana schools, which regard it as the embodiment of the ultimate doctrine. It teaches the salvation of all beings, and it reduces the three vehicles which carry the human soul across the sea of life and death to nirvana to one. Its first translation into Chinese dates from the third century A.D.

LOUQUO A Carib deity. He was supposed to have died, come to life again after three days, and gone to heaven.

LUA A Roman goddess to whom captive weapons were dedicated and then burned.

LUBARA A Babylonian god of pestilence and disease.

LUCINA In Roman religion, the goddess of birth, the surname of Juno, Diana, or a daughter of Jupiter and Juno. Her festival, celebrated on March 1, gave matrons an opportunity to assemble in her temple and implore a happy posterity.

LUDKI Among the Wends, a Baltic deity who presided over the home.

LUG In Celtic mythology, Lug was a god whose functions were similar to those of Mercury. His festival, Lughnasad, the Feast of Lug, fell in Britain on August 1. The name Lammas is derived from this festival.
One of Lug's centers was the town of Lugdunum, that is, Lug's town. This is now the city of Lyons.

LUMAWIG CULT A Bontoc cult centered on ancester worship.

LUNUS A variant name for the Phrygian god Men.

LUPERCALIA A Roman festival dedicated to Faunus or Pan. The Luperci ('wolf-warders'), clad only in goatskins, ran around the Palatine Hill. The rite was intended to protect domesticated animals from wolves. The Luperci also struck women with goatskin thongs to insure fertility.

LYNA In Norse mythology, a goddess who looked after things intrusted to her care by Frigga.

M

MA A Cappadocian deity who was equated with Bellona, the Roman goddess of war. The worship of Mâ was dominant in the Taurus mountains. As a fertility goddess as well, she had kinship with Cybele and also with Anahita, the divinity of the Mazdeans.

MAA KHERU In Egyptian religion, this means 'the right word.' It was a kind of open sesame that permitted the spirit of the dead to enter the halls of the Nether Regions and to assume the powers of the gods.

MAAT In Egyptian religion Maat was the goddess of truth and justice. Her symbol was the ostrich feather. When the dead are conducted before Osiris in the underworld, the heart of the dead is weighed in the balance against an ostrich feather.

MAAT-ATEF In Egyptian religion, one of seven funerary deities.

MACHU PICCHU A mountain in Peru which towers above the sacred shrine of Vilcapampa. The Incas had two capitals, after Cuzco fell to the Conquistadors, Vitcos and Vilcapampa. The latter was a magnificent sanctuary never seen by the Spaniards. Vitcos was the military headquarters of the Incas who tried to preserve the Inca heritage after the arrival of Pizarro. The ruins of Vilcapampa may be a part of a temple built by Manco Capac to honor his ancestors. Ancestor worship was practiced by the Incas long after Manco Capac had established himself as their Inca.

MACUILXOCHITL In Aztec religion, the god of pleasure and patron of the blind. He is related to Huehuecoyotl.

MAENAD In Greek religion, a nymph who attended Dionysus. Also, a woman who celebrated the orgiastic rites of the god of wine.

MAGDALENIAN AGE Archaelogical evidence from the Magdalenian age, which is the age of cave paintings, suggests that the primitive inhabitants of Europe held dynamistic conceptions of the world in which they lived. The hunters of the Magdalenian age portrayed on the walls of their caves the killing of animals and mimetic dances in which men wore animal masks.

MAGI In Zoroastrian religion, master adepts in all things of the Spirit, initiators in the Mysteries, and judges at the Trial by Ordeal.

MAGIANISM A cult practiced by Iranian polytheists. This form of Iranian religion represented Ahura Mazda, Mithra, and Anahita in the form of images. Darius fought against the Magian priests and Herodotus wrote about their religion. In Hellenistic times Magianism was combined with paganism and astrology.

MAGIC In ancient pagan religions, magic practices played an important role. They were associated with mystery rituals in Rome, Egypt, and in the religions of the Near East. The techniques involved in magic ceremonials included sympathetic magic, the use of amulets and charms, invocations to the infernal deities, necromancy, divination.

MAGNA DEA A Latin expression meaning 'The Great Goddess.' This name was assigned to the goddess Ceres for her bountiful harvests.

MAHABHARATA The longer of the two great epic poems of India and the longest epic in the world. The work of many hands, it was largely completed by the beginning of the

Christian era. It relates the struggle between two branches of the house of Bharata. The didactic Bhagavadgita, one part of the Mahabharata, has become India's best loved devotional work.

MAHADEVA A name applied to the Hindu god Shiva.

MAHAT A Sanskrit word meaning 'The Great One.' It is the first principle of universal intelligence and consciousness. In the Puranic philosophy, it is the producer of Manas, the thinking principle.

MAHATTATTWA In the Puranas, the first of the seven creations — Mahatowarat, Chuta, Indriya, Mjkhya, Tiryaksrotas, Urdhwasrotas, and Arvaksrotas.

MAHAVAIROCANA The Buddha of the mystical school of Buddhism. He 'illuminates the whole world as the sun does' and all phenomena are his manifestations.

MAHAYANA A branch of Buddhism with elaborate ritual and images. Developed in northern India from the second century A.D., this theistic branch survives in China and Japan.

MAHREM The Ethiopian god of war.

MAIA In Roman religion, an ancient goddess, also called Majesta. She was the consort of Vulcan. Offerings were made to her on May 1. She was later confused with the Greek goddess Maia, mother of Hermes.

MAKARA A Sanskrit word meaning 'The Crocodile.' In Hindu mythology, it is the vehicle of Varuna, the water god.

MAL'TA GODDESS CULT The occurrence of a great number of male and female figurines of Western Asiatic type in prehistoric times suggests that at Mal'ta, near Lake Baikal, Siberia, the Great Goddess had a male partner.

199

Maltese temples were sometimes built in pairs, expressing both elements of the fertility cult.

MAMA Among the Incas of ancient Peru this title, which means 'Mother,' was applied to the four sister-wives of the four brothers called collectively the Ayar. These wives were named Occlo, Huaco, Cura, Raua.

MAMA-CUNA The High Priestess or the convent of the Chosen Women or 'Virgins of the Sun' in Macchu Picchu, the hidden sanctuary of the Incas of Peru.

MAMITU A Babylonian goddess of fate.

MAMMETUM A Mesopotamian goddess who decided the destinies of man. She may be equated with the Greek *Moira,* fate.

MANA In Polynesian and Australasian religions, an extraphysical power ascribed to persons or objects behaving in a striking manner. This immaterial power is viewed as the embodiment of the elemental powers which, collectively, constitute the order of the universe. A similar idea is expressed by various words in other languages: *Orenda* in Iroquoian, *Manitu* in Siouan Algonquin, and *Hasina* in Madagascan.

MANANAN In Celtic mythology, a god who was the patron of seamen and merchants. His abode was the Isle of Man. He was the son of Lir, the Irish god of the sea, and acquired many of Lir's attributes.

MANAS A Sanskrit word designating the mind or mental faculty which makes man an intelligent and moral being. Esoterically, it designates the sentient reincarnating principle in man.

MANAS SANYAMA In Yoga practice, perfect control over the mind.

MANCO CAPAC A Peruvian god. He was the lawgiver and taught the Peruvians to worship the sun.

MANDALA A geometric design consisting of an inner circle enclosed in a square with four entrances. Sometimes called a magic circle, its symbolism derives from the yoga doctrine which teaches that the soul can unite with the divine by meditation and concentration. The Tantric sects believe that the mandala is the dwelling abode of the deity, who resides in the innermost circle and can be evoked by various incantations. C. G. Jung and others have offered psychological interpretations of the mandala.

MANDEANS Members of a Gnostic sect that makes John the Baptist the central figure and baptism the main rite. John the Baptist is regarded as the Messiah. The ancient texts of the sect, written in a peculiar script and dialect of Aramaic, have recently been studied. The sect arose in southern Iraq some five hundred years B.C., under the influence of Dosithaean, Marcionite, and Manichaean teachings.

The sacred literature was the Great Book. The religious beliefs of the Mandeans were compounded of Jewish, Christian, and pagan elements. Variant names for the Mandeans are Nasoraeans and Sabians.

MANE In the Celtic Eddas, the name of the Moon.

MANES In Roman religion, spirits of the dead. Graves were dedicated to the manes. Their worship was practiced at three major festivals: the Feralia, Parentalia, and Lemuria. Sometimes the term *manes* is used for the realm of the dead itself. It was also applied to the deities of the Nether Regions: Dis, Orcus, Persephone.

At a later date the manes were identified with the Di Parentum, the ancestors of the family.

MANI In Nordic mythology, the personification of the moon. Revered as a deity. Teutonic sacrifices took place preferably during the New Moon or the Full Moon.

MANI The Persian founder of the religious system of Manicheanism. Born c. 216 A.D., near Ctesiphon in Mesopotamia, he later traveled in Central Asia, India, and China. Mani was subject to visions and revelations, like many religious founders. On his return to Persia, he was persecuted by

201

the Magi, who represented the official religion, and was imprisoned and finally executed.

Mani's commandments were a synthesis of the Old Testament, the Sermon on the Mount, and Buddhism. He was opposed to warfare and stressed the value of purity of thought and act.

Mani's father was Patek. Mani spoke mainly Aramaic, but also Persian, in which language he composed one of his books.

He died in 276 A.D. His doctrines spread West to North Africa, to Egypt and, later, to China.

MANICHEANISM This religion, founded by the Persian Mani in the third century A.D., was a syncretism of Mazdaism, Buddhism, Christianity, Gnosticism. Manicheanism was based on the principle of dualism, which reflected the conflict between god and evil, light and darkness. Liberation from evil was to be achieved by practicing the virtues taught by Mani. There were two categories in this religious system. The Elect or Perfect lived virtuously, in chastity, and practiced celibacy. They were assured of salvation in the afterlife. The other category consisted of the Imperfect, the Hearers, who might marry but had to confine their sexual indulgence. They might be reborn among the Perfect. The ultimate aim of the Hearers was to attain this status of the Elect. There were twelve chief priests. An annual feast, commemorating the Passion of Mani, was associated with fasting, supplications to Mani for forgiveness of sins.

In spite of hostilities, Manicheanism persisted as an active religion until the fifth century. In the later Middle Ages its tenets infiltrated into areas of Central Europe. In China Manicheanism, in its essence, was adopted into secret cults.

MANISM Belief in mana, common to many primitive religions and characteristic of much popular religious thinking today. Manism assumes that the body is inhabited by a spirit which can exist independently as a shade or ghost.

MANITU In Algonquian languages, a word used to one of the

202

powers or spirits which inhabit persons or objects and endow them with magical attributes.

MANJUSRI A bodhisattva symbolizing wisdom and generally placed on the left side of Sakyamuni in temples. His most famous center is the Mountain of Five Terraces (Wu-t'ai) in Shansi, China. This mountain is the Mecca of many Buddhists.

MANNUS An ancient Teutonic deity. The progenitor of the Teutons.

MANO In Gnosticism, the Lord of Light, the second Life of the second or manifested trinity.

MANTHRA In Zorastrian religion, the Holy Word by which Creation was accomplished.

MANTIS Among the African Bushmen, he is the first being who created all things. A mischievous, buffoon-hero in popular lore, he became the center of a cult and was credited with making fire and giving all things their names. According to legend, Mantis was carried by a bee over the dark primeval waters, laid to rest in the heart of a white flower that appear above the formless waste, and impregnated with the seed of the first human being. He had sprung from the African soil as an invisible egg and had crawled on the earth as a worm before his transformation into an insect. Finally, he was devoured by his wife in the act of procreation. As the object of a cult he is called Cagn or Caggen.

MANTRA In Vedic Hinduism, a term applied to hymns and prayers addressed to the gods. The Gayatri mantra is the most popular one.

MANTRA SHASTRA Brahmanical writings on the occult science of incantations.

203

MANTRIKA SAKTI The occult potency of mystic numbers, sounds, or letters in the Vedic mantras.

MANTUS Among the ancient Etruscans, he was the god of the Lower Regions.

MANU The Sanskrit word means 'man' and refers to one of a series of progenitors of mankind. In this he shares honors with Yama in the Vedas. In the Brahmanic story of the Flood, Manu is saved and becomes the father of post-diluvian humanity. Manu and each of his successors ruled over the world for a Manvantara (one complete cycle). The Manu of the present Manvantara is the seventh and the reputed author of the Code of Manu. Both Manu and Yama were sons of Vivasvant.

MANU In Egyptian religion, the mountain of the sunset from behind which Ra, the sun god, rises daily at dawn.

MANUAL OF DISCIPLINE This manual contains the tenets of the Essenes, an ancient Jewish sect that explained good and evil in terms of Zoroastrian dualism represented by the beneficent deity Ahura Mazda and his opponent Ahriman, the Spirit of Evil.

MANYO-SHIU Compiled near the end of the eighth century or the beginning of the ninth, the *Manyo-shiu* ('Collection of Myriad Leaves') contains four hundred poems, many of which celebrate the splendors of the Japanese landscape. It is a part of the sacred literature of people whose religion is fundamentally a form of nature worship.

MARA In Hindu mythology, the god of temptation who tries to turn away Buddha from his path.

MARAMA In Tahunaism, one of the names under which Na Vahine was worshipped.

MARCUS AURELIUS A Roman emperor whose *Meditations* on Stoic philosophy have been the object of reverent devotion through the ages. The Emperor Diocletian instituted a pagan ritual for him as one of the gods. Born at Rome in 121 A.D., he was deified upon his death in 180 A.D., and his statue joined the *Dei Penates* of the Roman household. Like Epictetus and Seneca, he stressed the unity of the universe and man's obligations as a member of the great whole. 'O Nature!' he wrote, 'From thee are all things, in thee are all things, to thee all things return.'

MARDUK (MERODACH) The chief deity of the ancient Babylonian religion. Originally a local sun god, he became the principal deity of the eastern Semites, creator and arbiter of all destines.
A tablet from the Cossaean period (1600-1200 B.C.) identifies Marduk successively with a long list of male deities, illustrating the principle that the transition from polytheism to practical monotheism occurs after people recognize that many different deities are manifestations of one high god whose domain is universal. Enlil is viewed as Marduk the ruler and decision-maker; Sin as Marduk the illuminator of darkness; Shamash as Marduk who metes out justice, etc.

MARGA The holy or sacred path leading to Nirvana.

MARI Site of an ancient Assyrian settlement near the Euphrates. Excavations by the French archaeologist Parrot and others have revealed a series of temples, palaces, and statues as well as more than twenty thousand tablets. The palace, the temples of Ishtar, Dagon, and Ninharsag, and the Ziggurat contain much pictorial documentation yielding insights into the Mesopotamian culture.

MARZYANA An ancient Polish goddess who presided over harvests.

MASSEBAH (MASSEBOTH) Among the Semites, an upright stone or pillar placed in a sanctuary to honor a hero or deity, or to commemorate an event.

MASHU A Babylonian word meaning 'twins.' It refers to a mountain with twin peaks. The sun god was believed to return to the world through the mountain at dawn. The gate was guarded by mythical monsters, half-scorpion and half-human.

MATHADHIPATIS Heads of various religious brotherhoods in India.

MATRIPADMA A Sanskrit word designating the mother-lotus, the womb of nature.

MATRIS A Sanskrit word designating the seven divine mothers, the female aspects of the gods.

MATRNS In Etruscan religion, a deity whose functions are obscure.

MATRONALIA A Roman festival that was held in honor of Juno, the consort of Jupiter.

MATSYA In Sanskrit, a fish. Matsya's avatar was one of the earliest incarnations of Vishnu.

MATURA In Roman mythology, a rustic goddess who presided over ripened ears of corn.

MATURNA A Roman goddess who presided over connubial fidelity.

MAUI In the Tonga Islands, he was the supreme deity.

MAWU In Dahomey, in West Africa, Mawu is worshipped as the sky goddess. She is the mother of Legba.

MAYA CULTURAL CENTERS The great Maya civilization flourished between 300 A.D. and 900 A.D., but Tikal, the greatest of its ceremonial centers, was inhabited as early as 600 B.C. Temples were built there before 200 B.C. Maya remains are found today in the lowlands of Guatemala and in surrounding regions. Every artifact points to the existence of a real cult, and traits of this cult still survive among the Mayas. The ceremonial centers differed greatly in size and importance, but all were concerned with the passage of time. At Bonampak, Copan, Palenque, Tikal, and many other centers, there was probably a large population made up mainly of the ruling class in possession of special knowledge and skills. Copan was probably the leading astronomical center.

The chief god of the Mayas was the old god, or god of fire, called Itzamna. Chac, the longnosed rain god, was sometimes represented as four Chacs, one for each of the cardinal points. There were also gods of the wind and the maize, thirteen gods of the upper world, nine gods of the underworld, gods of the sun, the moon and venus, a god of death, and many others. Four divinities known as *bacabs* stood at the cardinal points, each appropriately colored (red for east, yellow for south, black for west, white for north), and held up the sky. Men offered to the gods precious objects like jade and portions of their own blood, drawn from different parts of the body.

The Mayas had reached a high level of culture in pre-Columbian times. They had developed a system of hieroglyphic writing, a calendar more accurate than the one now in use, and architectural techniques permitting them to achieve remarkable results with stone.

MAYA FESTIVALS Such festivals were always preceded by long periods of ascetic practices, including continence and fasting, on the part of the priests and initiates.

MAYAHUEL In Aztec religion, the goddess of the maguey and its products, patroness of pulque and drunkenness, and sister of Tlaloques and Centzontotochtin.

MAYA PYRAMIDS Among the Maya of Yucatan temples to the gods were built on the tops of pyramids.

MAYA RELIGION The religion of the ancient inhabitants of Yucatan. Their religion was based on vegetation cults, similar to those of the Aztecs. Mayan religion postulated a dualism, consisting of beneficent deities dwelling in heaven and, on the other hand, malefic spirits whose abode was the underworld.

Among the most important deities were Itzamna, the sky god and Kukulkan, god of the winds. Kukulkan was the creator, the civilizing force. Among the Aztecs, he was identified with Quetzalcóatl, the plumed serpent. Yumtoax was the god who presided over the maize. Chac was in charge of rain, death, the sun, and the stars.

MAYA STELES Maya ceremonial centers were concerned primarily with the passage of time under the appropriate gods. The steles are memorials constructed to mark intervals of time. They probably constitute impersonal markers of calendrical or astronomical phenomena or events linked with religious ideas. Archeological findings indicate that they were the objects of a cult which still survives in Central America. The steles of Copan, about twelve feet high, probably represent rulers of the center. Each of the nine steles has a dignified figure in high relief on the front and hieroglyphic inscriptions recording dates on the back.

MAYRS In Teutonic mythology, they were three deities who presided over childbirth.

MAZATECA The frog and snake cult among the Aztecs.

MAZDAK The founder of the Persian cult of Mazdakism. Mazdak began his work late in the fifth century A.D., when his native country of Persian was in a chaotic condition marked by war, oppression, and general discontent.

Mazdak quickly began to exert a powerful influence on the Persian people. He preached extreme doctrines, in tune with the times. After a few months, his followers multiplied by the hundred thousand, at every level of society.

He was possibly the first great revolutionary in history. He not only preached communism in material possessions. He also proposed, as Plato did in the *Republic,* an equal division of women among men.

The king, Kawadh, recognizing the danger of this movement, attempted, during the last thirty years of his reign,
to ameliorate the social conditions in his country.

Kawadh's son, however, Khusrav I, liberated the Persians
from Mazdak's movement. He realized the threat of Mazdak's teaching to the state religion and to the political state
as well. He therefore suppressed Mazdakism. He brought
back prosperity and justice to the country and thus elimin-
ated the need for Mazdakism.

Mazdakism was a successor of Mani, the founder of Manicheanism. Mazdak's approach was social, but essentially
it was a religious force. His teaching threatened the existence of Zoroastrianism. Hence he was violently attacked
by Zoroastrian priests and writers. He was called by them
Ashemaogha, a distorter of the truth. Zoroastrians also
called him 'accursed.'

He preached violent communism, absolute community of
possessions, including women. He also advocated self-
restraint, which the Greeks called sophrosyne, and renunciation of sensual pleasures, including animal food. The
latter proscription was a factor in the Greek Dionysiac
rites. For his views on food, Mazdak was called 'the devil
who would not eat.'

The universal cause of all strife and hatred, he asserted,
was due to the desire for pleasure and material possessions.
He stressed the two principles of Good and Evil that per-
vade all life. This precept was in harmony with Manicheanism. Lastly, he enjoined rigid purity of the elements — fire,
water, and earth.

Mazdak's end was tragic. He was treacherously murdered.
His teaching, however, despite difficulties, persisted for
several centuries longer.

MBANJE A herb smoked by the tribes of central and southern
Africa to ward off evil influences.

MBIPITSJIN In the Asmat headhunting cult, a piece of skin,
removed separately from the nose and upper lip of the
victim during the scalping process.

MBORI The supreme being of the Azande.

MDOKI An evil spirit of the Congo.

ME In Sumerian religion, a code of rules assigned to each *dingir* or cosmic entity for the perpetual operation of the universe.

MEDEA The famous sorceress of classical mythology was honored as a goddess at Corinth. See Absyrtus.

MEDER In the ancient religion of the Semitic population of Ethiopia, the goddess of the earth and fertility.

MEDICINE-MAN Among Australian aborigines, the medicine-men initiate the tribal members into the mysteries of rituals and myths. They practice meditation, telepathy, and hypnotism. They are, in addition, seers, treat sickness, and give protection against magic practices.
The term is frequently applied to the priests and shamans of the Indian tribes of North America.

MEDITATION SCHOOL OF BUDDHISM Buddhist meditation developed in the Ch'an School in China and better known to the West as *Zen*.

MEDITRINA A Roman goddess who was in charge of medicine.

MEDITRINALIA Among the Romans, a ceremony associated with the goddess Meditrina. At this festival the participants drank old and new wine.

MEFITIS An Italian goddess of sulphurous fumes. She had a cult throughout Italy, particularly in volcanic areas.

MEGABYZI The high priests of the goddess Artemis. They were eunuchs, and served in her temple at Ephesus.

MELANEPHOROI Sodalities associated with the Egyptian cult of Isis.

MELANESIAN DEATH RITUALS The Asmat headhunters maintain that even after death the deceased warrior, on reaching the realm of souls, will boast of his feats in an attempt to make the spirits more cautious. There may be a solemn unveiling of a carved memorial prow in a canoe named after the dead warrior, preceded by offerings of food and the performance of prescribed rituals by the surviving brothers-in-law.

MELEK The Canaanite word meaning 'king.' The Ammonites use the noun, in the form Milkom, as the name of their national god. The god of Tyre is called Melqart, 'king of the city.'

MELKART The patron deity of Tyre. He was the Phoenician equivalent of Hermes (Mercury).

MELLONA In Roman methology, a rustic goddess who invented the art of making honey.

MEMPHIS In the Egyptian temple at Memphis sacred Apis bulls, on their death, were entombed.

MEN Men was a Phrygian god whose original name was Manes. His worship was centered in Anatolia. He is depicted with a crescent moon over his shoulders. To some extent he reflects the attributes of Attis, with whom he is sometimes identified. He embraces both heaven and earth. Among his functions are healing, prophecy, and the protection of tombs. During the third and fourth centuries B.C., metics, that is, non-Greek residents in Attica, as well as slaves were his votaries.

MENAGYRTAE A variant name for the Galli, the priests of the goddess Cybele.

MENAT A magic amulet worn by Egyptian gods, goddesses, kings, priests, and officials. Inscribed with representations of a goddess and a serpent, it was supposed to insure fertility and was buried with the wearer in order to renew his sex powers in the outer world.

MERCURIUS In the writings of the alchemists, Mercurius (or the planetary spirit Mercury) is the god who discloses the

211

secret of the art to the initiates. He is also the soul of bodies, spirit that has become earth, spirit that transforms the material world. Identified with Hermes Trismegistus, he is also symbolized, like *nous* or *pneuma,* by the serpent and called the mediator, the original man, and the Hermaphroditic Adam.

MERCURY A Latin god whose cult was derived from that of the Greek Hermes.

MERI An African god, originally worshipped in Punt (probably Somaliland), introduced into the Egyptian pantheon after the nation became a world power.

MEROE The ruins of the ancient capital of the Sudanese kingdom of Kush (538 B.C.-350 A.D.), ranked among the great monuments of the ancient world. The ruins lie about a hundred miles down the Nile from Khartoum and testify to the existence of a flourishing civilization whose religious life centered around the cult of Ammon, god of the sun.

MERTI In Egyptian, this expression means 'The Two Eyes.' This is the name of the two Egyptian goddesses Isis and Nephthys. In the form of two serpents, they appear on the head of Ra, the sun god.

MERU The Land of Bliss of the earliest Vedic times.

ME'S In Sumerian religion, the divine laws that governed the entire universe since its creation.

MESHIA AND MESHIANE The Adam and Eve of the early Persians.

MESLAMTAEA (NERGAL) A chthonian god in the Sumerian pantheon. His temple in Cuthah, called 'He Who Issues from Meslam,' indicates that he may have been a tree god originally. The son of Ehlil and Nihlil, he appears in hymns as a warrior. As Nergal, he is ruler of the underworld and husband of Ereshkigal.

MESOPOTAMIAN RELIGIONS The ancient religions of the Akkadian-speaking Babylonians and Assyrians go back to the Sumerians of Southern Mesopotamia.

To the Sumerians the gods existed for the benefit and advantage of mankind. They were eternal and more powerful and effective than human beings. In other respects they were conceived anthropomorphically. In form, in their material needs such as food and habitation they were like man.

The superior gods were associated with the natural resources of the country. On a lower level were the minor gods, and in the lowest scale was man himself.

The relations of the Sumerians to their deities corresponded to the relations between a member of the family and the head of the family himself. The Sumerian thus had his personal god, who gave help in the personal requirements of the votary and who acted as an intermediary between the Sumerian and the higher gods.

With these higher gods, man came in contact in the same way as a subject before his lord. Marduk and his father Enki, two powerful deities, could be appealed to in time of great crisis.

The gods might help in sickness and disaster, but not in the matter of death. 'When the gods created man they assigned death to him, life they kept in their own hands.'

At death, man entered 'the great dwelling,' a shadowy region below the earth. His position in this region depended on the manner of his death and his burial, the number of children he left behind, and the nature of the sacrifices that were offered at his grave.

The gods owned the Sumerian cities and delegated their control to human stewards. The steward, the *ensi*, received his orders from the god of the city through the medium of omens and dreams. The *ensi* then executed these orders in terms of the domestic and the foreign policy of the city. The abode of the god was the temple. There he lived with his divine family, his attendants, and his followers. The divine attendants governed the human house-servants, who prepared and served the god's food and kept the temple in acceptable order.

In addition to administering the city and the temple, each

god was closely associated with some element or phenomenon relating to man's physical and mental environment. For instance, the Akkadian Anim, Heaven, was lord of the city of Uruk and god of heaven. Enlil, Lord Wind, Lord of Nippur, was god of wind and storm. Ninhursag, Lady Mountain, a Mother-Goddess, was Queen of Kesh and goddess of mountains. Utu, the Sun, who owned the cities of Larsa and Sippur, was god of the sun and of justice. Ningirsu, Lord of the city Girsu, was also Lord of Lagash and god of thunder showers and spring floods. Dumuzi was a god of the pasture. Nergal, Lord of Kutha and his consort Ereshkigal were rulers of Hades.

In protohistorical times, the god was not only an anthropomorphic being symbolizing a phenomenon but actually the phenomenon itself. In the mystery cult the initiate aspired to enter into the powers of the god and as a man produce the same phenomena as the god himself produced. This attitude on man's part prevailed at the great cult festivals in the agricultural communities of the Sumerians. The divine marriage was another widespread rite. Every New Year the king assumed the identity of Dumuzi (Tammuz), god of vegetation, and as the divinity the king sexually joined the goddess Inanna, who was incarnated in a priestess.

Another important rite was associated with the death and rebirth of vegetation in the spring. This rite involved the cult of Tammuz and Ishtar. The death of Tammuz was lamented by his consort Ishtar, who voiced her jubilation on his rebirth in spring.

Another feature of Mesopotamian religion was the battle fought each New Year between the gods and the forces of chaos, resulting in the return of order to the universe.

MESOPOTAMIAN TEMPLES The temple was dedicated to the god. Here he lived and worked and from here he supervised the temple estate. But the god always retained his divine personality, in which the temple itself participated. When the temple of Nigirsu at Lagash greets the god, the heavens tremble with the tumult and all lands are awestricken.

In rituals designed to placate an angry deity, the temple has an utterance, and even the brickwork may intercede for the suppliant. Temples in Mesopotamia often appear as divine powers themselves. They give protection and hear petitions just like the deity himself.

METEMPSYCHOSIS The passing of the soul at death into the body of an animal or a person. Outside of India, the doctrine was held by the ancient Egyptians, the Orphics, and by the later Greek thinkers, Pythagoras, Plato, and Plotinus.

METIS The first wife of Zeus, daughter of Oceanus and Tethys, and goddess of prudence.

METRAGYRTES A Greek term that denotes the mendicant priests attendant on the goddess Cybele. They wandered around in large bands, begging their way, to the accompaniment of ritualistic dancing. When in their ecstatic moods, they made prophetic announcements. Usually they were eunuchs. They were known in Greece, Rome, and in Syria. The Roman novelist Apuleius, who flourished in the second century A.D., presents a vivid picture of these votaries in Books 8-9 of the Metamorphoses.

METZLI In Aztec religion, the deity who presided over the moon and vegetation.

MEXICO Before the conquest of Mexico by the Spaniards, the Aztecs dominated the country. The religion of the Aztecs was a syncretism of the people subjugated by the Aztecs and of the earlier indigenous inhabitants such as the Toltecs and the Olmecs.

MEZZULLA In the Hittite pantheon, the daughter of Taru and Wurusemu.

MIALISM A type of witchcraft involving communication with the spirits of the dead. It is practiced in Jamaica.

MICRONESIAN RELIGION The Micronesians put less emphasis on religion than do the other peoples of Oceania. They believe in the existence of a personal soul which departs from the body at death and seeks its fortune in

215

the spiritual world, that certain places command reverence, and that the ghosts of the dead may haunt the living. Burial rites and mourning are prescribed according to local custom.

MICTLANCIUATL In Aztec religion, she was the goddess who presided over The Place of the Dead. Her consort was Mictlantecuhtli.

MICTLANTECUHTLI In Aztec religion, he was the god of the dead.

MIDGARD In Norse mythology, Midgard is the earth, that lies midway between Asgard, which is heaven, and the misty kingdom of Hell, the home of the dead.

MIDGARD SERPENT In Norse mythololgy, a snake-like monster, offspring of the evil god Loki. Lying in the sea, it is coiled around the earth. At the end of the world it will arise and kill Thor with its poisonous breath.

MILAMALA Among the Trobriand Islanders, a seasonal feast marked by the return of the spirits of the dead.

MILKOM The national god of the Ammonites.

MILU In Hawaiian religion, he is the god who presides over the dead.

MIMIR In Norse mythology, the god of eloquence and wisdom. By drinking the waters of the well at the root of the world ash, Yggdrasil, he gained knowledge of the past and future.

MIN In Egyptian religion, Min was the god of sexual reproduction. His place of worship was at Coptos. He was represented in ithyphallic form.

MINERVA An ancient Italian goddess, probably of Etrurian origin. Her chief temple, on the Aventine, was the center of the worship of the Roman guilds. She was regarded primarily as a goddess of the handicrafts. Under Greek influence, she was later identified with Athena.

MINOAN PANTHEON The religion of the prehistoric Greeks was a nature creed. It is possible that the Minoan-Mycenaeans venerated one great goddess of nature under various aspects. They are known to have worshipped a goddess named Eileithyia, a snake goddess, a dove goddess, a goddess of healing, a goddess of the Tree Cult, a goddess of the mountains, a war goddess, and a goddess of the seas. The snake goddess was the patron of the underworld, fertility, and the domestic cult. There was also a mistress of the animals and her companion. All of these divinities may represent different features of one Great Nature Goddess.

MINOAN RELIGION The source of pre-Greek Minoan religion was Crete. The externals were humble: no magnificent temples, only rural shrines. The double axe, probably a sacrificial instrument, is the symbol of the religion. Among the deities was a snake-goddess, symbolizing the goddess of the Underworld. Later, there was a merging of Minoan-Mycenaean religion and culture.

MINOS A judge of the shades in Hades, he was the son of Zeus and Europa.

MINUSCULARII These were minor Roman deities presiding over small daily matters.

MINUTIUS Among the Romans, a minor deity. He was invoked in trifling matters.

MINVRA The Etruscan form of Minerva.

MIRTHLESS STONE In the mystery cult of Demeter, the mirthless stone was the stone on which Demeter mourned the disappearance of her daughter Persephone.

MIRU In the Hawaiian pantheon, a member of the fourth heavenly trinity. He was lord of the spirit world.

MISTLETOE The parasitic plant was sacred to the Druids and is connected with many pagan rites. In Brittany it was hung in stables to protect livestock. In Scandinavian mythology, it killed the god Balder. In Sweden it was said to have the power to reveal the existence of gold. It was cut by the Druids, who may have viewed it as the genitalia of the oak tree. In popular belief, it was supposed to be the source of life. In Frazer's *The Golden Bough*, the myth of Balder, vulnerable only to an arrow made of mistletoe, is interpreted as a symbolic account of a fertility drama of death and resurrection.

MISTRESS OF THE ANIMALS A goddess who was worshipped in prehistoric Greece in Minoan-Mycenaean times.

MITAMA In Shinto, some gods are represented as having *mitama* 'august jewels or souls' which reside in the shrines dedicated to them. Thus the shrine at Isé is not inhabited by the goddess of the sun but by her mitama. At shrines, they are represented by a *shintai*.

MITHRA In Iranian religion, Mithra is the spirit of heavenly light. He is invoked as the Sol Invictus, the Invincible Sun. In inscriptions that have been unearthed in the Middle East and in various parts of Europe, the dedication to him runs: To the Unconquerable Sun, the Invincible Mithra.
He is the Lord of Heavenly Light, the God of Truth. He wars against the forces of evil, destroying the wicked. Sacrificial offerings to him included animals and birds. The immolations were accompanied by libations, ritual prayers, and liturgies. Initiation into the Mithraic cult required on the part of the aspirant purifications and flagellations. Only men could become votaries. Mithra was absorbed into Zoroastrianism. Along with Ahura Mazda, the Supreme Deity, Mithra and Ahura govern the universe. Ahura is Heaven, while Mithra is his agent. In his aspect as a warrior Mithra is directed to destroy all demons and even to come to grips with Ahriman, the Spirit of Evil.
After the disappearance of the Persian Empire, Mithraism extended into Roman territories and took a strong hold on the Roman soldiery stationed in Britain, in the Danube

218

regions, and in the Middle East.

In the second century A.D. Mithraism became highly popular among cultured Romans and was even embraced eagerly by the Emperors and their Imperial courts. Mithraic temples have been excavated in England, Central Europe, and elsewhere.

Mithra is represented most frequently, in sculpture, on vases and artifacts, as a youth wearing a Phrygian cap and plunging a dagger into a bull.

Initiation into Mithraism demanded rigid austerities. There were seven stages of advancement into the inner mysteries. Each stage was designated by a name of mystical significance, as follows: Corax, Cryphius, Miles, Leo, Perses, Heliodromus, Pater. Bread, water, and honey were used in the services, along with supplications, sacrifices and baptism on the blood of a bull or a lamb. The ultimate purpose of these initiation was the attainment of a state of happiness in the afterlife.

In Rome Mithraic priests were known as *Patres Sacrorum,* Fathers of the Sacred Mysteries. There were also *Matres Sacrorum,* Mothers of the Sacred Mysteries. Many ancient authorities discuss the popularity and the appeal of Mithra and his cult. Among them may be noted the Greek historian Herodotus, Plutarch the Greek biographer, Porphyry the Neoplatonic philosopher, Origen, and St. Jerome the Church Father.

Mithraism was one of the last of the oriental mystery cults to reach the West. It became the chief rival of Christianity before it was officially suppressed toward the end of the fourth century A.D. Its death struggle was prolonged. Altars to Mithra, dating from the first to the fifth century, are common in Egland.

MITHRAIC PRIESTS In the Mithraic cult, certain priests were mystically designated as lions, and the priestesses were known as hyenas. Other names given to the priests were crows and sacred crows. Special festivals were associated with these priestly appellations: the Leontica, the festival of of the Lions: the Coracica, the festival of the Crows: the Hierocoracica, the festival of the Sacred Crows.

219

MITHRAIC SANCTUARY Wherever possible, in the Mithraic cult, the sanctuary was an underground grotto or cave.

MITHRA THE FATHER In the Mithraic cult, Mithra is conceived as the Father, while the son is Sol. Together, they are one, 'the great god Helios Mithra.'

MITRA In the religion of the ancient Aryans, the defender of the sanctity of contracts and treaties. A solar deity associated with Varuna, he was later identified with the Persian Mithra.

MIXCOATL A prehistoric Aztec star god, patron of the hunters. Originally a lightning god, he was called 'cloud serpent' and credited with the making of fire.

MJOLLNIR In Norse mythology, this is the name of the god Thor's hammer.

MKOS A Slavic god who presided over commerce.

MLOKO The great annual festival of the Apa Tanis. It is devoted to the worship of Kilo and Kiru.

MNEMOSYNE In Greek mythology, the goddess of memory, a Titaness, the mother of the Muses by Zeus.

MNEUIS In Egyptian religion, a sacred bull that was worshipped in the temple of Ra, the sun-god. Mneuis is identified in his worship with Apis.

MOCCUS In Celtic mythology, the god of swine. His rites centered in remote glades.

MOGON A Celtic god who was worshipped in the North of England.

MOHANES Among the Indians of Peru, the shamanistic medicine-men.

MOHENJO-DARO Site of an ancient city in the Indus Valley of utmost importance in the study of the origin of Hinduism. Excavations indicate that a highly developed culture existed in India as early as the third millenium B.C., long before the Aryans invaded the region.

MOI The Vietnamese name for the hill people who have retained pagan cults. They have practiced cannibalism and the ritual eating of human livers.

MOKSHA In Hinduism, the general term meaning salvation.

MOKUM A female earth-dwelling deity worshipped by the Apa Tanis of the Himalayas.

MOLEK (MOLK) A Hebrew word which meant 'king' and is now used to designate a ritual sacrifice, whether real or a substitute. The practice mentioned in the Old Testament as 'the abomination of the Ammonites,' is associated particularly with first-born males. Plutarch described the ritual sacrifices practiced in Carthage.

MOLOCH He was a Semitic solar deity: probably of Phoenician origin. His symbols were two pillars and a bull. Human sacrifices, fire-worship, and self-mutilation formed elements in his cult.
Children were the most frequent victims of the sacrifices. Moloch himself was known to both the Israelites and the Canaanites.

MOMOS A Greek deity, son of Night and Sleep. He was regarded as a jester and mimic.

MONTU In Egyptian religion, a war-god of Hermonthis. He is represented as a man with a falcon's head surmounted by a solar disc.

MOROM A fertility rite conducted by priests of the Apa Tanis. Grains of rice are scattered on the fields to be cultivated, and boys prance about with huge bamboo phalli.

MORS In Roman religion, the personification of Death, represented as the daughter of Erebus and Nox.

MOT In Canaanite religion, he was the god of lifelessness, of the Underworld. He was also called Resheph, the Ravager, the demon of plague and pestilence. Another appellation was Horon, He of the Pit.
As Resheph he was the demon of plague, identified with the Mesopotamian Nergal. By the Phoenicians Mot was equated with the Greek god Apollo in his manifestation as a god of pestilence.

MOTHER EARTH In the religion of the ancient Aryans, Mother Earth was the consort of Dyeus, the father of gods and men.

MOTHER-GODDESS In pagan religions the Mother-Goddess was of supreme importance as the source of fertility. She was Ishtar among the Assyro-Babylonians. In Phoenicia she was known as Astarte. In Syria she was Atargatis. In Phrygia she was Cybele. In Greece, she was Demeter. The Egyptians knew her as Isis.

MOUNTAIN OF ASSEMBLY In Canaanite religion, this was the abode of the gods, called 'the holy ones.' They were conceived anthropomorphically as members of a human family. The chief deity was El, the creator, the supreme god. He was represented as a bull, and was ceremonially so called.

MOUNT IOUKTAS In ancient Crete, a mountain where bloodless sacrifices were offered at the shrine of the Earth-Mother.

MOUSTERIAN BURIALS Religious practices and beliefs seem to have existed since the Paleolithic period. Evidence of ceremonial burials dates from the Mousterian age, perhaps as long as 30,000 years ago, and points to belief in a future life. The name of the period is derived from Le Moustier, a cave at Le Moustier, in Dordogne in southwestern France.

MOUTH A Phoenician god of the dead. Also called Pluto.

MTRH In Canaanite religion, this term denotes a bridegroom. It refers to a priestly official who acted as the bridegroom in a sacred marriage rite.

MU The earliest progenitors of the Polynesian peoples who settled in Hawaii. The priests or *tahunas* taught that the word now familiar to westerners as Hawaii originally referred to a huge continent that had existed since prehistoric times in the Pacific Ocean, and that the present islands are former mountain peaks of the submerged continent. The Mu were defined by the tahunas as earliest inhabitants of Hawaii. Two orders of the Mu were still living in the islands in the nineteenth century. The evil Mu wore hideously painted masks made of gourds and served as the henchmen of the wicked tahunas. The Holy Mu included priests and benevolent chiefs who carefully preserved the ancient rites.

MUDRA A system of occult signs made with the fingers and first used by Buddhists of the Yogacharya school. These signs imitate ancient Sanskrit characters.

MUISAK SOUL The Jivaro of eastern Ecuador believe that only a person who has had an *arutam* soul, a soul that protects its possessor from death except by contagious disease, is capable of forming a muisak. The muisak soul is an avenging soul that comes into existence when a person who has seen an arutam is killed. The avenging soul of the deceased, created at the moment of his death, leaves the body through the mouth. Its sole objective is to kill the murderer.

MULUKUAUSI Among the Trobriand Islanders, these are invisible sorceresses, dangerous on land and especially dangerous at sea. Possessed of truly ghoulish instincts, they swarm and feed on the insides of the dead.

MULUNGU Among the Yaos of Nyasaland, Mulungu is the Great One. He created the world and presides over human affairs.

223

MUMBO JUMBO Among the Mandingo tribes of the Sudan, the tutelary genius who protects a village against evil spirits.

MUMMIFIED OSIRIS In Egyptian funeral papyri, the god Osiris is depicted in mummified form, wearing a white crown.

MUMMU The creative utterance or life force mentioned in the Akkadian myth of creation in connection with Apsu. Apsu consults his Mummu and receives advice on how to destroy Nudimmud. Mummu may also be identified as a personification of the phalos.

MUNIN In Norse mythology, the crow that belongs to Odin. The name Munin means 'memory.' At dawn Munin traverses the world. In the evening it returns and, perched on Odin's shoulders, relates what happened on earth.

MUSAWARAT Site of a Kushite temple completed before the end of the first century A.D. The ruins lie between the modern city of Khartoum and the ancient city of Meroe. Probably the residence of a god-king or goddess-queen, the site has yielded evidence of a well-developed cult.

MUSES In Greek and Roman religion, the nine daughters of the supreme god Zeus. They each preside over a special field in the arts, science, and literature. Calliope was in charge of epic poetry: Clio, of history: Euterpe, of lyric poetry: Melpomene, of tragedy: Terpsichore, of dancing: Erato, of love poetry: Polyhymnia, of sacred poetry: Thalia of comedy: Urania, of astronomy.

MUSHADAMMA In Sumerian religion, the god who is the great builder.

MUSPELLSHEIM In Norse mythology, this is the home of the god Surtr, who destroys the universe.
It is the land of fire, whence issue fiery clouds and twelve rivers.

MUSUBI In ancient Japanese religion, the god of growth.

MUT An Egyptian deity associated with Khonsu and Ammon. A mother-goddess, she was the third member of the divine triad of Thebes.

MUTI The stock of medicine used by the African *hakata* or witch doctor.

MUTILATIONS Inflicting injuries on the body for religious or superstitious reasons are common practices among savages and primitive peoples.

MYLITTA In Babylonian religion, she was the goddess of pro-creation and childbirth. In this respect she was akin to Ishtar. In her temple in Babylon every Babylonian woman was required, as a religious duty, to prostitute herself at least once to a stranger.

MYSTAGOGUE In Greek religion, he was a priest whose duty was to instruct aspirants into the mystery cults.

MYSTERY CULT OF SAMOTHRACE A Greek mystery cult that was observed on the island of Samothrace.

MYSTERY RELIGIONS Certain pagan religions received initiates by secret rites that were not publicly divulged. The secret knowledge thus acquired by the aspirant would insure advantages in his present life and in the life after death.
The most important mystery religions were those of the Greeks, Phrygians, Syrians, Egyptians, Persians.
Among the Greeks the rites celebrated at Eleusis were the most famous. They were associated with Demeter and Persephone and interpreted a vegetation concept.
Other Greek mysteries were celebrated at Andania and on the island of Samothrace. The Dionysiac mysteries were observed in different places. The ceremonies, which were orgiastic, required the drinking of the sacred wine, the eating of the raw flesh of the sacrificed animal, drinking its blood. The ultimate purpose of the cult was an assurance of immortality.
In Phrygia the mysteries were connected with Cybele, the

Mother-Goddess. As the Nature goddess she mourned the death of her young consort Attis and rejoiced on his return to earth. The mystery similarly involved a vegetation myth. In Syria the mysteries, again involving a vegetation myth, centered around Adonis, the consort of the Nature-goddess, who dies and is reborn.

The Egyptian mysteries of Isis and Osiris were popular throughout the Graeco-Roman world.

The last mystery religion that was immensely popular in the Roman Empire was Mithraism, the cult of Mithra and his conflict with Ahriman, the Spirit of Evil. Initiation ceremonies were elaborate and demanded a great deal of preparation and austerity. There were sacramental rites, ablutions, sacred meals. In seven stages of advancement, symbolizing the passage of the soul after death through the seven heavens into the abode of the blessed, the initiate reached the ultimate inner mystery. Women were excluded from membership in this cult.

MYSTES The Greek term for a mystic. A member of a religious cult who is initiated into its mysteries.

MYSTICAL SCHOOL OF BUDDHISM A branch of Mahayana Buddhism. It considers the universe itself to be the Great Sun Buddha.

MYTH-CHANTS Among Australian Aborigines, myth-chants are totemic rites. The rites symbolize the past and the lives of heroic figures. The ceremonies involve singers and ecstatic dancing.

MYTHOLOGY In ancient pagan religions, the relation between man and the gods was interpreted by means of myths. The creation myth of Babylonia is illustrated by the conflict between Marduk and Tiamat. The Egyptian sun myth, the myth of Isis-Osiris, of Orpheus, are all designed to explain man in terms of the cosmic and the creative forces of the universe.

MYTHS The Greek word *mythos* means a tale. Myths were fanciful, imaginative stories that pictured the operations of natural phenomena in terms of anthropomorphic beings. Later, myths evolved into dramatic presentations of these vivid tales of gods and men. Another aspect in the concept of the myth was an attempt to interpret man's activities, his personal longings, his purpose in life, his relation to the divinities who appeared to rule the cosmos. Mystery cults centering on some particular local or universally conceived divinity evolved, with the object of discovering how man could make contacts with such a divinity, how he could commune with him, and how the divinity would help in clarifying the meaning of life, in steering men toward personal salvation, in expounding the possibilities and even the promises of a future life. Votaries of a deity were initiated into secret rituals so that they would comprehend the cosmic scheme. Contacts with the deities were achieved by elaborate ceremonials, liturgies, fastings and ascetic practices, and purifications. There were sacred dancing performances, while magnificent processional parades, led by the priesthood, were a notable feature, together with chants and supplications and temple services.

N

NAASSENES One of the Ophite group of Gnostic sects. Serpent worshippers, they considered the constellation of the Dragon as the symbol of their Logos.

NABATAEANS A sect almost identical with the Mandaeans. They had more reverence for John the Baptist than for Jesus. Maimonides called them astrolaters.

NABU An Assyro-Babylonian deity. He was associated with the city of Borsippa. He presided over learning and eloquence. He was the son of Marduk and the consort of Tashmetum.

NAGA in Hindu mythology, a member of a race of semihuman serpents, ruled by Shesha, the sacred serpent of Vishnu. They inhabit Patala, a magnificent subaqueous kingdom.

NAGA The best preserved of all the ruins of the ancient Kushite civilization. The ruins contain an engraving of a lion god with four arms and three heads, possibly a survival of the ancient cult which gave Egypt its deities.

NAGLFAR In Norse mythology, the ship, built from the nails of the dead, on which the forces of Hel sail to attack the Aesir at Ragnarok.

NAGUAL An individual guardian spirit or totem among Central American tribes. A person and his nagual, usually an animal, have the same soul. The notion of the nagual was elaborated into a mystery cult opposed to the religion of the conquerors of these tribes.

NAHUA The language of the Aztecs of ancient Mexico.

NAIAD In Greek and Roman mythology, one of the nymphs believed to inhabit and animate fountains, rivers, springs, and lakes.

NAISKOS In Greece, an aedicule in the form of a temple. It was designed to hold a sacred image or symbol.

NAKATOMI In Shinto, the priestly class of men.

NAMJIPI In the Asmat headhunting cult *namjipi* is the name for the soul of a body that is not yet dead.

NAMTAR A Sumerian word designating fate or destiny.

NAMU In Sumerian religion, a city-god of the region near Ur. His cult stressed rites of lamentation and the search for a god who had disappeared. In time the cult blended with the cult of Dumuzi. He was the son of Ningishzida and Ninazimua. He was primarily a vegetation god.

NANABOZHO Among American Indians, this was a spirit who created the earth and its inhabitants. His abode was in the North, in the ice country.

NANAK Born a Moslem in 1469 A.D., Nanak founded the Sikh faith in India. His faith combines both Hindu and Moslem tenets. Many of his writings are included in the Granth, the sacred book of the Sikhs.

NANDI The sacred white bull of Siva and his vehicle.

NANGGA In the Fiji Islands, a deity who was hostile to unmarried men and women.

NANNA The Sumerian moon god, whose worship was centered in the city of Ur. He was the father of Ishtar, the goddess of love.

NANSHE A Sumerian goddess of truth and mercy. She is associated with the city of Lagash.

NAO In the Asmat headhunting cult, the technique of butchering.

NAOS A small Egyptian shrine in which the spirit of a deity was supposed to be present at all times.

NAPIWA Among the Blackfoot Indians, an anthropomorphic white god.

NARADA One of the seven great Rishis, one of the most mysterious personages in Brahmanical writings, which ascribe to him some of the most occult hymns in the Rig Veda.

NARAYANA In Hindu mythology, the Mover of the Waters, a title of Vishnu in his aspect of the Holy Spirit.

NARVE In Norse mythology, a son of the evil god Loki. He was devoured by his brother.

NASCIO Also called Natio. A Roman goddess who presided at the birth of a child.

NASTROND In Nordic mythology, the shore of the dead. The frozen Underworld, where the damned experience the extremes of punishment.

NASU In Zoroastrian religion, a female demon that feeds on corpses of the dead.

NATIVE AMERICAN CHURCH In 1918, groups practicing the peyote religion were incorporated as the Native American Church. See Peyotism.

NATURE WORSHIP In primitive pagan religions, almost all the deities were nature forces, the heavenly bodies, animals, plants. Man had to adjust his needs to his environment in order to secure necessary food for sustenance. Man found that in many manifestations Nature was beneficial but at times also hostile and destructive. Man needed fruits, fresh water, winds, the sun, rain. When he received these aids

231

to his well-being, he expressed his gratitude in mystery rites and appealed to the powers associated with such cults. If the powers responded to his prayers, these powers became manifest divinities, endowed with particular attributes and functions.

NA VAHINE In Tahunaism, the daughter of Teave and member of the divine triad composed of the goddess Uri Uri, Eri Eri, and Teave. Her name means 'Lady of Peace,' 'Goddess of Serenity.' When Teave decided to establish a royal family to rule over his kingdom on earth as well as his celestial kingdom, he manifested himself as a female divinity, taking the shape of his daughter Na Vahine, who became the goddess Uri Uri and the feminine generative force of the sun. She became the mate of Tane and the Holy Mother of Heaven. She was also known as the Goddess of Infinity and worshipped by the name of Maram, Moon Goddess.

NAVAHO CEREMONIALS Among the Navahos, ceremonies have special designations. There are Blessingway rites, Gameways, Holyway rites, Ghostways. Each ceremonial involves specific rituals. The rituals include exorcistic practices, invocations, chants, songs, prayers. The ceremonies lasted four days.
Navaho rites are largely directed toward the curing of diseases and sickness.

NAVAJO RELIGION The main aim of Navajo religion is the restoration of universal harmony, once this harmony has been disturbed. The Navajo universe contains the ghosts of the dead and many personalized powers, called the Holy People. The sun may be the dominant deity, but the most beloved is Changing Woman, whose sons, the Hero Twins, slew the monsters which were threatening to destroy universal harmony. In addition, there are plants, animals and natural phenomena who once were people and may still assume human form: Big Snake, Cactus People, Thunders, etc. Ritual and myth enable the Navajos to exert a stabilizing influence on a world which threatens to disintegrate.

NDGENDI In the Fiji Islands, the supreme deity to whom sacrifices were offered.

NEBEBKA In Egyptian religion, a judge in the Hall of Osiris in the underworld.

NEBO In Babylonian religion, the god of wisdom and writing. His worship was centered at Borsippa. His functions were akin to those of the Egyptian god Thoth. Nebo's symbol was the stylus.

NECROMANCY A method of communication with the spirits of the dead. Necromancy was practiced by the Greeks and Romans and the pagan peoples of Asia Minor.

NEDU In Sumerian mythology, he is the chief guardian of the entrance to the Lower World, and corresponds to the Greek god Charon, the ferryman who rowed souls across the river Styx.

NEEDFIRE In Teutonic folklore, a fire kindled to remove injury from the herd and promote prosperity. Of heathen origin, probably during a time of plague, the practice involved extinguishing hearth fires and relighting them from the new fire. The custom dates back to prehistoric times and survives in some modern settings, particularly in the lighting of fires on St. John's Day.

NEFERTEM In Egyptian religion, the god who was the son of Ptah. He is depicted as a bearded figure, with a lotus flower on his head.

NEHALENNIA A Teutonic goddess of fertility.

NEHEH Also called Heh. The Egyptian god of eternity. He is represented as a man sitting on the ground. In his hand he holds the symbol for millions of years.

NEITH In Egyptian religion, goddess of the hunt.

NEKHEM In Egyptian religion, the sanctuary of the mother-goddess Nekhebet, the protectress of Upper Egypt and of the royal house.

NELI The Apa Tani land of the dead. It is supposed to be under the earth.

NELKIRI In the religion of the Apa Tanis, the guardian spirit of the land of the dead stands at the entrance to his domain. Nelkiri interrogates each newcomer and determines what his status in Neli will be.

NEMBUTSU In Japanese Buddhism, the name of the process of repeating Buddha's name and meditating on him.

NEMEAN GAMES Greek games held every two years in honor of Zeus.

NEMESIS In Greek mythology, the goddess of public indignation against the breaking of the moral code. In later times, a deity who punished those who were guilty of hubris, excessive pride or arrogance.

NEMOSTRINUS A Roman deity who presided over groves and forests.

NENECHEN The Supreme Being of the Mapuche Indians. A major aspect of the fertility rites known as the *nillatun* is the offering of food to the Nenechen and to other divinities and ancestral spirits.

NEOLITHIC FEMALE FIGURINES The female principle predominated during the Neolithic period. Clay and ivory figurines of the Venus type have been found near Nineveh, Tepe Gawra, Warka, and elsewhere. Those found near Nineveh are shaped in a squatting posture suggestive of childbirth, and in all of them prominence is given to the maternal organs. Figurines found in the Indus valley may have been used in the practice of a Mother Goddess cult.

234

NEOPLATONISM A mystic philosophical religious system. It was compounded of Platonic doctrine and religious mysticism. It was established by Plotinus (205-270 A.D.), who founded a School in Rome. In his expository treatise entitled the *Enneads* he postulated that God is the One, the Source, the Undivided Unity. From him flows a succession of emanations of gradually diminishing splendor. His most famous pupil was the philosopher Porphyry.

NEPHTHYS In Egyptian religion, a goddess who was a sister of Isis and consort of Set. On her head she wore the hieroglyphic form of her name.
She acted as assistant to Isis.

NEPRI In Egyptian religion, he was the god who presided over the grain.

NEPTUNE In primitive Roman religion, a deity associated with the perpetuity of springs and streams. He was later assimilated to the Greek Poseidon and became the chief god of the sea.

NEREIDS Sea-nymphs, daughters of Nereus and Doris. Their worship was generally in seaports Mediterranean seaports. Fifty in number, they lived on the bottom of the sea, arising at times to aid ship-wrecked sailors. Thetis, the mother of Achilles, was the most famous Nereid. All had the gift of prophecy.

NEREUS A marine deity of the Mediterranean Sea, offspring of Pontus and Gaea, and father of the Nereids.

NERGAL The Sumerian god of the Lower Regions, husband of Ereshkigal. He may be equated with the Greek god Pluto who ruled the Underworld. Nergal, like the Biblical Satan, originally dwelt in heaven.

NERTHUS Also called Hertha. In Teutonic religion, she was the goddess of fertility. Slaves were sacrificed to her by drowning.

NESHAMAH In the Cabala, as taught by the Rosicrucian order, one of the three highest essences of the human soul. It corresponds to the Sephira Binah.

NETHUN In Etruscan religion, the god corresponding to Neptune.

NGANGA A witch doctor or sorcerer to whom the natives of central and southern Africa attribute special powers. He generally works with a *shave* or spirit advisor and has at his disposal a stock of medicines as well as his *hakata*. The hakata is a set of carved bones, sticks, or pieces of ivory used in divination.

NICHEREN SHOSHU OF AMERICA A cult recently introduced into the United States from Japan and now numbering about two hundred thousand members. The rapidly growing movement stresses moral rectitude and spiritual insights leading to the achievement of world peace. The name of the cult means 'The True Church of Nicheren.' See Soka Gakkai.

NICKEN In Baltic mythology, he was a god who presided over the sea.

NIDABA A Sumerian goddess who drew up treaties and boundaries. She was also in charge of the food and drink of the gods.

NIDANA In Buddhism, a chain of causation consisting of twelve links: birth, age, consciousness, will to live, love, perception, sense of touch, the organs of sensation, individuality perfect knowledge and ignorance. The understanding of these twelve links prepares the mind for Nirvana.

NIDHI Nine treasures belonging to the Vedic god Kubera and guarded by nine demons. Personified, they are worshipped by the Tantrikas.

NIFLHEIM In Norse religion, Niflheim was the Underworld, cold and dark. Here the dead dwelt among the nine subdivided regions. The presiding deity of Niflheim was Hela.

NIG-GIG A Sumerian term equivalent to the word *tabu*. It designates the dynamistic power associated with unusual persons or objects as well as with divinities.

NIHI-NAME In Shinto, the annual festival of firstfruits.

NIHONGI Compiled in 720 A.D., the *Nihongi* ('Chronicles of Japan') is written wholly in Chinese and contains alternate versions of myths and events recorded in the *Kojiki*.

NILE The Nile, like many sacred rivers, was thought by prehistoric men to be the earthly continuation of the Milky Way. From it emerged the sun-egg, made from the mud by Khnemu, the creator, who was also the primeval watery abyss.

NILE GOD In Egyptian religion, the Nile god was worshipped under two aspects: as Hapy in the South, and as Hapy of the North. He is represented with female breasts, symbolizing fertility.

NILLATUN An elaborate fertility rite practiced by the Mapuche Indians. One major aspect of the nillatun is the sacrificial offering of food to the supreme being, the pantheon, and ancestral spirits. Four sessions of sacrifices, dances, and prayers, and a special dance to dramatize the relationship between the living and the dead chiefs, are supposed to mark each day of the nillatun.

NIMANAKAYA In Buddhism, Trikaya. In Theosophy, the state of an adept who wishes to help mankind and, after death, chooses semipreservation of his personality rather than nirvana.

NIMRUD (NIMROD) Described in the Book of Genesis as 'a mighty hunter' and the first on earth to be 'a mighty man.' Nimrod resembles the legendary Babylonian hero Gilgamesh.
The ruins of Nimrud, a suburb of Nineveh, supposedly built by the mighty hunter, contain many buildings and sculptures of interest to students of ancient religions.

NINATTA and KULITTA In Hittite religion, the two most important female attendants at the court of the goddess Shaushka, who is an aspect of Ishtar.

NINAZU A Sumerian underworld deity. He was the spouse of Ningirda, daughter of Enki.
In late Sumerian liturgies, this is the name given to Tammuz. It means 'Lord of Healing.'

NINEVEH One of the capitals of ancient Assyria, situated on the east bank of the Tigris in northern Iraq. Excavations have yielded the greatest library of cuneiform tablets ever found, among them the Epic of Gilgamesh, which contains nearly all the familiar elements of the biblical account of the Deluge. Two temples have been discovered, that of Ishtar, goddess of love and war, and that of Nabu, god of writing.

NINGIRDA In Sumerian religion, the daughter of Enki and wife of Ninazu.

NINGISHZIDA In Sumerian religion, a city-god in the vicinity of Ur. He was an underworld divinity and, originally perhaps, a tree god. He was the son of Ninazu and Ningirda.

NIN-GIZZIDA In Sumerian religion, the father of Tammuz. The name means 'The Lord of the Faithful Tree.'

NINGMA The form of Tibetan Buddhism which immediately followed Bonism but preceded Langdarma is called Ningma, the ancient.

NINHAR A city-god in the Sumerian pantheon. In the region of Ur, he was god of thunder and rainstorms. The son of Nanna and Ningal, he was the husband of Ninigara, the goddess of the dairy. He was represented as a roaring bull.

NINHARSAG A Sumerian goddess, originally associated with the cities of Adab and Kesh as the 'Lady of the Stony Ground.' She became a mother-goddess, queen of the gods, and creator of all growing things. She appears not only

as the goddess of animal birth in early representations but
also as the mother of all children. Her husband is Shulpae.
Their son, Mululil, appears to have been a dying god, like
Tammuz, and to be the have been the object of yearly
lamentations. Later, as Nin-Khursag, 'she gives life to the
dead,' she was the guardian of fields and herds which supplied milk giving nourishment to the sacred herd of the
temple of Lagash. Her usual symbol was the cow. Other
names of the godess are Ninhursag, Ninhursaga, Ninmah,
and Nintu.
Functionally, she is identifiable with the Roman Venus.
The attributes of Venus are thus described by the poet
Lucretius (c. 94-55 B.C.):
O mother of the descendants of Aeneas,
darling of men and gods, fostering Venus!
Beneath the gliding stars of heaven
you throng the sea with ships and fill
the productive lands. For through you
every living thing is conceived and rises
and beholds the light of the sun.

NINIB An Assyro-Babylonian deity who was god of war, hunt-
ting, and healing. His worship centered in Kish and Nippur.

NINIGIKU In Mesopotamian religion, another name of Ea, lord
of wisdom and creator of the universe.

NINKARRAK In Babylonian religion, the goddess of healing.

NINMAH Babylonian goddess of the underworld.

NINMAR A Sumerian goddess, daughter of Nanshe and granddaughter of Enki.

NINSHUBUR In Sumerian religion, the messenger of the goddess
Inanna.

NINSUN A Sumerian goddess, originally imaged in the shape
of a cow. She embodies all the qualities associated with
cows. She was the wife of Lugalbanda and mother of
Dumuzi, the 'wild bull' of the cowherds, whom she lamented
in the annual observance of his death.

239

NINTU Also called Araru. A Sumeran goddess who fashioned 'king and lord.'

NINURTA In Assyrian religion, he was the son of Enlil. He was the war god. He also presided over storms, and was a guardian of the boundaries of fields. He was in addition a patron of physicians.

NIORD In Norse mythology he is also called Njordhr. He is the god of the ocean and the winds. He is also the patron god of sailors. Skadhi is his consort. Niord is akin to the Greek god Aeolus, who also was in charge of the winds and storms.

NIRRITI In Hindu mythology, a goddess of death and decay.

NIRVANA In Buddhism, the extinction of the threefold fire of *raga, dosa,* and *moha* (passion, hatred, delusion). When this fire dies out, the Buddhist attains a beatific spiritual condition and freedom from the necessity of future transmigration.

NIPPUR The cult center of Enlil ('lord of the storm') in central Babylonia. From the earliest historical times it was regarded as a neutral sacred city to which different parts of the country sent votive offerings. Afterwards, the Babylonians identified Marduk with Enlil. Still later, the Assyrians equated Enlil with Assur and made his name synonymous with the Canaanite Baal.
Most of the Sumerian literature known to exist was discovered at Nippur. One tablet is inscribed with a fragment of a deluge myth differing from the version at Ninevah.

NISABA The Mesopotamian goddess of grain. She is equated with the Greek goddess Demeter, whose functions were identical. Among the Romans Demeter was identified with the goddess Ceres. She became the patroness of writing.

NISIR In Babylonian mythology, the mountain on which Utnapishtim's ark came to rest after the Flood.

NITHHOGG In Norse mythology, a dragon that lives in the well Hvergelmir, in Niflheim, gnawing at the root of Yggdrasil, the great ash-tree that symbolizes the universe.

NIUBU An Apo Tani priest. He approaches gods and spirits on behalf of those faced with a personal crisis.

NIX In Teutonic mythology, this was an evil water-spirit. It was capable of assuming a half-human, half-fish form.

NJORD One of the Vanir, Norse divinities of fertility. He was also worshipped as god of the north wind. See Niord.

NOCCA An ancient Gothic god; identified with Neptune.

NODOSUS In Roman mythology, a rustic god who was in charge of knots and joints in stalks.

NORDIC TREE In Norse mythology Odin, the supreme deity, achieves knowledge of the runes and of the drink of immortality by hanging from the tree, Yggdrasil.

NORITO Shinto prayers recited by priests or by high government officials. The ritual is believed to have magical effect.

NORNS In Norse mythology, they were three maidens—Urd, Verdandi, and Skuld—who constituted Fate. They were akin to the classical concept of Fate, namely, the three sisters called Clotho, Lachesis, and Atropos. The Norns determined the manner of death of mankind.

NORSE CYCLE In Norse religion, everything that exists—gods, men, animals, plants—is doomed to disintegration and chaos. From this chaos the cycle of creation begins again. This concept coincides with the Stoic view of the conflagration of the cosmos, followed by a new cycle.

NORSE GODS In Norse mythology there were twelve principal deities: Odin, Thor, Balder, Hermod, Tyr, Forseti, Bragi,

Heimdal, Hodur, Vidar, Uller, Vali. They constituted a group called the Aesir. A variant Norse pantheon included these gods: Njordr, Tyr, Bragi, Loki, Hoenir, Kuasir, Freyr, Heimdal, Hoder, Vidar, Vali, Uller. The goddesses were the following: Fulla, Sjofn, Lofn, Vara, Syn, Gerda, Rinda, Freya, Frigg, Jord, Saga, Sith, Idun, Hlin, Bil, Sigyn, Fir, Nanna, Gefjon, Snotra, Gna, Sol.

NORTIA In Etruscan religion, a deity that was originally associated with a particular family and later on became widely popular.
The center of her worship was at Volsinii. She was identified with the Roman goddess Fortuna.

NOVENSIDES A group of Roman divinities whose functions are obscure. Presumably, the name given by the ancient Romans to new gods received from other peoples.

NOX In Roman religion, one of the most ancient deities. She was the goddess of night. Her union with her brother Erebus produced Aether (air) and Dies (day).

NUDIMMUD In the Akkadian myth of creation, Apsu received advice from his Mummu on how to destroy Nudimmud, his offspring. Apsu was ultimately slain by Nudimmud, who wrapped up Apsu's Mummu and laid it crosswise on his body. Nudimmud later mated with Damkina, 'Lady of the Earth.'

NUDIPEDALIA In Roman religion, an annual festival during which the participants walked barefooted, in commemoration of a public disaster.

NUER RELIGION The Nuer religion, practiced by some three hundred thousand tribesmen living on the banks of the Nile in the southern Sudan, reflects an awareness of the omnipresence of spirits. These spirits are put into two categories, the free and the earthbound, those of the upper regions and those of the world below. Kwoth is the god of the heavens, an invisible and ubiquitous spirit, the creative force of the universe, the explanation of all things. The Nuer are very religious and attribute their suffering to neglect of their duties to various spirits.

NUMEN In Roman religion, the divine force ascribed to an object or a person held in awe. There were numina of rivers, trees, fields, etc.

NUNDINA A Roman goddess who presided over the ninth day of a child's age. On this day the infant was named.

NUSKU A Sumerian-Assyrian god of fire. He also personified the moon. His worship was centered at Harran. His symbol was a lamp. He corresponds to the Babylonian Giro, also the god of fire.

NUT In ancient Egypt, the sky-goddess who was separated from her husband, Geb, the earth-god, by Shu, the air-god.

NYAKALA An Amba goddess, seen by the tribesmen as being the most powerful member of the whole supernatural host. By sacrificing to her, Amba women hope to overcome sterility.

NYAME An Akan god who, without the help of a male partner, gave birth to the universe.

NYIKANG Leader of the Shilluk in their heroic age, he led them to their present homeland in the southern Sudan. The spirit of Nyikang is believed to have passed from king to king down to Dak Fadiet, the divine ruler elected in 1945. He is the medium between man and God.

NYJA A Polish deity whose functions are not known. Sometimes identified with Pluto.

243

NYMPH In Greek and Roman mythology, one of the lesser divinities of nature, often represented as beautiful maidens dwelling in the ocean, a fountain, or a grove. Favorites with the greater divinities, they were the guardians of human beings.

NYORO GHOST CULT The Nyoro attribute misfortune to sorcery (*burogo*), nonhuman spirits (*mbandwa*), or the activity of a ghost, the disembodied spirit of a person who has died. Ghosts are associated with the underworld (*Okuzimu*) and may appear in dreams, but they are never seen. When a sick person suspects that a ghost has caused his illness, he relies on a local diviner (*muraguzi*) to diagnose his trouble and identify the ghost. The ghost must be induced to 'mount into the head' of the affected person, then destroyed or kept at bay. The muraguzi, if he could not destroy the ghost, might perform rituals or specific acts requested by the ghost.

NZAMBI In the Congo, a sky-god.

O

OANNES A Babylonian deity, part fish and part man, known in legends transmitted through the fragments of Berossos. He is said to have appeared from the sea, bringing to the Babylonians letters, science, and civilization. He was represented with a fish-like body, two human heads and two hands and feet.

OBAKU SHU A branch of the Meditation School of Buddhism in Japan.

OBEAH (OBI) A cult prevalent in the West Indies, particularly in Jamaica. Similar to Vodon (Voodoo), it uses corpses and is therefore associated with Satanic sorcery. Its rites and practices include elements of ophiolatry.

OBELISK An upright monolithic pillar. Like many other elements of the Egyptian religion, it may have been a phallic symbol.

OCCATOR In Roman mythology, a minor deity. He presided over the harrowing of the fields, and his worship was celebrated at the time of harrowing.

OCCULTISM A name given to a group of rejected sciences: astrology, horoscopy, palmistry, alchemy, etc.

OCEAN In Norse religion, the encircling Ocean was made from the blood of the giant Ymir.

OCEANID In ancient Greek mythology, a sea-nymph, the offspring of Oceanus, the ocean god, and Tethys. The Oceanids were said to number three thousand.

OCHER The widespread practice of coating corpses with red ocher seems to have existed since the beginning of the Paleolithic period. Perhaps the red color is associated with life-supporting blood and represents an attempt by survivors to make the body of the deceased again serviceable for its owner's use. The red powder is found in almost all Paleolithic graves, yet its use was in no way necessary for burying a corpse. It was also scattered on the floors of caves, such as the Lascaux caves, in southern France. Though its exact significance remains a mystery, it clearly was linked with religious rites.

OCYPETE In Greek and Roman mythology, one of the Harpies.

ODACON A Syrian deity whose functions were identified with Dagon.

ODIN In Norse mythology, the one-eyed supreme god, the God of Gods, the All-Father, the Lord of Hosts, the Many-shaped. As Alfadur, he is the ruler of heaven and earth, but not the primal Creator.
He is also designated by some fifty other descriptive titles. As god of agriculture, a harvest offering is dedicated to him. He is the arbiter of life and death, war and peace. As war-god, prisoners taken in war are sacrificed to him. His home is in Asgard, the Nordic Olympus, and his palace is Hlidskialf. His other functions include the invention of runes. Like the Greek Apollo, he was the inspiration of poets, and also presided over the magic arts. The magic cauldron of his uncle Mimir gave him wisdom.
From his throne he surveys the universe, like a Nordic Jupiter. He is represented as an old, white-bearded figure riding the winds on a white horse and bringing tempests and havoc in his wake. In another aspect, he is a mighty warrior. He was responsible for provoking the first universal war.
In Teutonic mythology his name is Wotan or Woden. Wednesday is derived from his name. His chief wife, his

Queen, is Frigga, and his son is Balder. Like Jupiter, he has a great many other offspring.

Odin formed one of the triad of Norse deities, the two other members being Thor and Freyr.

Although a god, Odin could not escape death. He therefore ordered his body to be burned, so that his soul would return to Asgard. Asgard itself corresponded to the Elysian Fields described by the Roman poet Vergil in his *Aeneid*.

ODIN'S HORSE In Norse religion, Sleipnir is the horse used by Odin for making his ascents and descents.

ODUR In Norse mythology, the husband of Freya. He was changed into a statue because he abandoned his wife after she had lost her beauty.

OEAIHU An esoteric term for the six in one or the mystic seven. The ever present manifestation of the universal principle.

OERA LINDA BOEK A Frisian manuscript that putatively contains esoteric knowledge.

OGAM A mystery language used by the early Celts.

The ancient Celtic form of writing is found on stone monuments in Scotland, Ireland, and Wales. It is thought to have been a system used by the Druids for secret magical communications.

OGENUS A Greek god who presided over old men.

OGMA (OGMIOD, OGMIOS) A god worshipped by the ancient Druids. He was the god of eloquence and the inventor of ogam writing.

OGOA An obscure Carian deity.

OHO-HARAHI In Shinto, the *Oho-harahi* ('Great Purification') ritual was celebrated twice a year. It was supposed to remove every trace of contamination pollution since its last celebration.

OHONAMOCHI In Shinto, an earth god worshipped today in the province of Idzuma. He was the offspring of Susa-no-wo and the father of many children, including the god of the harvest and the goddess of food.

OHO-NIHE In Shinto, the Oho-nihe ('Great Tasting') was regarded as the greatest of the sacred ceremonies. An elaborated version of the annual festival of firstfruits, it served to inaugurate the reign of a new Mikado.

OKI A North American sky demon.

OLDEST GOD In Egyptian religion, in the *Book of the Dead,* Ra the sun god is regarded as the oldest of the deities, identified with Temu, an indigenous solar god of Egypt.

OLMECS They were early inhabitants of Mexico who were subjugated by later cultures, including the Aztecs, who absorbed the religious beliefs of the Olmecs.

OLYMPIAN GAMES Greek religious games held every four years at Olympia in honor of Zeus.

OLYMPUS The highest mountain in Greece, between Macedonia and Thessaly. It was the abode of Zeus (Jupiter) and the principal deities, the Olympian gods, who were also called the Immortals.

OM (AUM) A mystic syllable used in Hinduism, occultism, primitive masonry, and syncretic cults practiced in modern youth communes which have recently sprung up all across the United States. The Hindu syllable originally denoted assent but is now the most solemn of all words heard in India. A mantra representing the triple constitution of the universe, it is used as an invocation, a benediction, an affirmation, and a promise. It is generally placed at the beginning of sacred scriptures and prefixed to prayers. The three component parts of the syllable are the Absolute

(Agni or Fire), the Relative (Varuna or Water), and the relation between them (Maruts or Air). The mystic syllable is called the Udgitta and is sacred with both Buddhists and Brahmins. It is chanted each evening before dinner by members of some youth communes after they have joined hands and stood for two or three minutes in silent meditation.

OMBIASY NKAZO In Madagascar, the name given to a medicine man.

OMBOS The cult center of Set, an early god of Egypt.

OMETECUTLI A supreme being worshipped by the Aztecs.

OMORCA An ancient Chaldean deity identified with the sea and Tiamat.

OPENING OF THE MOUTH A ceremony which originated among the early inhabitants of the valley of the Nile. Ancient formulas were recited during the performance of ceremonial rites to reconstitute the body of a person who had died and restore to its *ba* and *ka,* its living soul and the ghostly double of this soul, given to the person at birth. Originally, the ceremony was performed on a statue and consisted in using holy water and other substances to purify the statue, presenting the foreleg of a slain ox to the statue, touching its eyes, nose and ears with various magical instruments, and pronouncing a formula which ended, 'the mouth of every god is opened.' Finally, the statue was invested with royal insignia and a sacred meal was served on the altar. The king had the sacred duty to perform the reanimation rites for his deceased father.

OPERTANEA These were sacrifices performed in honor of the goddess Cybele. Her votaries were enjoined to preserve scrupulous silence during the rituals.

OPHIOLATRY The cult of the serpent. This cult was prevalent in ancient Greece where the serpent was regarded as a domestic deity.

249

In Egypt the serpent was sometimes a god of evil. As such he was crushed by Horus. Among the Romans, too, both Jupiter and Apollo destroyed the serpent.

In many primitive religions the serpent is an object of tabu and is associated with magic rites.

In another aspect the serpent was revered for his healing attributes. Among the Gnostics, he was the Master of Wisdom. In pre-Columbian America, he was the plumed serpent Quetzalcóatl.

OPHITES A Gnostic sect that originated anciently in Syria. The members considered the serpent as the symbol of the supreme emanation of the Divinity.

OPS In Roman religion, an ancient Italian goddess of plenty, fertility, and power. Later, she was identified with the Greek Rhea and made the consort of Saturn.

ORA The word pronounced by the Hawaiian god Teave to initiate the process of life in the region of Po.

ORACLE HEAD In the alchemical tradition, the oracle head seems to point to an original human sacrifice. Such sacrifices may have been made for the purpose of summoning up familiar spirits. A severed head, prepared according to prescribed rites, was supposed to reveal to people their inmost thoughts and to answer questions addressed to it. Gerbert of Reims, who later became Pope Sylvester II, was believed to have a golden head with oracular powers. The alchemical head may be connected with the teraphim, considered by Rabbinic tradition to have been a decapitated skull or a dummy head.

The oracle head was also known in ancient Greece and may go back to the severed head of Osiris, which was linked with the notion of resurrection. Aelian swore that the head of Archonides was preserved in a jar of honey by his friend Cleomenes of Sparta, who consulted it as an oracle. Similar powers were attributed to the head of Orpheus.

ORACLES In ancient religions these were utterances of a god through the medium of a priestess attached to the deity's temple. The characteristic of an oracle was that the interpretation was ambiguous and obscure. Responses could therefore harmonize with questions in a number of different or even contradictory ways. In this manner the integrity and veracity of the divine oracle could not be impugned. The manner of the response varied. Sometimes it was, as at Dodona in Greece, the rustling of oak leaves. Or it might be the utterance of a priestess at the temple of Apollo in Delphi. Or a dream at Epidaurus.

The two most famous shrines where oracular responses were given were the temple of Zeus at Dodona and the temple of Apollo at Delphi. The Delphic oracle gained a reputation as the most powerful influence throughout all Greece.

In Italy, the Sibyl's Cave under the temple of Apollo at Cumae and the temple of Fortuna at Praeneste were notable.

ORAL TRADITIONS Among the Druids of ancient Gaul, the traditions and sagas of the people were committed to memory in verse.

ORBONA A Roman goddess who protected orphans.

ORCUS In Greek religion, he was the god of the Lower Regions. He is identified with the Roman Dis.

OREAD In Greek mythology, one of the Nymphs presiding over mountains and hills.

ORENDA Among the Iroquois Indians, this expression denoted the principle of life.

ORIENTAL GODDESS IN ROME The first Oriental deity worshipped by the Romans was the goddess of Phrygia. She was the goddess associated with the city of Pessinus and Mt. Ida. In the West, she was called the Mighty Mother of the Gods. She was the Phrygian Cybele. In Italy her worship endured for some six centuries. In 205 B.C., when Hannibal threatened Bruttium, torrents of stones terrified the Romans. The sacred Books advised that the enemy would be driven off if the Great Mother of Ida, that is Cybele, were brought to Rome. Roman ambassadors took back with them a black aerolite, the abode of the goddess. The stone was carried by Roman matrons to the Palatine Hill, where it was installed formally in 204 B.C. In honor of the goddess, annual festivals, known as the Ludi Megalenses, were instituted.

ORMAZD In the Zoroastrian religion, the supreme god, the principle of good, creator of the world, "the wise lord," and guardian of mankind. He is the opponent of Ahriman, the spirit of evil.

ORPHEOTELESTAI In ancient Greece, they were imposters who traveled from place to place offering initiates in the Orphic cult redemption on payment of a fee for which they recited certain formulas.

ORPHEUS In Greek mythology, Orpheus was a Thracian poet and minstrel, whose music held a supreme charm. He almost succeeded in freeing his wife Eurydice from Hades, but, although forbidden by the gods, he looked back at her before reaching the upper world and so lost her.

ORPHIC HYMNS The Orphic mystery rites of ancient Greece were expounded in hymns putatively composed by Orpheus himself. The precepts therein were intended to cleanse the initiate of impurity. They also contained explanations of the genesis of the gods and men, as well as directions for man's redemption through self-denial and ascetic practices.

ORPHIC MYSTERIES These mysteries, founded by Orpheus, were secret rituals associated with the cult of Dionysus. Orphism taught morality, a pure life, and promised reincarnation in the life after death. Details of rituals are obscure, but it is known that initiates were required to obstain from meat, beans, and sexual intercourse.

OSIRIS In Egyptian religion, the great god of the underworld, sun god, and judge of the dead. The son of Geb and Nut,

he was the brother and husband of Isis. The Greeks identified Osiris with Dionysus, the symbol of fertility and life.

OSSIPAGO A Roman deity who presided over the development
of flesh and bone in infants.

P

PACHACAMAC The principal deity among the Incas of Peru. He is supposed to have existed from the beginning of time and to have created man by saying, 'Let man be.'

PAGANISM IN GREECE The pagan religion of ancient Greece was polytheistic. It conceived a multiplicity of deities concerned with the universe. It was also anthropomorphic, depicting the deities in human form and character.

Divinities were added to the native Greek pantheon as invaders swarmed over the mainland and as cultural contacts arose with other territories that imported new gods and new cults.

The supreme god, Zeus, was not the primal Creator. He was the father of the gods and of men, but he was not omnipotent or omniscient.

The Olympic gods comprised twelve deities, six male and six female, with Zeus as the foremost of them all.

There were secondary deities also, both male and female, spirits and demons: in all, some 30,000.

Worship of the gods aimed at winning their favor and goodwill. The approach was through offerings of produce of the fields, sacrifices, and prayers.

PAINAL In Aztec religion, the war god and messenger of Huitzilopochtli. Priests dressed as this god ran through towns to announce a call to arms.

PALENGENESIA The Greek mystery religions consisted of symbolic rites whose meaning was esoteric and whose aim was to inspire the initiate with a mystic experience that led him to palengenesia or regeneration.

255

PALENQUE A cultural center of the classic Maya civilization. It excels in low-relief carving as well as in stucco modeling. The Temple of the Sun stands on a low pyramid, in contrast to the towering pyramids of Tikal. Hieroglyphic matter in the Temple of the Inscriptions is a notable feature. This center, located in Chiapas, Mexico, has a sacred character and must have been constructed under the supervision of a ruling caste whose esoteric knowledge and ability set them apart from the peasants.

PALEOLITHIC CULT OF THE DEAD Available evidence concerning the disposal of the dead suggests that a cult of the dead existed from the beginning of the Pleistocene period and that it became associated with the cult of the Great Mother. Preservation of the skull and extraction of the brain, ceremonial interment, the presence of flint implements, animal bones, ochreous powder, shells and other ornaments at burial sites, all available data point to the existence of religious rites and beliefs.

Scores of sepulchers dating from the age of the reindeer have been discovered in Europe. The deceased usually was interred in a pit, with a few stones to protect his head. Ornaments included shell hairnets, necklaces, and delicately carved objects of bone or ivory. At Laugerie-Basse, Dordogne, cowries were placed in pairs on the forehead, feet, etc. The shape of the shells suggests a connection with the female principle and their employment as fertility charms. Thus the distribution of these shells may have been for the purpose of giving life to the deceased. Firm trussing of the body immediately after death may have been a cautionary measure, intended to protect the living against the dead, but the care taken in the ritual disposal of the body indicates that respect and concern for the dead went beyond fear. See Ocher, Blood, Shells.

PALEOLITHIC RELIGION Paintings and artifacts dating from the Old Stone Age testify to primitive man's dual involvement with his kindred and superhuman powers. All available evidence points to the existence of a coherent religious conception proclaiming man's intimate relationship with the divine. Deep in caves which could be entered only at great risk, primitive man left paintings which may have had great religious significance. Ancient burial sites yield further evidence of primitive religious life.

PALES A Roman rustic goddess. She presided over shepherds and their flocks.

PALICI Two Roman deities associated with two sulfurous pools in Sicily.

PALLAS ATHENA (MINERVA) In classical legend, the goddess of wisdom.

PAMYLIA An ancient phallic ceremony, observed in honor of the birth of Osiris.

PAN (FAUNUS) An ancient Greek god of herdsmen. He is represented as partly human, partly hircine. He was a follower of the god Dionysus.

PANDA A Roman deity who opened roads.

PANEGYREIS In Greek religion, assemblies of Greeks in a sanctuary dedicated to a god. The Olympic and the Pythian Games constituted panegyreis.

PAPA In the Hawaiian pantheon, a member of the fourth heavenly trinity. She was queen of the kingdom of nature and the mate of Vatea.

PARACELSUS The name adopted by Theophrastus Bombastus von Hohenheim (c. 1490-1541), one of the most famous physicians and occultists of the Middle Ages. He regarded the life of man as inseparable from that of the universe and disease as the result of a separation of the three mystic elements of which man is compounded — salt, sulfur, and mercury.

PARADISE In Sumerian religion, paradise was destined for the immortal gods, not for mankind.

PARCA In Roman religion, a birth goddess corresponding to the Greek concept of *Moira.* See Fate.

PARE In Tahunaism, a verse or chant transmitted orally through the centuries by the high priests of the religion. The word also means a veil or cloak that obscures or conceals an esoteric meaning. It meaning was revealed only to selected members of the House of Teave and to adepts who taught the hula in temples.

PARIHAI In Hawaiian mythology, the consort of Paritu.

PARITU In Hawaiian mythology, one of the progenitors of the Paritu dynasty He sprouted from the Tree of Life in Po at the beginning of the twelfth era of Creation.

PASTOPHORI In the temples of Isis and of Serapis in Rome, the pastophori were the priests who carried the shrines in processions.

PATELINA In Roman mythology, a minor goddess who was in charge of the grain after it appears out of the pod.

PATELLARII Minor Roman deities.

PATINA A Roman goddess who taught infants to eat and drink.

PAUT In Egyptian religion, the company of the gods who helped Osiris as judge in the Judgment Hall of the Dead.

PAX A deified personification of peace, to whom the Romans often erected shrines on making a peace. She was equivalent to the Greek goddess Irene.

PEAK SANCTUARIES By the middle of the Minoan period (3,000-1100 B.C.) mountain peaks were used for worship. Bonfires apparently formed part of the cult of a nature divinity. The existence of such a cult is attested by discoveries in Crete.

PECUNIA A Roman goddess who presided over money.

PELE In the Hawaiian religion, she is the goddess who presides over volcanoes.

PELONIA In Roman mythology, a goddess whose function was to repel enemies.

PENATES In Roman religion, the spirits that protected the food storehouse in the home.

PEPENUTH An ancient Saxon deity whose functions are obscure.

PERCUNUS A Teutonic deity. See Perkunas.

PERDOITE A Teutonic deity who presided over seamen and fishermen.

PERGUBRIOS A Teutonic deity who presided over the produce of the earth. His festival was held in March.

PERKUNAS An ancient Baltic divinity, regarded as a thunder-god. A fire was always maintained in his honor.

PERSEPHONE In Greek religion, the daughter of Demeter, the earth-mother, and Zeus. Abducted by Hades (Pluto), she was allowed to spend only the summer months with her mother, becoming the symbol of the vegetation powers of nature.

PERSIAN RELIGION Persian religion extended in very early times to Babylonia and other areas of the Middle East. Among the oldest deities known to the Greeks were the two major divinities Ahura Mazda and Mithra. Herodotus, the Greek historian, Plutarch the Greek biographer, and the Roman Cicero make references to Persian religious rites.

PERT EM HRU The Egyptian *Book of the Dead,* a guide to the Nether Regions for the souls of the dead and a kind of manual of instructions.

PERUN In the old Baltic religion, he was the thunder god.

PETA A Roman goddess who presided over requests made to the gods.

PET TA FUAT In Egyptian religion, these were the three divisions of the world. They are akin to heaven, earth, and hell.

PEYOTISM In the old, pre-Columbian peyote cult, a spineless cactus plant called peyote *(peyotl* in Nahuatl) was used by Indians in Mexico and the United States to obtain visions and induce supernatural revelation. It was widely used to induce trances during tribal dancing rites. The modern peyote cult, which probably originated out of an Apache peyote rite, spread rapidly during the last half of the nineteenth century and became the most widespread indigenous religion of North America. It is a syncretistic cult stressing prayer, quiet contemplation, and peyote as a symbol of spirits and a sacrament. Peyotist doctrine is based on belief in the existence of power (mana, the Holy Spirit or Holy Ghost), spirits or personifications of power (the Christian trinity and Indian spirits such as the Indian Thunderbird or the Christian dove), and incarnations or material embodiments of power in the form of peyote, water, and the foods used in the morning communion breakfast. The main features of the peyotist ethic are brotherly love, concern for the family, self-reliance, and avoidance of strong drink. The peyote rites has four major components: prayer, singing, eating the sacred plant, and contemplation. It is through contemplation that the worshipper rises to the level of spiritual sublimity and communes with God.

PHALLICISM A form of nature worship in which the generative principle in nature is symbolized by the male organ or phallus. The custom is characteristic not only of primitive religions but also of sophisticated cultures. Anciently prevelant among the Semites, it was later adopted by the Greeks. Often occurring as a form of sympathetic magic, it may assume an orgiastic character in ceremonies, as in the *Sakti puja* of the Indians.

PHANES In the mystery cult of Orpheus, Phanes was a deity who issued from an egg made by Night. Phanes is also known as Phaëthon Protogonos, the First-Born and as Erikapaios. He is the Creator of all things. He is represented with the heads of various animals. His mother is Night.

PHERSIPNEI The Etruscan name of the goddess Persephone (Proserpina).

PHOENICIAN RELIGION In the Phoenician pantheon the supreme deity was El, and his consort was Ashirat. Baal or Hadad was the King of the gods. He presided over storms. His usual designation was Baal Shamen — Lord of Heaven. Ashirat (Astarte) and Anath were goddesses of fecundity.

PHORCUS A sea deity to whom a harbor of Ithaca was devoted, son of Neptune, and father of Medusa and the other Gorgons.

PHRYGIAN MYSTERIES A ritualistic cult that was practiced in the Mediterranean littoral. It centered around Cybele, the Great Mother of the Gods, her lament on her lover Attis' death, and her jubilation on his rebirth in spring. The cult symbolized a vegetation myth.

PHYTALUS In Greek mythology, a demi-god who welcomed Demeter when she came to Eleusis.

PICUMNUS and PILUMNUS Among the Romans, twin minor deities. They presided over nuptial auspices.
Picumnus discovered fertilizer.

PILA One of two gods to whom the Apa Tanis sacrifice fowls. Pila and Yachu are associated with the escape or ransom of prisoners of war. They are promised sacrificial fowls in exchange for their help.

PILLAR CULT In Minoan-Mycenaean times in ancient Greece, columns and pillars were venerated as divinities. Pillars were even regarded as personifications of the deities themselves.

PILLARS OF SHU In Egyptian religion, these are the pillars of heaven.

PILUMNUS In Roman religion, he was a minor deity. He is credited with inventing the art of kneading dough and baking bread. He protected children.

PISAMAR A Baltic deity whose functions are obscure.

PISTIS SOPHIA A Gnostic treatise. It was written in Egypt and belongs in the third century A.D. Its contents deal with Gnostic mysteries and the purification of the soul by means of these mysteries.

PITRIS In Hindu mythology, the ten Prajapatis or progenitors of the human race. In popular theology they are said to be created from Brahma's side.

PITS Pits were dug in mystery cults and in other religious ceremonies. Liquids were poured into these pits, as offerings to the gods of the Lower Regions.

PLAGUE The Babylonians ascribed plagues to seven earth-spirits who were born without parents in the encircling Ocean.

PLATO Many nobler forms of mysticism are derived from the writings of Plato (427-347 B.C.), who laid the foundation for much subsequent philosophy.

PLATONIC CREATOR In Plato's dialogue, the *Timaeus,* the Creator is the Demiurge, the Craftsman. He produces a world based on eternal order. The Demiurge is also the creator of the other gods and the offspring of the gods.

PLUTO A euphemistic name for the Greek god of the underworld. He was the son of Cronus and Rhea, husband of Proserpine, and brother of Zeus and Poseidon. Black animals were sacrificed to him, particularly at Elis, where he was Hades, god of the dead.

PLUTUS Greek god of wealth, blinded by Zeus in order that he might distribute his gifts without prejudice. He was the son of Iasion and Demeter.

PO One of the names for the Hawaiian equivalent of Hell. The word can also mean the divine region of man's origin and the exalted realm of spirit which can illuminate the *tahuna's* mind even as his physical body sleeps. Native priests insisted that the Hawaiian people could trace their origin to Po, the Region of God.

PODOGA An ancient Baltic deity whose functions are not known.
Possibly a god of the air.

POLOTU In Polynesia, the legendary or mythical island of certain gods and of the elect after death.

POLYDAEMONISM Worship of many local deities linked with trees, plants, and other objects. Characteristic of ancient Semitic populations, it is typical of the nomadic way of life. Tribal deities had no fixed abode and were unlikely to spread beyond the region occupied by a tribe. The prestige of local deities varied with the ascendancy of the tribes to which they belonged.

POMONA An old Italian goddess of fruit, orchards, and gardens. She had a special priest at Rome, the *flamen Pomponalis,* and a sacred grove, the Pomponal, near Ostia. See Vertumnus.

POP and KOD In the Papuan story of the beginnings of mankind, Pop appeared first. He saw a pair of turtles copulating and decided that he needed a mate. He created a sea cow

263

out of white mud, added two legs, and lay down to sleep. The next morning, he held the figure up to his face and coughed into its mouth.

POPOL VUH This was the sacred book of the Quiche Indians, a branch of the Mayans. The expression means collection of the council. It consists of information on traditions, history, religion, mythology.

POREVIT A Slavonic five-headed god.

PORTUNUS In Roman religion, he was the god of harbors.

POSEIDON (NEPTUNE) In ancient Greek mythology, god of the sea. He is identified with the Roman god Neptune. In some areas of the Greek mainland Poseidon was the god who presided over earthquakes and horses.

POSTVORTA and ANTEVORTA Two Roman deities who presided over the past and the future, respectively.

POTINA A Roman goddess who presided over infants. She gave them milk to drink.

PRAJAPATI In the Vedas, he is first an epithet of Savitar and Soma, then an abstract god and the apotheosis of the creative activity of the universe. In the later period of the Brahmanas, he becomes the chief deity.

PRAJAPATIS In Hindu mythology, the progenitors or givers of life to all on this earth.

PRAKRITI In the Sankhya system of Hindu philosophy, nature in general, as opposed to Purusha. These are the two primeval aspects of the one unknown deity.

PRAPATTI-MARGA In Hinduism, the way of salvation by complete surrender to God.

PREANIMISM The theory that primitive people had a definite concept of the supernatural before they reached the stage of animism.

PRE-EXISTENCE This is a belief that postulates the existence of the soul before its incarnation in the human body. The ancient Egyptians and the Manichaeans held this view.

PRESERVATION OF THE DEAD In ancient Egypt, it was the custom to preserve the body of the dead. The custom prevailed from pre-dynastic times down to the seventh century A.D.

PRIAPUS In classical mythology, he was the god of procreation and fertility. He is represented as a deformed figure in an ithyphallic pose.

PRIESTLY DUTIES In Assyro-Babylonian religion, the priesthood performed a great variety of functions. The priests maintained the cultural tradition of the people. They regulated the system of measurements. They reduced rates of interest. They granted loans without interest. They regulated the calendar. They recorded and interpreted astronomical phenomena. The priestly scribes collected, copied, and expounded the religious literature. They also provided texts for the study of the Sumerian language, which was regarded as a sacred tongue. They trained young priests in the art of divination.

PRIESTLY ROUTINE In Assyro-Babylonian religion, the priests were required to prepare food for the gods, organize the order of daily or festal rituals, and supervise the activities of the deity from morning to night, when the sanctuary was closed.
In the kitchens adjoining the temples, feasts were prepared and served two or three times daily. Drink, including water for washing the fingers, was also a matter of concern for the priests.
The consumption of the food destined for the deity was assigned to the priests who were enclosed in a tent around the divine image. The actual consumption of food by the god was a religious mystery, forbidden to the laity.

265

PRIESTLY SERVICE In Egyptian religion, all over the land the sequence of temple service was virtually identical. Acts of purification, involving both priests and statues of the gods, were followed by offerings, then by a procession of the gods. Each ceremony was accompanied by music and dancing and the chanting of hymns.

Offerings consisted of animals, vegetables, fruit. Sometimes part of the sacrificial animal was eaten ceremonially. At Memphis a bull was so used, and at Thebes a ram. In other, earlier times antelopes, wild goats, and gazelles were immolated.

For the people in general, there were shrines in their own homes, as well as wayside sanctuaries.

Festivals and feasts were common. The festivals were related to fertility cults, to harvests, and to special temple banquets. Each god had his own calendar that was supervised by the priestly attendants. One festival, celebrating the deification of the ruler as Osiris, was held every thirty years.

PRIEST-RULER Among the Maya of Yucatan the ruler performed a dual function. He was high priest as well. This dual funciton is comparable to the status of Julius Caesar, who was both High Priest and head of the state.

PRIMITIVE RELIGION A term applied to the supernatural elements within the whole complex of life. Belief in spirits and associated patterns of behavior have been called *animism*. Spirits may inhabit objects or bodies and may control the well-being of individuals and groups. Specialists (shamans) may communicate with the spirit world. An interesting feature of American religion is the development of the notion of guardian spirits. Preanimistic religion, sometimes called animatism, stresses *mana*, or supernatural power as conceived by the Melanesians. Worship of a 'high god' or supreme being has been observed among primitives as well as among advanced cultures.

Primitive people often have complicated theories about the origin of the universe and divine powers. These mythologies vary widely. Ritual, sacrifice, exorcism, and prayer are essential elements of many primitive religions. Magic is important in the lives of primitive people, but most of them make a distinction between natural means of achieving goals and magical means. Finally, tabu is an important element of most primitive religions.

Outstanding among the many theories of primitive religion is that of Emile Durkheim, who thinks that from the psychological point of view, society is the real god. The most distinctively religious behavior is a part of group activities, such as religious festivals. The totem animal is the symbolic representation of the true object of religion, which is too abstract for the primitive mind.

PRIPEGALIA A Baltic deity whose functions are not known.

PROAA A Teutonic deity who presided over justice.

PROPHETES In the temples of Isis and of Sarapis in Rome, the prophetes were priests skilled in sacred science.

PROSTITUTION Sacred prostitution of both sexes was practiced by the Syrians and Anatolians. In the second millennium B.C. the Syrian goddess was commonly represented as a naked woman holding fertility symbols, such as snakes and lily stalks. The name applied to eunuchs by the Western Semites also meant 'male prostitute.'

PROVEN A Baltic deity whose functions are obscure.

PTAH Egyptian god associated with the city of Memphis. He is represented in human form. He was the creator, also the dispenser of life and inventor of crafts. Among the Greeks he was identified with Hephaestus, the craftsman-god.

PUJA A form of worship, performed daily by every devout Hindu. In the temple it is performed by a Brahmin priest. In the home, it is sometimes performed by a priest but generally by the householder.

PUDUHEPA Wife of the Hittite king, Hattusilis III.

PULOTU A deity of Samoa whose functions are obscure.

PURANAS A collection of Sanskrit writings dealing with cosmogonic, theological, astronomical, and physical knowledge. In Hinduism, they comprise eighteen books of religious poems. They constitute the sacred literature of Hindu popular religion and are the sources of popular belief concerning origins, time, the gods, and the Vedas.

PURE LAND A school of Buddhism founded in China by Hui-yuan (334-416 A.D.) and in Japan by Honen (1173-1212 A.D.). The most popular school in China and Japan, it aims at birth in the Pure Land, the western heaven of Amita.

PURIFICATION Purification rites were performed in ancient pagan religions for various purposes. Sometimes the objective was to avert the influence of black magic or to cure sickness. In essence, purification was a cleaning procedure. This entailed baptism in water, in blood, a change of garments — all directed to a spiritual purification achieved during the mystery rites.

PURURAVAS The son of Buddha, born of Soma (the moon) and Ila. He is reputed to have been the first to produce fire by friction of two pieces of wood.

PURUSHA In Hindu philosophy, the male or evolving principle, spirit as opposed to matter, the source of creation. The Sanskrit word means 'man.'
The hymm to Purusha (in the Rig Veda X, 90) is said to be the starting point of Indian pantheism. Purusha is the Cosmic Man whose sacrifice by the gods becomes the origin of all things. There is but one fundamental world-ground, an all-encompassing unity. The pantheistic tendency eventually triumphed over the monotheistic tendency represented in Prajapati. In the Sankhya system, the word designates an individual soul. An infinite number of purushas exist distinct from matter (*prakriti*) and act upon matter.

PURUSHASPA In Zoroastrian religion, he was the father of Zoroaster himself.

PURUVIT A Baltic deity whose functions are obscure.

PUSAN (PUSHAN) In Vedic Hinduism, one of the lesser sun gods, probably introduced by a pastoral tribe. He is a shepherd, protector of flocks, and pathfinder. He helps people to find lost objects.

PUTATII Minor Roman deities.

PYRAMID TEXTS The early Egyptians had faith in the glorious after-life of their kings. Beginning in the Fifth Dynasty (c. 2400 B.C.), the walls of the interior chambers of pyramids were covered with hymns and magic spells to be used by the deceased king as he ascended to heaven and union with the sun god. The practice was inaugurated at the pyramid of Onnos, the last king of the Ffth Dynasty. The texts are among the longest and oldest religious inscriptions known. Some of them probably go back to the predynastic period. They are the principal source of knowledge concerning the earliest religion of Egypt.
These texts contain magic spells, which were used by each new ruler in order to become identified with the god Osiris.

PYTHAGOREANISM A system of philosophy founded by Pythagoras of Samos in the sixth century B.C. The Pythagoreans evolved an esoteric philosophy of which the supreme concept appears to be number. They held that the soul was timeless, changeless, self-existing, and at times the prisoner of successive bodies. They also believed in metempsychosis and considered earthly life to be merely a purification of the soul, which retained full memory of its earthly incarnations. They also advocated the eternal repetition of all things, and they originated the doctrine of the harmony of the stars.

Q

QENNA In Egyptian religion, she was the goddess of matter that has been revivified.

QEBHSENNUF In Egyptian religion, one of seven deities linked with funerary rites.
Also one of the gods of the four cardinal points, he watched over the intestines of the dead.

QETESH An Egyptian goddess of love. She is depicted as a nude woman standing on the back of a lion, with flowers in her hand. She is identified with Hathor.

QUETZALCOATL An Aztec god of the winds. He is the creator of men and the god of the waning moon. He is also the 'feathered snake' god.
Quetzalcoatl is a counterpart of Tezcatlipoca.
He is represented as a white-skinned, bearded figure. He is regarded as the inventor of the calendar, as the god of life, and the god of the East.

QUILLA The world-god of the Incas of Peru.

QUIRINUS In Roman religion, the name by which Romulus was designated after his deification.

R

RA The Egyptian sun god, who was worshipped particularly in Heliopolis, the City of the Sun. He is represented with a falcon's or ram's head, or with a sun disc over his shoulders. He was linked with Ammon. A variant form of his name is Re.

RADEGASTA A Slavic deity whose functions were similar to those of the war-goddess Bellona.

RAGA One of the five afflictions in Yoga philosophy. The Sanskrit word means 'passion.'

RAGNAROK In Norse religion, the end of the world, bringing a new age of righteousness on a new earth. The new age will involve a conflict between the gods and the evil giants, resulting in the defeat of evil.

RA'I RA'I In Hawaiian mythology, a goddess born of the mind of Tane in the sublimest realms of the celestial spheres. She was chosen by the Goddess of the Sun to give birth to the first human beings in the Garden of Sunshine: Mure, Tu Rua, Ha'i, Haria, and Hatia. Ta Rua plucked and ate the sacred *ape,* a plant resembling the taro, although her mother had forbidden her to do so. For the first time Ta Rua became conscious of the masculine beauty of her brothers, Mure and Hatia. The two brothers joined Ta Rua and Ha'i in their defiance of the divine decree. Children born of the union of brothers and sisters were at first hidden from Ra'i Ra'i, who finally found them. When these children grew up, they too ate of the forbidden fruit. Tane hurled a rain of stones upon his disobedient progeny but the population of Rua grew as generation succeeded generation in the land of the Mu.

Tane gave his first-born son, Mure, to Haria, still an obedient virgin. From their union sprang the noblest line of royal Hawaiian chiefs.

RANGI The name by which the great Sky Father is known among the Maoris.

RAMS Worship of the ram may have originated in North Africa or in Central Africa. The sacred animal was the symbol of Ammon, the sun god. The Mandingos of the West Sudan believe that the god of storm and thunder assumes the shape of a ram. The Baoulé of the Ivory Coast use the mask of a ram to represent Niannié, the personalized sky. Shango, the Yoruba god of storm and thunder, is represented by a ram's mask. As the symbol of Ammon, the ram became a divine Kushite figure. In Dahomey, divine rams in different forms have various significations. In the Cameroons and deep in the Congo, wood-carvers still are fashioning rams.

RAN In Teutonic religion, the goddess of the sea. In her palace dwelt those who had been drowned.

RASHNU In Zoroastrianism, Rashnu symbolized Justice, the Spirit of Truth. Rashnu forms a triad with Mithra and Sraosha to judge the dead.

RATA In the Hawaiian pantheon, one of the members of the third heavenly trinity. She was the daughter of Tane and the mate of Rono.

RAUNI An ancient Finnish goddess. She was the consort of Ukko.

RAYS In Akkadian literature, the undefined but elemental power or force possessed by all gods. One god might deprive another of his supernatural functions by stealing his Rays. Similar notions are expressed by *Mana* in Melanesia and by *Ton* as the word is used by the Dakotas.

RAYMI A festival celebrated by the Incas of Peru in honor of the Sun. The ceremony was held in June, at sunrise.

RELIGION OF EGYPTIANS Among the tenets of ancient Egyptian religion were a belief in the immortality of the soul, a faith in the continuous existence of the ka, and a belief in the efficacy of magic rituals and funerary sacrifices. Lastly, there was an acceptance of the Judgment of Osiris, that determined rewards for the righteous and destruction for the wicked. The rewards consisted of eternal life and happiness.

RELIGIOUS CENTERS In Egyptian religion, many cities were the centers of religious cults and were closely associated with some particular deity. Among such cities were Abydos, Thebes, Memphis, and Heliopolis.

REN In Egyptian religion, *ren* means the name of a person. The Egyptians regarded the name as a part of the person that must be guarded and preserved, as it had it an innate protective virtue in itself.
In family life a son was bound to preserve the name of deceased parents in order to maintain the continued existence of the parents in the afterlife.

RENNUT In Egyptian religion, she was the goddess in charge of the harvest.

REPHAIM In Canaanite religion, they were the denizens of the Lower Regions.

REPTILES In the Gilgamesh epic, the serpent stole the magic plant that conferred immortality. Because of its ability to shed its skin, the snake was widely considered to be immortal. The Zulus believed that two lizards were entrusted with messages concerning immortality; the second lizard, arriving last, canceled the immortality which had been conferred by the first. In East Africa, a snake stole the secret from a bird.

RESHEF An important Phoenician deity. In a cuneiform text from Ugarit, he is identified with Nergal, the Babylonian god of hell.

As a Syrian war-god, he was also the deity who presided over lightning, fire, and pestilence. He was absorbed into the Egyptian pantheon.

In Canaanite cult, the name Resheph was given to Mot, the genius of aridity and lifelessness.

RESURRECTION OF THE DEAD In the Sumerian religion, the spirits of the dead could be evoked from Fur, the realm of the dead.

RHEA In Greek mythology, she was an earth-goddess. She was associated with Crete. She was regarded as the mother of Zeus.

RHODES In Rhodes the principal cult was that of Helios, the sun-god.

RIG VEDA The oldest literary monument of the Indo-European races. It is one of four Vedas composing the most ancient sacred literature of India. It consists of 1,017 hymns, composed by many different generations and transmitted orally for a long period before it was recorded in Sanskrit, beginning as early as the fifteenth century B.C.

RIKSHA In Hindu writings, each of the twenty-seven constellations forming the Zodiac.

RIMMON Assyrian deity whose worship centered in Damascus.

RIND In Norse mythology, she is a goddess of the Norse pantheon.

RINVIT A Slavic deity, of obscure functions.

RISHABHA A sage supposed to have introduced the Jain doctrines into India.

RISHIS Those to whom the sacred vedas have been revealed. In Vedic literature the term denotes those persons through whom the mantras were revealed. Later, it came to mean adepts or inspired ones.

RITA In Vedic Hinduism, the concept of cosmic and ethical order. The concept almost certainly reaches back into ancient Indo-European thought. Varuna is the guardian of Order in the Rig Veda.

RITES A rite is a prescribed form of conducting a ceremony of profound significance. Confucius pointed up the importance of rites in any society when he said: 'Ceremonies are the bond that holds the multitudes together, and if the bond be removed, those multitudes fall into confusion.' In another passage of the *Book of Rites,* he is quoted as having said that ancient kings 'instituted ceremonies to direct men's aims aright.'

RITES OF INANNA In Sumerian religion, the goddess Inanna, who is the Semitic Ishtar, had a cult that required the participation of hierodules, who were sacred prostitutes attached to the temples, as well as eunuchs and perverts of various types.

RIVER GODS In ancient Greek mythology, rivers were identified with particular gods. The father of all rivers was Oceanus, the river that encircles the entire world. An important river god was Inachus, father of Io.
Altars were set up to such gods and sacrifices were performed by casting horses and bulls into streams. Among the Romans the Tiber river was a deity, in human form. So too with the Nile among the ancient Egyptians.

ROBIGUS A Roman god of the fields. He protected wheat against rust.

RODIGAST In Teutonic mythology, a war god.

ROIAKURILUO Among the Bororos of Brazil, this was a funeral lamentation.

ROMA In ancient Roman religion, the city of Rome was personified and worshipped as Dea Roma. She had temples in Asia Minor as early as the second century B.C. She was introduced into Egypt after it became a Roman province in 30 B.C.

ROMAN RELIGION Primitively, Roman religion was animistic, that is, it acknowledged the existence of spirits indwelling in trees, rivers, springs. There were also spirits associated with the home and the farm. With the development of the state, the spirits assumed new functions. For instance, Jupiter, god of the sky, became a god of justice.

Etruscan and Greek influences brought an anthropomorphic conception of the deities. The old Roman gods were frequently identified with Greek gods, with regard to functions and attributes.

Roman religion was extremely ritualistic. It stressed the formal and ceremonial features of all religious acts in which the Romans participated.

During the Empire, the old indigenous religious beliefs were gradually abandoned. The mystery cults of the East became influential, particularly among the common people but in time among the ruling classes as well and even in the Imperial court.

These Oriental cults appealed strongly to the emotions and furthermore they brought an assurance of happiness in the afterlife. The cults included the Eleusinian Mysteries, the cult of Cybele, or Isis and Osiris, of Mithra, and of Sabazius.

ROMAN TEMPLES The earliest Roman temple contained, in Etruscan-Italic tradition, three cells as private rooms for the triad of Jupiter, Minerva, and Juno. A very ancient type of temple was the small, round structure, like the temple of Vesta at Tivoli.

The most impressive temple is the Pantheon, rebuilt by the Emperor Hadrian.

The temple itself was not, either among the Greeks or the

278

Romans, a place of assembly for the people.

ROMULUS In the legendary history of Rome, he was the son of Mars and Silvia, a vestal. The founder and first king of Rome, he was deified after his death and worshipped under the name of Quirinus.

RONGO A Polynesian god of the same general type as Tu, Tane, and Tangaloa.

RONO In Tahunaism, one of the three sons of Tane. He was lord of the east and one of the 'Four Major Male Pillars of Creation.'

ROPI A rite performed by the Apa Tanis. The rite accompanies the disposal of human trophies. These trophies include hands, eyes, or tongues which are severed from the bodies of enemies and stored in a *nago* shrine until the performance of the rite. The idea underlying the practice is the belief that the dead man will be prevented from seeing his enemy again. The Apa Tanis also sacrifice an animal to their war gods at the conclusion of a successful raid against the enemy, thus fulfilling a promise made prior to the raid at a *lapang* sacrifice.

RUDRA In Vedic Hinduism, a storm god of minor importance, celebrated in three hymns in the Rig Veda. He represents the destructive or maleficent aspects of the storm.

RUMINA In Roman religion, an obscure goddess. She presided over mothers who were suckling their young. At her shrine offerings of milk were made.

RUNCINA A Roman goddess of weeding.

RUNES (FUTHARK) The word 'rune' means 'mystery' in its earliest usage in English and related languages. From the outset, runes were associated with magic, divination, and other rites. The runic alphabet later became the storehouse of pagan Germanic rites. The twenty-four runes of the common Germanic *futhark* (alphabet) were used to evoke or ward off the power continued in their ɩames. In Germanic mythology, Woden hung upon the world-ash Yggdrasil for nine nights, tormented by hunger and pain, until finally he glimpsed the runes which he then seized and passed on to men. Runes are credited with the power of resurrecting the dead and are associated with health, fertility, love, etc. Belief in rune-magic survived until the seventeenth century.

RUSINA A Roman rural goddess.

S

SABAZIUS He was a Thraco-Phrygian deity, who was sometimes identified in Greek mythology with Dionysus and in Roman religion with Jupiter. His cult was predominant in Lydia and Phrygia. In the late fifth century B.C. Sabazius was also worshipped at Athens. His cult was linked with that of Cybele. Symbolically, he was represented by a snake. The snake was also a central feature in the mystery cult of Sabazius. Sculpturally, he was depicted in Phrygian costume, bearing the eagle and the thunderbolt of Zeus. His Greek designation as *kurios Sabazios,* Lord Sabazius, has led some scholars to consider him as the Jewish God, the Lord Zebaoth.

SABBAT An assembly of demons, sorcerers and witches. In the medieval demonology, the witches' sabbat was celebrated at a crossroad or in some deserted place. At their midnight assembly, the attendants cast spells, plotted mischief, and engaged in orgies.

SACRAMENTAL SACRIFICE In the Thracian cult of Dionysus the women votaries, the Maenads, rent a goat or a bull, ate the raw flesh, and drank the blood. They were thus united with the divinity himself.

SACRA PRIVATA In ancient Rome, these were ceremonials of family worship. The father served as priest and the children as acolytes in rites honoring the Lares (spirits of ancestors), Penates (household divinities), and Vesta (goddess of the hearth).

SACRA PUBLICA In ancient Rome, ceremonials held on March 16 to mark the coming of age of young males. After putting on the *toga virilis* at the family altar and in the public

281

forum, the youth was taken to the Capitol and public sacrifices were made to the gods.

SACRED ANIMALS In ancient Egypt bulls, cats, ibises, hawks, snakes, rats, mice, toads, as well as beetles were held sacred. Their remains were mummified and preserved.

SACRED BABOON In Egyptian religion, the baboon was the sacred animal attached to the god Thoth.

SACRED BODY Among the Romans, a particular deity was associated with a part of the human body. The head was sacred to Jupiter. The chest was in the care of Neptune. Mars favored the waist. Cupid was attached to the eyes. Memory had charge of the ears. Fides claimed the right hand. The rear part of the body was in control of Pluto. Venus presided over the loins. Mercury was associated with the feet and Misericordia with the knees. Thetis presided over the ankles and the soles of the feet, while the fingers belonged to Minerva.

SACRED GAMES In Greek and Roman religion, certain games were held as solemn public festivals that honored the gods. In Greece there were Olympian, Pythian, Isthmian, and Nemaean Games.
Among the Romans, the principal Games were the Ludi Apollinares, glorifying Apollo; the Ludi Augustales, honoring the Emperor Augustus; the Ludi Capitolini, held in honor of Jupiter Capitolinus; the Ludi Cereales, athletic sports dedicated to Ceres.

SACRED GROVES In ancient pagan religions, in addition to temples, altars, and 'high places,' groves served as sanctuaries for the worship of the gods. They were also meeting-places for the initiates in the mystery cults. Here they performed their rituals and ceremonies. Such groves were considered to be the special haunts of divinities and thus acquired a particular sanctity.
Notable among such religious retreats were the groves associated with the Druidic worship and sacrifices held annually in Central Gaul.

SACRED IMAGES In Assyro-Babylonian religion, images of the deities were made of rare wood, plated with gold, and provided with large inset eyes. The images were robed resplendently and equipped with the divine insignia characteristic of the deity. These insignia included miters studded with jewels, and also pectorals. The image was then set on a pedestal, under a canopy. Beside the image stood the divinity's sacred symbol or animal.

The image could be transported, on the shoulders of temple attendants, or in a chariot, or in a special barque. The image was then set up in the precincts of the temple, or within the city, or even outside the city walls.

SACRED LITERATURE OF EGYPT The sacred writings of Egyptian religion consists of the Book of the Dead, the Pyramid Texts, the Litanies of Seker, the Festival Songs and Lamentations of Isis and Nephthys.

SACRED POOL Among the Mayans, the Sacred Pool near the Temple of the Serpent-God Kukulcan was the scene of many human sacrifices.

SACRED STONES The strange size or shape of some stones prompted pagans in antiquity to attach some mystic property to the stone itself and finally to endow it with divinity and consequent reverence.

SACRED TREES In prehistoric Greece, between 1600-1100 B.C., trees and even branches had a divine sanctity. They were venerated as vegetation deities. Among such trees were fig-trees, palms, cypresses, pines.

SACRED WRITINGS The Zoroastrians claimed that their sacred writings, the Zend Avesta, were a divine revelation. The sacred writings of Egypt and Babylonia are filled with ritual magic, spells, incantations, hymns to the gods, funerary rituals, festival songs.

SACRIFICES Sacrifice, whether in the form of a human victim, an animal, or an object, was prevalent in ancient pagan rituals. It was practiced by the Assyro-Babylonians, the

Egyptians, the Greeks and Romans, the Zoroastrians, the Aztecs, Mayans, Incas and many tribal communities in Asia and in the Pacific Islands.

In Greek and Roman religion, offerings to the gods in very ancient times consisted of cereals, vegetables, fruit, milk, honey, cheese, oil.

The most popular offering was a blood sacrifice of animals, birds, sows, dogs, horses, asses, and occasionally fish.

Human sacrifices belong to primitive practices. They were associated too with cannibalistic features.

Among American Indians sacrifices often assumed a more or less innocuous form. Objects were thrown into a fire, or rocks were placed at certain assigned spots, or wounds were self-inflicted. During the Sun Dance all such practices constituted 'sacrifices.'

SACROCANNIBALISM The custom of partaking piously of the flesh of the deceased is considered to be a sacred duty among the Melanesians of New Guinea. A variety of this custom may be exemplified by the Australians and Papuans, who smear the body with the fat of the deceased.

SADHANA In Tantric Buddhism, a ceremony to enable the worshipper to see and gain control of any god. Sadhana is also used in Hinduism to identify the means used by the mystic to attain to samadhi.

SADHU A Hindu ascetic or holy man.

SADHYAS In Hindu mythology, one of the names of the twelve great gods created by Brahma. The Sanskrit word means 'divine sacrificers.'

SAGA In Norse mythology, the goddess of history. She corresponds to Clio, the Greek goddess of history.

SAGO A dry starch prepared from a palm tree, a staple food in Indonesia. It is also mixed with the brains of the victim in ceremonies associated with the headhunting cult of the Asmat in New Guinea. The brains are eaten exclusively by the old men of the tribe.

One of the initiation rituals takes place in a sago wood

284

and consists of the ritual pounding of the striped trunk of a sago tree. An Asmat myth relates the sago tree to headhunting by telling how Biwiripitsj's son was killed to improve its pith (from which starch is prepared).

SAHE-NO-KAMI In Japanese religion, these are phallic deities and represent an abstract quality in nature. Since 1868, by order of the government, most phallic emblems have been removed from public view.

SAHU In Egyptian religion, the immaterial body of a deceased person. The sahu was believed capable of ascending to heaven and dwelling among the gods.

SAINT-GERMAIN The Count of Saint-Germain died about 1784. Of disputed origin, he claimed to have lived two thousand years and to have known Christ and the apostles. He is reputed to have been a great linguist, musician, and seer. He also claimed extraordinary powers of alchemy, including the ability to transmute metals and make diamonds from pure carbon. He lived in France, England, and Russia before moving to Schleswig, where he engaged in magical practices with the landgrave Karl of Hesse.

SAKRADAGAMIN In Hinduism, the second of the four paths leading to nirvana. The literal meaning of the word is 'he who will receive birth only once more.'

SAKYA The form of Tibetan Buddhism which followed Ningma and preceded Kagyud.

SAKYAMUNI A name of Gautama Buddha.

SALACIA A Roman goddess of the sea. She was the consort of Neptune.

SALII In Roman religion, the Salii were the priests of Mars, the war-god. Among their functions were the care of the *ancilia,* the twelve sacred shields, and ritual dancing and chanting. They comprised a body of twelve members, later, increased to twenty-four. These priests officially

285

wore war-dress, and carried a sword at their side. On certain prescribed days they marched in procession through the Roman streets. The march was followed by an evening feast.

SALVATION In Zoroastrian religion, salvation is attained through good thoughts, good words, good acts. The righteous man is rewarded with eternal life, while the evildoer is condemned to destruction.

SAMADHI The final stage reached by the Hindu mystic. It is a superconscious state in which the distinction between subject and predicate disappears and the One Self is realized. Moksha offers a foretaste of the final state of emancipation.

SAMA-VEDA One of the four Vedas of early Hinduism. It contains only seventy-five original stanzas, the rest being taken from the Rig Veda. It was used by the priest who sang the sacred strophes at the Soma sacrifice.

SAMHAIN In Celtic religion, a festival associated with the New Year and the Harvest.

SAMOAN RELIGION The gods were thought to have resigned their sacredness to the Samoan chiefs, who retained enough sanctity to cause anyone who touched their clothing to become sick. Each family had a god, a *tupua,* which was embodied in some animal. There were no temples, no religious festivals, no sustained interest in religion, according to Margaret Mead, who spent considerable time studying the Samoans.

SAMRU In Persian mythology, this was the bird of immortality; it was akin to the phoenix and to the Egyptian bird called the bennu.

SAMSARA In Hinduism, the world or universe in which the law of rebirth functions. The wheel of life, the endless round of birth and rebirth, or transmigration, ceases to operate only when moksha or salvation is achieved.

SAMU In the Asmat headhunting cult, the word designates the spirits of the decapitated.

SAMUQAN In Babylonian religion, the cattle god. He is said to have had a shaggy hide like that of a wild ox.

SANGU An ancient Mesopotamian priest. He stood at the head of the temple community and appeard as bailiff of the city god, usually the chief god, who owned the land around the temple. *The sangu's* assistant, the *nubanda* or steward, supervised the administration of community.

SANKHYA One of the six traditional systems of Indian philosophy. Probably the oldest, it was founded by Kapila, who repudiated the monism of the Upanishads and denied the existence of God. The sankhya system is dualistic. It explains creation in terms of the union of nature or matter (prakriti) and soul or ego (purusha) and teaches five principles of existence. Matter is real and exists eternally; soul is without qualities or part and can only be described negatively. There are many souls, and they excite matter, initiating the cyclic evolution and devolution of the universe, a process which continues throughout eternity.

SANNYASI In Hinduism, one who has entered upon the fourth stage of life through which high caste Hindus were supposed to pass: student, householder, forest dweller, and homeless mendicant. The sannyasi is a holy man or ascetic who has consecrated himself wholly to the quest for moksha.

SAOSHYANT The Zoroastrian Messiah. Three are to come, each inaugurating a new order of things. The last one will help to purify and regenerate the universe, eliminating all evil. The souls of the righteous will arise, while the souls of the wicked will be purified. The Resurrection will then be consummated.

SAPA INCA Among the Incas of Peru, a title which means 'Only Inca.' It was applied to the ruler of the Incas.

SARAMA In Hindu mythology, the divine watchdog of Indra.

SARAPEUM A temple dedicated to the Egyptian god Sarapis at Alexandria. It was one of the wonders of antiquity.

SARAPIS An Egyptian deity. Among the Romans, he was usually called Serapis. He combined the attributes of Osiris and Apis. He was the god of the Underworld and of healing. In Alexandria he had a remarkable temple, known as the Serapeum. He was also worshipped in Greece and Rome, and was variously identified with Jupiter, Dionysus, and other deities. He was associated too with the cult of Isis and Harpocrates and Anubis-Hermes.
In the fourth century A.D. his cult was suppressed by the Christians.

In Greece, cult societies, called Sarapiastai, were votaries of the god. Many extant inscriptions contain the words 'There is one Zeus Sarapis.'

SARASVATI (BRAHMI) The goddess of speech and consort of Brahma.

SARONIDAE Among the Druids of ancient Gaul, they were the judges and the teachers.

SARRITOR In Roman mythology, a god who presides over raking.

SARVASTIVADA (SABBATTHIVADA) A school of Buddhism which flourished in northern India in the fifth century B.C. It regarded all elements and time as real.

SATANISM The worship of Satan, also called diabolism, takes the form of a cult, real or fictitious, which travesties Christian rites, as in the Black Mass. The practice of satanism may represent defiance of Christianity or an incantation of black magic. From the fifteenth through the seventeenth centuries, belief in a material Arch Fiend was so widespread, particularly in rural areas of Europe, that many prohibitions were promulgated and hundreds of sorcerers were condemned to death or banishment.

SATARAN In late Sumerian liturgies, the name given to Tammuz. The word means 'The Serpent Goddess.'

SATOR In Roman mythology, a deity who presided over sowing.

SATYASIDDHI The Satyasiddhi school of Buddhism, based on the work of Harivarman (about 250-350 A.D.), arose in India. It was introduced into China in the fifth century and into Japan in the seventh.

SATYRS In classical mythology, divinities who were partly animal in form, partly human. They were associated with the fields and woodlands, and were followers of the god Dionysus.

SCAPEGOAT A term derived from the late Hebrew practice of placing the sins of the people upon the head of a goat and allowing the animal to escape into the wilderness. Other animals were used in China, Babylonia, and Japan. Some ancient societies transferred the guilt of the community to a human victim who was killed.

SCARAB In Egyptian religion, this was the image of the scarabaeus beetle. It was the symbol of resurrection.

SCARABAEUS In Egyptian religion, the dung beetle. It is symbolic of the male generative principle. The image of the scarabaeus was often engraved on rings.

SCHEMHAMPHORAS The mystical divine names (seventy-two) discussed in the Cabala.

SEBAU In Egyptian religion, the name of a host of demons in the Underworld.

SEBEK In Egyptian religion, a crocodile god of the Fayum, represented as a man with the head of a crocodile.
Like other early gods, he was later identified with the supreme god, Ra. Later called *Suchos*, which see.

SECRET NAMES The gods of Egypt had several sacred and secret names. Ra's hidden name, for example, was revealed only to Isis.
Marduk, the Babylonian god, had fifty names.

SEDNA In the religion of the Eskimos, Sedna is the Sea Goddess. The shaman journeys to the depths of the sea to placate Sedna when she withholds the sea animals that the Eskimos require for their sustenance.

SEGETIA A Roman goddess who presided over the seed in the ground.

SEKER In Egyptian religion, a funerary god, worshipped at Memphis and often identified with Osiris and Ptah. He was represented as a mummified man with the head of a sparrow hawk. Also called Sokaris.

SEKHET HETEPET In Egyptian religion, the Elysian Fields, the paradise where souls may have a 'homestead for ever with wheat and barley therefor.'

SEKHMET Egyptian lion-headed goddess, wife of Ptah. She was the eye of Ra, capable of destroying all enemies. Endowed with magic powers, she was also goddess of medicine.

SEMELE Also called Thyone. An Olympian goddess. Her cult centered in Thebes, in Greece.

SEMITALES In Roman mythology, the gods who presided over roads.

SEMO SANCUS DIUS EIDIUS A Roman deity who may have been a corn or sky god and witness to solemn oaths.

SEMOTHEES Another name for Druids.

SEMUNES Minor Roman deities. They were assumed to have presided over sowing. They were associated with the chants of the Fratres Arvales, a Roman priestly college charged with agricultural rites and ceremonies.

SENECA The Stoic philosopher stood on the very threshold of Christianity and profoundly influenced early Christian thinkers. Born at Cordova about 4 B.C., he came to Rome at an early age and later served as Nero's tutor. 'All this universe which ecompasses us is one,' he wrote, 'and it is God.' He had no fear of death, believing that 'the soul at death is either sent forth into a better life . . . or mingled with nature again.' He died by his own hand in 69 A.D., at Nero's command, after he had been falsely accused of complicity in a conspiracy.

SENTINUS A Roman deity who presided over the intellectual stimulus of children.

SEPA In Egyptian religion, a name for the god Osiris, husband of Isis.

SEPHER SEPHIROTH A Cabalistic treatise on the gradual evolution of God from negative repose to active emanation and creation.

SEPHIRA In the Cabala, an emanation of God; any of the ten potencies or agencies through which God manifested his existence in producing the universe.

SEPHIROTH The ten emanations of God in Cabalistic teachings. The highest is formed by the concentration of the Ain Soph Aur (Limitless Light) and each successive Sephira produces by emanation another Sephira. The Ten Sephiroth are Kether (Crown), Chokmah (Wisdom), Binah (Un-

291

derstanding), Chesed (Mercu), Geburah (Power) Tiphereth (Beauty), Netzach (Victory), Hod (Splendor), Jesod (Foundation), and Malkuth (Kingdom).

SEPTERION A religious festival held every ninth year at Delphi in honor of Helios (Apollo) to commemorate his triumph over Python or darkness.

SEPT (SOTHIS) In Egyptian religion, he was the star-god.

SERAPIS In Egyptian religion, a god who combined the attributes of Osiris and Apis. At first a symbol of the Nile, and therefore of fertility, he became the object of a cult which enjoyed great prestige under the Ptolemaic dynasty at Alexandria and spread throughout the Hellenistic world. Also Sarapis, which see.

SESHAT In Egyptian religion, the goddess of writing and learning, worshipped at Memphis and Heliopolis.
She also presided over architectural knowledge
She was associated with Thoth as sister or wife. Also known as Sesheta or Safekht.

SET In Egyptian religion, the wicked god Set, brother of Horus killed his father Osiris and after a prolonged conflict was killed by Horus. Horus and Set symbolized the powers of Light and Darkness. He is represented as a human figure with an animal head. To the Greeks Set is known as Typhon. A temple was dedicated to Set by the Hyksos, an invading people who entered Egypt from Syria in the eighteenth century B.C.

SETHIANI A pre-Christian Gnostic sect described by Hippolytus as a society whose life was based on three principles: Light, Darkness, and Spirit. The sect probably tried to reconcile Judaism with Hellenism.

SETHLANS In Etruscan religion, a local deity worshipped at Perugia. He may have corresponded to Vulcan.
SETSUBUN A festival of spring celebrated by the Japanese.

Beans are thrown to drive away evil spirits and promote the growth of crops.

SEVEN ARITS In Egyptian religion, these are the seven stables that constitute the dwelling-place of Osiris in the Other World.

SEVEN BEINGS In Egyptian religion, seven Spirits, identified with the Eye of Ra, the sun-god. The number seven has been associated with the seven stars of the Great Bear.

SHAHAR and SHALEM In Canaanite religion, they were the gods of Dawn and Sunset respectively. They are called 'the heavenly ones.'

SHAI In Egyptian religion, he is the god of destiny. He is associated with the weighing of the souls of the dead in the Other World.

SHAKTA In Hinduism, a worshipper of Shakti, the personification of the female creative force.

SHAKTI In Hinduism, the active producing principle (prakiti), manifested in the wives of Siva (Durga, Kali, Parvati).

SHAKUBUKU The practice of winning new converts to the Soka Gakkai religious cult. Every member of the cult is expected to convert new members wherever he goes. Most of the converts in the United States are now non-Japanese, but the first converts were Japanese-Americans or Americans who had married Japanese citizens. See Soka Gakkai.

SHALEM In Canaanite religion, the personification of the sunset.

SHAMAN Among Siberian tribes, the shaman is a healer and a conductor of souls. He descends into the Lower Regions to capture the soul of a patient, or to accompany the soul of the deceased into the Infernal Realms. To bring back the soul, three routes are possible for the shaman: a subterranean descent into Hell; immersion into the Ocean depths; ascent to Heaven.

SHAMANIC INITIATION Among the Siberian tribes, the Ostyaks, Yakuts, Tunguses, Dolgans, Samoyedes, shamanic initiation involves an ascent. The aspirant is required to climb three trees placed in a row. Then he passes over the tops of the other trees. He also climbs a birch tree, with a sabre in his hand. Symbolically he has thus achieved a passage into the farthest Heaven. This ascent is experienced by the shaman by means of an ecstatic trance.

SHAMASH The Mesopotamian god of the sun who dictated to Hammurabi, upon a mountain-top, his code of two hundred and eighty-two laws. He was the son of Sin and appears as Utu or Babbar on early Sumerian lists of gods. On one list of the divine triad, he appears with Adad (Hadad), the storm god of the air, and Sin (Nanna), god of the moon.

SHAMS In Arabian religion, one of the names given to the god of the sun.

SHANGO The Yoruba national god. He appears with a ram's mask and is also considered to be the god of storm and thunder.

SHANG-TI In Taoism, the title of the highest deity.

SHAPASH In Canaanite religion, this goddess is the female counterpart of Shemesh, the sun.

SHARA In Sumerian religion, a deity who presided over the city of Umma.

SHARUMMA In Hittite religion, a god who is the son of Teshub and Hebat.

SHAUSHKA A Hittite goddess, identified with Ishtar.

SHAWABTI See Ushebtis.

SHE CHI In ancient Chinese religion, the gods of the ground and the grain. Today She Chi is worshipped in an open altar near a tree at the head of a village.

SHELLS Shell necklaces and headdresses were common in Paleolithic times. An abundance of shells adorns many burial sites. Certain shells, such as the cowrie, seem to suggest the female principle and to have been widely used in fertility rites. Cowries had evidently been placed in pairs on various parts of bodies found at Laugerie-Basse, Dordogne, in southern France.

SHEMESH In Canaanite religion, the sun-god. He was also the god of justice. His attendant spirits were Sedeq and Mishor.

SHENIU In Egyptian religion, a chamber in the Underworld where the enemies of Ra the sun-god are tortured. Another similar torture chamber was called Mesqet.

SHESMU In Egyptian religion, the headsman of Osiris. His nightly duty was to dismember the bodies of the wicked dead, after the completion of Osiris' Judgment.

SHIMEGI In Hittite religion, a sun-god.

SHINTAI In Shinto, a round stone placed in a shrine to represent the *mitama* (double) of a god or goddess.

SHINTO Until the fifth century, the national religion of the Japanese was a simple form of ancestor-worship combined with nature-worship. The name Shinto, of Chinese origin, designates the cult which existed at the time writing was introduced in the fifth century and which had has survived in modified forms until the present.
The Shinto mythology traces the divine ancestry of the Mikado and his people back to the creation of the world. These divine ancestors (*kami*) possess many human characteristics. Moreover, not only human beings but animals and plants, mountains and streams, all things which are thought to possess extraordinary powers, are called *kami*. The sacred books of Shinto are the *Record of Ancient Affairs* (712 A.D.) and the *Record of Japan* (720 A.D.). These books have not resulted in a system of theology but preserve the ancient lore of Japan and provide a basis

for a code of ethics which may be stated simply in these words: "Follow the pure impulse of your heart."

The existence of immaterial spirit is recognized in Shinto, but the concept of a future life is vague.

The ancestor and hero worship of Shinto was incorporated into Buddhism, which does profess knowledge of a future life. Hero worship is maintained mostly in shrines built of unpainted wood. The worshipper at the shrine sounds a gong to call the attention of the unseen deity to whom he offers food and drink.

Until 1868 two living persons were held to be divine: the Mikado and the high-priest of the Izumo O Yashiro, called the 'Living God.'

SHAVE In central and southern Africa, the spirit advisor of the witch doctor or *nganga*.

SHIVA (SIVA, CIVA) Regarded as one member of the Hindu triad (Trimurti), he is one of the supreme deities of Hinduism, representing the principle of destruction. His universal symbol is the linga, a phallic emblem. Under this symbol he is worshipped in his capacity as the creative energy of the universe. He is the central object of worship in the Shivaite sect of Hinduism. Nandi the bull is frequently associated with his worship. In his philosophical aspect, he is represented as the great ascetic seated in eternal contemplation. Many Hindus worship his consort (Shakti) under various names: Kali, Durga, Devi, Parvati, Uma.

SHRADDHA In Hinduism, an ancestral rite performed by relatives until a new body has been provided for the spirit and the spirit has been enabled to progress from lower worlds to higher and back to earth. The practice of this rite in some form is almost universal in India.

SHU (SHOU) In Egyptian religion, a solar deity typifying the atmosphere. He leans on the earth (Geb) and holds aloft the canopy of heaven (Nut), creating space for mankind to live and breathe. He is represented as a man bearing a feather on his head. His consort was Tefnut.

SHURIYAS A god worshipped by the ancient Kassites, equivalent to the Indian Shuryah (Surya).

SIBYL A female prophetess who appears in Greek and Roman mythology. The name acquired a generic sense, and there were some ten sibyls, located in various regions, in Italy, Samos, Persia, Delphi, Libya.
The utterances of the Sibyl were inscribed originally on palm-leaves and were collected for consultation in times of emergency. These Sibylline Books were destroyed during the burning of the Capitol in Rome in 83 B.C.

SICUN Among the Dakota Indians, the essence of a deity. The Sicun is thought to be present at the birth of each child.

SIDDHARTHA The given name of Gautama Buddha. Literally, 'he who has attained his aim.'

SIF In Norse religion, the wife of Thor and guardian of the home. Loki cut off her beautiful hair, compelling Thor to get her a new head of hair made of gold.

SIGN OF TANIT A symbol used by the priests of Carthage. Its primitive form was a trapezium closed by a horizontal line at the top extending beyond its adjacent sides (like the extended arms of a human body) and surmounted in the middle by a head-like circle. The trapezium often became an isoceles isosceles triangle. Of disputed origin, the figure appears as a good-luck symbol on the floors of houses and on stelae. It was used for more than a thousand years to express the hopes and beliefs of the Punic civilization.

SIGYN In Norse mythology, the wife of Loki. She catches the venom dropped by the serpents which hang over him in the cavern in which he is chained.

SIKHISM The tenets and practices of a Hindu sect that arose in India as a result of the coming of Islam. It was founded by Guru Nanak about 1500 A.D. in the Punjab. Initiated

297

as a reform movement, it developed into a powerful military organization. Nanak was a follower of the poet Kabir. Both taught that the way of salvation was through bhakti, the way of faith or devotion. They also taught the oneness of God, whom they called Ram, Brahma, Govind, and Hari, which was another name for Vishnu and the one preferred in Nanak's songs. The faith prohibits idolatry, pilgrimages, the use of witchcraft, caste distinctions, etc. It preserves the Hindu belief in rebirth and seems to promise salvation to all.

SILENUS In Greek religion, one of a type of woodland deities, probably of Anatolian origin. The principal one is represented as the oldest of the Satyrs, son of Hermes or Pan, and companion of Bacchus. To him is ascribed the gift of prophecy.

SILVANUS In Roman religion, a rural deity, guardian of woods, forests, and fields. He was the object of private, rather than of public, worship.

SIMIOS In the Aramaean pantheon, the son of Hadad and Atargatis.

SIMON MAGUS A contemporary of Philo and the earliest Gnostic known to Irenaeus, author of a *Refutation of the Gnostics,* and to Hippolytus, another heresiologist. He is mentioned in the Bible as a magician who offered money to the Apostles in exchange for the gift of the Holy Spirit. He is supposed to have been the founder of Gnosticism.

SIMURGH In Persian mythology, a gigantic bird, the 'all-knowing bird of ages,' said to possess oracular powers. The half-phoenix, half-lion creature was the guardian of the ancient Persian mysteries. It has seen the world thrice destroyed and is expected to reappear at end of the Manvantaric cycle.

SIN In the Mesopotamian pantheon, the wise moon god who revealed the future to the adept. Identified by the Sumerians with Nanna.

In Mesopotamian religion, sin was the most natural way for a demon to enter the body of a man. Moral and ritual offenses were put in the same category. A man who sinned was abandoned by the gods, whereupon demons entered his body and made their presence felt in disagreeable ways. Priests used specific exorcisms to drive out the invading demons.

SIONA In Norse mythology, a goddess of love.

SISTRUM An oval metal frame with cross metal rods. A musical instrument that was used in the rites of Isis-Osiris.

SIVAISM The predominant religion of Hindus in various regions of India. It is based on the worship of Siva (Shiva) the supreme god of many Hindu sects.

SKALDSKAPARMAL In Norse mythology, books of directions for poets. These form part of the Younger Edda, one of the two sources on Norse religion.

SKANDHAS In Hinduism and Buddhism, the impermanent elements which enter into man's constitution at the time of his incarnation. Every human being has five attributes, known as the Pancha Skandhas: rupa (form), vidana (perception), sanjna (consciousness), sanskara (action), and vidyana (knowledge).

SKULL WORSHIP Skulls play an important role as sacred relics and as objects of worship among primitives. Among Polynesians and Melanesians, skulls of ancestors are worshipped in order to establish connections with spirits of the dead. Like the head of Osiris in Egypt, the skulls of ancestors may also serve as tutelary deities. The head or its parts, each of which may stand for the whole, can be used as magical food or as a means of increasing the fertility of the soil. Paleolithic tribes probably assumed that soul-substance resided in skulls and had the properties of a vitalizing agent. They may have practiced organized cannibalism, severing the heads of victims and extracting the brain for ceremonial sacrificial consumption. Numerous skulls and headless bodies that have been discovered in Paleolithic sites suggest that the corpses had been decapitated, buried until they had decomposed, and then exhumed. Afterwards, the heads had been carefully preserved and used in rites much like those practiced today in Borneo.

SKY GODS Among such primitive people as the Australian aborigines, High Gods or Supreme Beings are the personification and guardians of the tribal ethic. They are assumed to have given the tribe its laws, then retired to their celestial abode. These High Gods stand alone and constitute one element among primitive religions which can be observed among the Australian aborigines, the Californian tribes of North America, the Fuegians, and certain negroids of Africa. They do not exclude lesser spiritual beings, localized gods, culture heroes, and totems, but they stand alone as representatives of the ultimate moral value of the universe. The transcendent Sky God is deeply rooted in the history of religion from the Neolithic period on, and there are a few possible indications of such a belief in Paleolithic times: oval pendants of bone and stone, identical in shape with the bullroarer, still used by the aborigines of Australia, discovered in Dordogne and in a Magdalenian site at Saint Marcel, France.

When the existence of a transcendent power was made the source of universal creative activity, the Sky God became the head of a pantheon and the personification of various aspects of nature. Everywhere the same linguistic form connects him with the sky, the clouds, and the rain. As Zeus or Dyaus Pitar, he was known under various names by the Indo-Europeans and was primarily the god of the sky and weather. He assimilated various other gods and assumed their functions, becoming the source of life, death, rain, and celestial fire in Egypt, where Horus, was 'the lofty one.'

SLEIPNIR In Norse mythology, Odin's swift eight-hoofed horse.

SMARAGDINE TABLE The *Tabula Smaragdina,* a work on alchemy published in the sixteenth century and attributed to Hermes Trismegistus, is said to condense the whole of magic on a single page. Certain Masons and Cabalists allege that it was found by Abraham's wife on the body of Hermes.

SMERTRIOS In Celtic mythology he was a god of prosperity, identified by the Romans with Mercury.

SMRITI In Hinduism, traditional accounts transmitted orally. They include legal and ceremonial writings.

SNAKE DANCE Among the American Indians, particularly the Hopi tribe, the snake dance is a symbolic appeal for rain. The dance extends into a celebration involving songs, pageantry, games, and feasting.

SNAKE GODDESS In Minoan times in ancient Greece, the snake goddess, The Lady of the Nether Regions, was a chthonic divinity of fertility.

SNAKE PEOPLE These were commonly of the American Indian Hopi tribe. In their ceremonial rites they made offerings to the spirits in a sacred spot called batni.

SNAKES In ancient Greek domestic cults, snakes were sacred. They were called Dioskouroi, Sons of Zeus.
In Egypt, snakes were house pets. The Minoan snake-goddess was also a house goddess who protected the family.

SNENANTH In Etruscan religion, a deity who had subsidiary functions to the major divinities.

SNOTRA In Norse mythology, a goddess who was noted for her wisdom.

SOBK (SOBEK) See *Sebek, Suchos*.

SOCRATES The Delphic oracle is supposed to have told Chaerephon that Socrates was the wisest of men. Born at Athens about 470 B.C., he identified virtue with knowledge and placed religion on the basis of pure humanity. He is said to have listened to a little voice or 'daimonion' which warned him against doing anything he ought not to do. He was accused of denying the gods worshipped by the Athenians, introducing new gods, and corrupting the youth. Before he died from the hemlock he had been condemned to drink, he is supposed to have said that 'no harm can come to a good man in life or death.'

SOKA GAKKAI A rapidly growing religious cult founded in Japan in the early 1930's by a teacher named Tsunesaburo Makiguchi. Its main temple, the temple of Taisekiji in Japan, is visited daily by more than ten thousand of its sixteen million members. An odd blend of militant Buddhism and fervent personalism, it stresses the perfection of the individual and society. Its Clean Government Party is the third largest political group within the Diet. Its adherents in Japan and in the United States, where it is known as the Nichiren Shoshu of America, chant the *Daimoku* in front of *Gohonzon* containing the *Dai-Gohonzon,* practice *shakubuku,* and look toward the establishment of world peace. Soka Gakkai means 'Value Creation Society.'

SOKARIS See Seker.

SOMA Fermented sap of a shrub, the favorite drink of the Vedic gods. Soma is also one of the main gods of Vedic Hinduism. The ninth book of the Rig-Veda is dedicated to him.

SOMNUS In classical mythology, a deified personification of sleep. He is described as the son of Nox (night) and brother of Mors (death).

SORANUS In Etruscan religion, a deity that was originally a god associated with a particular family and then became popular among the people.

SORCERER An adept in the occult, bound to Satan in return for knowledge and skill in magic. Traditionally, the adept is represented as having a fixed stare. He is supposed to keep his power so long as his feet touch the ground.

302

Among Eskimos, certain adepts can create animals out of bone, infants' corpses. They can endow them with the power of flight and the capacity to inflict injury.

SOSOM Among the Kaya-Kaya in New Guinea, the bull roarer god. The practice of tying a slat of wood to the end of a thong so as to produce a roar when the thong is whirled is supposed to be of extreme antiquity. The Australian aborigines also use the bull roarer in religious rites.

SOULS The Egyptians pictured the soul as the image of a person as he might exist in the mind of an acquaintance. In Babylonian religion, souls were thought to wear dresses made of feathers. In the Hervey Islands of the South Pacific, the natives assume that fat men have fat souls, tall men tall souls, etc. The Bavili speak of the voices of the dead living on in the heads of relatives. To the Andamanese souls are like reflections in mirrors. The Fijians thought they saw the souls of the departed in a deep hole in the ground.

SOUL-SPIRIT Among Eskimos, everything has a soul-spirit. This includes animals, tools, clothing.

SOSIOSH The Mazdean Savior who, like Vishnu, Maitreya Buddha, and others, is expected to appear on a white horse to save mankind at the end of the cycle. See Saoshyant.

SOVIJ A Baltic god of the dead.

SOW In Egyptian religion, Nut in the form of a sow was a protective divinity.

SOWAN The first of the four paths that lead to nirvana.

SPENTA MAINYU In early Zoroastrianism, one of the names of Ahura Mazda (Ormazd). The Holy Spirit is seen as the cosmic rival of Ahriman (Angra Mainyu), the Evil Spirit.

SPHINX A monster with a human head and the body of a lion. The Great Sphinx at Giza had the features of King Khafre

(26th century B.C.), the builder of the second pyramid there. Originally built with the sole intention of worshipping the pharaoh, who was both human and divine, the Sphinx was taken into the theology of the sun god, beginning with the New Kingdom (1570-1075), as a representation of Harmachis, the morning sun.

SRADDHA In Hinduism, devotion to the memory of the manes of dead relatives.

SRADDHADEVA An epithet of Yama, the god of death and king of the Nether Regions.

SRAMANA In Buddhism, priests, ascetics, and postulants for nirvana. The term is a corruption of an expression meaning 'they who have to place a restraint on their thoughts.'

SRAOSHA A Zoroastrian deity who symbolizes obedience, the divine law. He protects the souls of the faithful against demons.

SRAVAKA In Buddhism, a disciple or chela.

SRI SANKARA ACHARYA A great religious reformer of India and a teacher of the Vedanta philosophy. He is regarded by the nondualists as an incarnation of Siva. He founded the Smartava sect among the Brahmans.

SRIVATSA A mystical mark worn by Krishna and adopted by the Jains.

SRIYANTRA The double triangle known as the seal of Vishnu and also as Solomon's seal.

SROTRIYA In Hinduism, a Brahman who practices the Vedic rites he studies, in contrast to the Vedavit, who studies them only theoretically.

SRUTI In Hinduism, sacred tradition based on revelation, opposed to traditional accounts imparted orally and known as Smriti. The Vedas are Sruti.

STAG In Hittite religion, the stag was the animal of the tutelary god of the fields.

STATANUS A Roman deity who taught infants to walk.

STATUA MATER A goddess who was worshipped in the Forum in Rome to preserve the area from burning or damage at night.

STERCULIUS A Roman god who presided over the enrichment of the soil.

STHANA In Hindu mythology, the place or abode of a god.

STILL-HEART In Egyptian religion, this was a name of Osiris.

STOLISTES Also called Ornatrices. In the temples of Isis and of Sarapis in Rome, the stolistes were priests who dressed the statues of the gods.

STONEHENGE A group of upright and horizontal stones located near Salisbury, England, and probably dating from the neolithic age. It is thought to be the ruins of an ancient shrine or temple connected with a neolithic cult and astronomical observations.

STONES In Canaanite religion, stones and pillars received the veneration of the people, as did trees and mountains.

STORJUNKARE Among the Laplanders, he was a deputy of the god Thor.

STRENIA An Italic goddess who was worshipped in Rome at the beginning of the New Year.

STRIBOG A Slavic deity whose functions are obscure.

STUPA A Buddhist mound forming a memorial shrine. It is usually erected over relics of Buddha, Arhats, or other great men.

STYX In Greek mythology, a river which flowed round the lower world seven times and had to be crossed by those who passed to the regions of the dead. Also, the nymph by whom inviolable oaths were sworn.

SUBIGUS A Roman god who presided over the consummation of marriages.

SUCCUBUS A demon who assumes the form of a female to copulate with human males in their sleep. The princess of all the succubi is called Nahemah.

SUCELLUS In Celtic religion, he was a chthonic god identified with Pluto. He was the god of the dead. In another aspect, he was a deity who presided over fertility.

SUCHOS Egyptian crocodile-god embodying the aquatic principle. His worship was highly popular, particularly in the Fayum area, of which he was the protector. His numerous temples in this region inspired the Greeks to call it Crocodilopolis. Crocodiles, in honor of the god, were adorned with jewels and hymns were chanted by priests. At the death of crocodiles, these creatures were mumified and, like royalty, given sacred burial. Also called Sebek.

SUDHA In Hindu mythology, the food of the gods. It is similar to *amrita*, the substance that confers immortality

SUDRA In Hindu mythology, the last of the four great castes that sprang from Brahma's body. The lowest or servile caste, it is said to have issued from the foot of the deity. The fourth and lowest ancient Hindu caste, formed mainly from non-Aryans, was assigned by classical law to perform menial work.

SUDYUMNA In Hindu mythology, an epithet of Ila, child of Vaivasvata Manu and the daughter who sprang from his sacrifice when he was left alone after the flood. An androgynous creature, Sudyumna was a male one month and a female the next.

306

SUKIAS In parts of Central America, these are witches.

SULFI They were Celtic deities who were worshipped by the Gauls.

SULIKATT In the Hittite pantheon, one of two famed warriors.

SUMER Ancient kingdom of the Sumerians, a race that dwelt in Mesopotamia and absorbed many of the ceremonials, rituals, and religious concepts of the Akkadians, who inhabited Babylonia.

SUMERIAN DEITIES In the Sumerian religion the pantheon comprised hundreds of deities. Many names of gods were recorded on tablets used in the Sumerian schools and also on sacrificial lists. The lists from Shuruppak (Tell Farah) in central Babylonia date from 2600 B.C. and name over seven hundred gods. A fragmentary list from Ur contains over forty names of deities. The Sumerians placed An at the head of the pantheon and En-lil ('lord of the storm') next to him. In Lagash, the chief god was called Ningirsu.

SUMERIAN FERRYMEN In Sumerian religion, three deities — the gatekeeper, the guardian of the Underworld river, and the ferryman conducted souls into the Lower Regions. These three corresponded to the Greek god Charon, who similarly rowed the souls of the dead across the river Styx into Hades.

SUMERIAN KING LIST A chronological list of the early Sumerian rulers, written not later than the middle of the Third Dynasty of Ur. It ascribes reigns of exaggerated length to the kings. From the time 'kingship was lowered from heaven' until the Flood, eight kings ruled for a period of 241,200 years: Alulim, Alagar, Enmenlu-Anna, Enmengal-Anna, Dumuzi (a divine shepherd), Ensipazi-Anna, Enmendur-Anna, and Unar-Tutu. Different names and longer periods are recorded by Berossos, a priest of Marduk at Babylon under Antiochus I (281-261 B.C.).

307

SUMMERIAN PANTHEON The principal gods of the ancient Sumerians were nature deities. From as far back as their written records god, the Sumerian theologians assumed the existence of a pantheon consisting of a group of living beings, human in form but invisible to the human eye, superhuman, and immortal. These deities controlled the cosmos in accordance with well-laid plans and prescribed laws. Every known phenomenon was associated with an anthropomorphic but immortal being, called a *dingir*, and the pantheon was thought to function as an assembly headed by a king. The most important groups in the assembly consisted of seven gods who presided over fate and fifty 'great gods.' The pantheon was further divided into the creative gods who controlled heaven and earth, sea and air, and noncreative gods created by these four. Each cosmic deity was assigned a *me*, a set of rules and regulations designed to keep each cosmic entity or phenomenon operating forever in accordance with a definite plan.

The goddess Nammu controlled the primeval sea. She gave birth to An, the male god of heaven, and to Ki, the earth goddess. An and Ki produced Enlil, god of the air. Enlil fashioned the moon, stars, and sun. He fathered the sun god Utu. With considerable help from Enki, god of the waters, Enlil and Ki produced all vegetable and animal life on earth. Man was the product of the combined efforts of Nammu, Ninmah, who is perhaps identical with Ki, Enki. All life was thought to result from a union of water, earth, and air.

SUMERIAN PARADISE In the Sumerian religion, paradise was intended for the gods only, not for mankind in general.

SUMERIAN PRIESTHOOD In Sumerian religion, the high priest was the spiritual head of the temple. Under him were a number of priestly classes, known as the *pashes*, the *lumah*, and the *ishib*.

Priestly services were also attended by a body of musicians and singers. A high priestess, in charge of priestesses herself, was the counterpart of the high priest. The functions of these priestesses, however, are unknown.

SUMERIAN TEMPLES The maintenance of ancient Sumerian temples required a vast and continuous revenue. This was partly secured by endowments and gifts from the ruler. There were at least hundreds of slaves and laborers who attended to the menial work around the temples. In the course of time, the temple priesthood absorbed large tracts of lands and the organization of the priestly hierarchy became secularized.

SUMUGAN A Sumerian deity who was called King of the Mountain. He was in charge of animal and plant life.

SUNASEPHA In Hindu mythology, the son of the sage Rishika, who sold him to King Ambarisha to be sacrificed to Varuna as a substitute for Rohita, the king's son. The Puranic Isaac is saved by Rishi Visvamitra.

SUN DANCE A ceremony, usually lasting eight days, that is characteristic of the Plains tribes of the American Indians. Smoking, fasting, and secret rites constituted part of the celebration. The underlying significance of the dance was an act of penance.

SUN DEITIES In Hittite religion, various deities associated with the sun were conceived. There was a Sun-Goddess of the Earth, a Sun-God of Heaven, a Sun-God of the Water.

SUN-EGG The ancient Egyptians believed that the sun first rose out of a wonderful island in the Nile, and that the sun-egg was made from the mud of the river bed by Khnemu, the creator.

SUNG-MING-SHU The Chinese tree of life and of knowledge.

SUNYA A Sanskrit word meaning illusion, in the sense that all existence is but a dream or shadow.

SUOYATOR In the Finnish epic poem, the *Kalevala,* the name of the Spirit of Evil whose saliva produced the serpent of sin.

SUN WATCHERS Among the Hopi Indians, the sun watchers are two officials who keep track of the seasons and notify celebrants of a forthcoming ceremony.

SUN WORSHIP Worship of the sun is widespread among primitive peoples. The sun has been personified as a great being, the eye of heaven, the source of life, etc. Sun worship probably reached its high point in Mexico, Egypt, and Japan, where the sun goddess Amaterasu is supposed to have been the founder of the royal family.

SUPREME SKY-GOD The ancient cults of Central Asia dwelt fundamentally on the worship of the sky god.

SURABHI In Hindu mythology, the 'cow of plenty,' a fabulous creation which yields every desire to its possessor. It is one of the fourteen precious things yielded by the ocean of milk when churned by the gods.

SURASA In Hindu mythology, a daughter of Daksha, the wife of Kashyapa, and the mother of a thousand many-headed dragons and serpents.

SURSUNABU In Babylonian mythology, he is the ferryman who rows across the waters of death. He corresponds to the Greek god Charon, whose functions were similar.

SURT Also called Surtr. In Norse religion, he was the fire god. He is destined to destroy the universe. This concept coincides with the Stoic view of the conflagration of the cosmos.

SURVIVALS Edward Tylor formulated the doctrine of survivals to account for the persistence of customs long after their religious significance has been forgotten. He pointed out that practices such as human sacrifice to appease the gods may disappear while a related superstition, such as the Bohemian belief that it is unlucky to save a man from drowning, survives. Meaningless customs are survivals, according to him, of practices that had a ceremonial intention when they first arose, 'but now are fallen into absurdity from having been carried on in a new state of society where the original sense has been discarded.'

SURYA (SHURIYAN) In Hindu religion, the sun god or the sun itself worshipped as the source of light and warmth. An important Vedic deity, he is represented as riding in a chariot drawn by seven horses.

SURYAVANSA In Hindu mythology, the solar race; one who claims descent from Ikshvaku. Rama belonged to the solar race. Krishna and Gautama Buddha to the lunar race (Chandravansa).

SUSANOWO In ancient Japanese religion, the storm god. He represents all that is dark, violent, or evil. His counterpart, Amaterasu, represents all that is light or good. Both are the offspring of Izanagi. With Amaterasu, he ruled the universe.

SUTEKH A West Asiatic god and special deity of the Hyksos. In Egyptian religion, this is another name for the god Set, who was identified with Sutekh while Egypt was ruled by Hyksos conquerors.

SUTRAS A late stage of Vedic literature presenting the essentials of the sacred writings in concise form. There are four kinds of sutras: 1) Srauta, or priestly sutras; 2) Grihya sutras, dealing with the domestic rites; 3) Dharma sutras, dealing with social duties; and 4) Sutras dealing with language, philosophy, magic, etc. A late collection of such rules or aphorisms is known as the Laws of Manu.

SVADILFARE In Norse mythology, the stallion belonging to Blast, the architect. With the stallion's help he constructs an impregnable fortress for the gods.

SVANTOVIT A Slavic god whose worship was associated with the island of Rügen.

SVARGA In Hinduism, a heavenly abode or paradise, especially the paradise of Indra.

SVAROG In Slavic religion, he was a sky- or thunder-god. He was identified with the Roman Vulcan.

SVETA In Hindu mythology, a serpent-dragon and son of Kashyapa.

SWAWMX In Burmese demonology, these are vampires.

SWASTIKA The name given by Bramin priests to the pramantha, a lighting stick which was turned in a small hollow formed at the intersection of two pieces of wood. The tips of the cross were bent at right angles and secured by four nails. It is found not only in ancient Persia and the ruins of Troy but also in China and Japan. It was used in the sun worship of the Kickapoos, and Pottawatomies. It is also called a fylfot.

SWORD Separation by the sword is a recurrent theme in alchemical literature. The 'philosophical egg' The sword is used to divide the 'philosophical egg,' to separate the elements, and to restore the primitive state of chaos in order to bring about the production of a more perfect body. It is prefigured in the flaming sword of the angel guarding paradise. Gerhard Dorn, a sixteenth-century alchemist, maintains that the sword was changed into Christ. In the Gnosis of the Ophites, the cosmos is supposed to be surrounded by a ring of fire which encloses paradise but is separated from paradise by a flaming sword.

SYCAMORE TREE In Egyptian religion, the Sycamore Tree of Heaven was the abode of the goddess Hathor.

SYMPATHETIC MAGIC In Egyptian religion, figures of wax or other material were used in magic rites to effect certain results, either beneficent for the performer, or malefic for an enemy.

T

TAAROA A Tahitian god believed to abide in the immensity of space and to have been the creator of Hawaii.

TA-AUTIS A Phoenician deity. He was identified with the Roman Saturn.

TABU (TABOO) Tabus may be used to prevent pollution or secure certain privileges. The tabu system is most highly developed among the Polynesians but exists or has existed among the Melanesians, Micronesians, Malays, Australians, and the aboriginal tribes of India, Siberia, Africa, and the Americas.

The word was borrowed from the Pacific area where tabu was expanded into a technique of social control. The subject has been studied by anthropologists since Captain Cook first used the word in his description of the Polynesians. Defined as a sacred interdiction laid upon the use of certain words or things or upon certain acts or contacts dangerous to the doer and ultimately to his group, tabu is generally enforced by social and supernatural sanctions. The tabu caution against contact applies almost universally to blood and death, and obviously serves to restrain or protect potential offenders. The most common Polynesian form of the word is *tapu*. Other forms are Paumotan *tafu*, Hawaiian *kapu*, Tongan *tabu*, and Malagassy *tabaka*. In peripheral areas the forms *tabu* and *tampu* are found. The alternate English spelling, *taboo*, fails to preserve either the form or the function of the Polynesian word, which is stressed on the first syllable and used only as an adjective.

TABUERIKI The chief deity of the Gilbert Islands.

TACITA In Roman mythology, a goddess of silence.

TAGES An Etruscan god of the Underworld.

TAGHAIRM In Celtic demonology, a method of divination. The seer clothed himself in the hide of a newly slaughtered bull and awaited the spirits near a waterfall or precipice. The name is also given to the sacrifice of cats to the demoniacal powers.

TAHITI A word said by Hawaiian priests to preserve the source of the origin of the Polynesians and their unity as a race. In the language of the ancient Hawaiians, the word meant: the point of origin of one who has departed from his homeland; the celestial sphere in which man originated; the unified group of which one is a member; or movement through time or space. The tahunas taught that their ancestors descended from heaven and that the wisdom of the race was preserved in their sacred temple chants and prayers.
According to the tahunas, Teave, the Primordial Lord of the Sun, created the seven planes or heavens which lie above the earth. The abode of the gds was the three upper planes, called Tahiti. The three planes were the blue heaven of the goddess Uri Uri, the golden realm of music, and the kingdom of the angels.

TAHMURATH In Persian mythology, the first man. His steed was Simurgh, the half-phoenix, half-lion creature or infinite cycle.

TAHUNAISM The theology of the Mu, the primitive inhabitants of Hawaii. The ancient Polynesian religion was abolished in 1819, six months prior to the arrival of the earliest missionaries. The chief divinities are Tane, the Heavenly Father; Teave, the Eternal Creator, and Uri Uri or Na Vahine, the feminine generative force of the sun. The wisdom and rites of the religion were preserved orally by the *Tahunas,* or priests.

314

The royal family tree of Tane is known mainly through the *Tumuripo*, Chant of Creation.' Teave, who evolved out of chaos, established his throne in the dome of Po. To establish a royal family to rule over his creation, he manifested himself as his daughter, Na Vahine. The son who emanated from him, Tane, became Na Vahine's mate. These three constituted the highest trinity in the Hawaiian pantheon. A second trinity was composed of the sons of `Tane and Na Vahine. A third trinity included their daughters. The fourth trinity was composed of Papa, Vatea, and Miru.

TAHUNAS Native priests of pre-Christian Hawaii. They had no written language but preserved the ancient wisdom and rites of the religion of Mu, or Tahunaism. Skilled in the arts of divination and spiritual healing, they passed on their teachings from generation to generation through many centuries. High priests were the historians, genealogists, and spiritual leaders of the Polynesian peoples of Hawaii. Low priests, called *tahuna ana'ana,* were skilled in necromancy. They were feared and hated because they used witchcraft to accomplish ruthless acts.

T'AI CHI In Chinese religion, the Great Ultimate or Terminus. It engenders the Two primary Modes, which in turn engender the Four Secondary Modes, which in turn engender the Eight Elements, which determine all good and evil, life in all its complexity.

T'AI I In Taoism, a deity identified with Hsuan-wu. Also, a branch of Taoism founded in the twelfth century to promote magic and realize the Three Origins of existence (Heaven, Earth, Man).

TAKULTU In Assyrian religion, an annual ritual ceremony at which a meal was offered to the gods.

TALAPOIN In Thailand, a Buddhist monk or ascetic, frequently credited with magic powers.

TALMIDAI HAKHAMEEN A class of Cabalists whom the Zohar calls 'Disciples of the Wise' and who became eunuchs for spiritual motives.

TAMAGISANGAK Among the inhabitants of Formosa, he is the deity who beautifies men.

TAMESIS In Celtic mythology, a river and lake deity.

TAMMUZ In Babylonian religion, a god of agriculture, spirit of vegetation, and lover of Ishtar, who with infinite pains retrieved him from the lower world after his death. His annual festival, occurring just before the summer solstice, was marked by a period of mourning for his loss, followed by rejoicing at his reappearance. His counterpart among the Phoenicians was Adonis.

TANAIM Learned Cabalists in ancient times.

TANAIS A Persian goddess whose function was to preside over slaves.

TANAROA One of the three sons of Tane and Na Vahine, major divinities in the Hawaiian pantheon. Tanaroa was ruler of the southern Pacific Ocean and one of the 'Four Major Male Pillars of Creation.'

TANE One of the primal gods of the Polynesian pantheon, variously regarded as god of forests and plants. In central and marginal Polynesia, he represents the procreative principle and the life-giving powers of nature.
Tane, the Heavenly Father of the pre-Christian natives of Hawaii, was known by a hallowed name which in the modern vernacular is pronounced Eli Eli. The name of the supreme god of *Tahunaism* preserves the spiritual identity of this divinity. The name means father, man, the male head of the tribe. Tane was the 'Lord who radiated rays of sunshine,' the fountainhead from which sprang the 'Living Water' or "Essence of Spirit' by which all creatures were nourished. He was the mate of Uri Uri and dwelt with

316

her in the House of the Sun at the zenith of space.

The spiritual union of Tane and Na Vahine produced three sons, Tanaroa, Rono, and Tu. With their father, they made up the 'Four Major Male Pillars of Creation.' Together with Teave, these four became the 'Five Supreme Beings.' With Uri Uri they made up the two highest trinities and were called the 'Holy Six.'

Tane and Na Vahine had three daughters, Rata, Tapo, and Hina. These three made up the third celestial trinity.

TANGALOA (TANGAROA) A Polynesian god. The only primal deity in Tonga, Futuna, Uvea, and Niue, he is also dominant in Samoa. Throughout Polynesia, he is associated with creation and frequently with great expanses, such as the sky or the sea.

TANHA In Buddhism, the thirst for life, desire to live, or clinging to life on this earth. Tanha causes rebirth or reincarnation.

TANIT A Carthaginian goddess, possibly identified with Astarte, but with a more prominent lunar character. Many Punic inscriptions begin with the stereotyped phrase: 'To the Lady Tanit, Face of Baal, and to the Lord Baal Hammon.' She seems to be closely connected with fertility and the protection of the dead. Sacrifices were made to her and to Baal Hammon.

In Carthage, she was the goddess of heaven and the moon. Her symbol was a crescent moon. Without the help of a male partner, she gave birth to the universe.

TANJUR A collection of Buddhist works, containing the commandments or word of the Buddha and many volumes on miscellaneous subjects, translated from Sanskrit into Tibetan and Mongolian.

TANTRAS Relatively late sacred writings of Hinduism. In their present form, they date from the seventh or eighth centuries A.D. They are used particularly by the Shaktas, who worship the female or creative principle of the universe. They contain many mystical and magical elements, and are a source of the rituals used in tantric worship.

TANTRIC BUDDHISM A system of esoteric beliefs and practices based on meditation of mystic syllables in accordance with rules laid down in various *tantras* (manuals). The goal of meditation was a state of mystical union with reality. The cults include so-called right-handed and left-handed sects, the latter rejecting the precepts of early Buddhism and indulging in orgiastic rites.

TAOISM The Chinese expression Tao Chia, denoting the Taoist School, did not appear until 97 B.C. But it was already a centuries-old movement. The essence of the teaching was the opposition between nature and man. Tao, The Way, was glorified. It postulated the pursuit of nature in its simplicity, together with tranquility and enlightenment. The purpose was directed toward long life and lasting vision. Taoism is a philosophical system. It advocates peace of mind, equality of things, unity of spirit.
Through the movement of the fang-shih, the priest-magicians, Taoism began to assume a mysterious, magic character involving alchemical concepts.
Taoist philosophers, in the fifth century A.D., established the ceremonies and the codes of the cult. In 440 A.D. Taoism became the state religion of China, to the detriment of Buddhism, which began to suffer persecution.
To the Chinese people in general Taoism is called the Religion of Mystery. It has distinctive features. It comprises a very populous pantheon. It has gods for every act, for every member of the body. It strives for blessings and long life by alchemical means. It embraces a large body of superstitions. In its literature it follows and imitates Buddhism.
The emphasis of Taoism is predominantly on ethical concepts. Lastly, Taoism has absorbed many sects and secret societies. In the fourteenth century there were four sects in Taoism, of which two are still in force. Virtually, Taoism offers materialistic as well as philosophical guidance, as Stoicism did in antiquity.

TAOIST TRIAD The Three Purities in Taoism are Essence (*ching*), Vital Force (*ch'i*), and the Spirit (*shen*). These also are called *San-ch'ing* or The Three Pure Ones of Taoism. The first, Wu-hsing T'ien-chun, lives in the Realm of Jade Purity, populated by holy men. The second, Wu-shih T'ien-chun, lives in the Realm of Superior Purity, populated by pure men. The third, Fan-hsing T'ien-chun, lives in the Realm of Great Purity which is populated by immortals.

TAPAS Mortification of the flesh, particularly as it is practiced by ascetic hermits and wanderers of India and Ceylon.

TAPO In the Hawaiian pantheon, one of the members of the third heavenly trinity. She was the daughter of Tane and wife of Tanaroa.

TARA In Mahayana Buddhism, a savior-goddess, Shakti of a Bodhisattva. In Hindu mythology, she is the wife of Brihaspati. Her abduction by King Soma led to the war of the gods with the Asuras. She personifies mystic knowledge and is the mother of Buddha (Wisdom).

TARANIS In Celtic mythology, he was the god of thunder.

TARHU In early Hittite religion, Tarhu is the most important god in the Hittite pantheon. He is the weather god, and has various appellations. In Hurrian his name is Teshub. In the Luwian language he is called Dattas.
Tarhu presides over rain and thunder storms. He is identified with Zeus as the supreme god.

TARHUND A name which appears in ancient texts, in hieroglyphic form, and surved until the classical period. It probably designates the Hittite weather god.

TARVOS TRIGARANNOS A Celtic deity whose functions are obscure.

TAT In the Egyptian Corpus Hermeticum, Tat is the son of

319

Hermes, with whom he holds conversations on mystical experience.

TA-TCHESERT In Egyptian religion, a name for the Lower Regions.

TATENEN In Egyptian religion, one of the most ancient gods of Egypt. He presided over the earth. Identified with Ptah of Memphis.

TAU CROSS A cross shaped like a T. It was used by the ancient Phoenicians as a magic symbol.

TAUROBOLIUM The sacrifice of a bull and baptism of a worshiper with its blood. The rite probably originated in the worship of Anahita, the Great Mother in the ancient Persian religion, and was adopted in the cults of Cybele, Attis, and Mithras. The initiate was supposed to secure the magic potency of a powerful animal by contact with its blood. Later the rite symbolized death and rebirth.

TAUVA'U Among the Trobriand Islanders, these are malignant beings. Invisible to ordinary human beings, they walk at night through villages, rattling gourds and clanking lethal wooden sword clubs. They sometimes change into reptiles and become visible. These reptiles, when injured or ill-treated, revenge themselves by death.

TCHAFUI In Egyptian religion, this denotes the twin souls of Ra and Osiris.

TCHATCHA In Egyptian religion, they were the chiefs who along with Osiris weighed the hearts of the dead in the Hall of Judgment. The Tchatcha consisted of Imset, Hapi, Tuamutef, Qebhsennuf.

TCHEFAU In Egyptian religion, this was the food of the gods. It corresponded to the nectar and ambrosia of the Greek gods.

TEACHING OF KAGEMNI The oldest book of Egyptian moral precepts. It dates from the Third Dynasty, about 4000 B.C.

TEAVE In Hawaii, the temple priests of the highest male religious cult taught that One Life was the Eternal Spirit of Teave, the Primordial Lord of the Sun (Ra), the Perennial Spirit of Fire, the Almighty Flame who created this world when he breathed forth the *manna* that pervades all. Teave evolved out of chaos and caused life to begin when he uttered the word *Ora* (Life of Ra) into the void and gloom of *Po*. Teave was the Father-Mother and ruler over the powers of Heaven, and his son was Tane. Teave manifested himself and his daughte Na Vahine, the third member of the divine triad.

TEFNUT In Egyptian religion, she was the wife of Shu.

TEHARONHIAWAGON Among the Iroquois, the god who personifies life.

TEKARPADA Among the inhabitants of Formosa, he is the rain god.

TELCHINES A variant name for the Galli, the priests of Cybele, The Great Mother of the Gods.

TELEPINU In Hittite religion, son of the Weather God. He was called The God who Disappears.
He was the son of Tarhu and Hatepinu, one of Tarhu's consorts.

TELESPHORUS A Greek god associated with Aesculapius.

TELETE In the ancient Greek Orphic mysteries, the celebration of the telete or initiation was introduced was mankind.

TELLUMO A Roman deity; the counterpart of Tellus.

TELLUS She is a Roman earth-goddess. Cows and pigs, symbolizing fertility, were sacrificed to her.

321

TEM HARMACHIS In Egyptian religion, a dual god. Within himself he united the attributes of the morning sun and the night.

TEMMANGU In Shinto, the god of learning and calligraphy, favored by pupils and their teachers. Born Sugawara-no-Michizane in 845, he attained a high rank in government and established a system of national education. A rival contrived to have him exiled. He died in exile in 903. Great calamities followed his exile and led to his deification.

TEMPLE According to the Greek historian Herodotus, the Egyptians were the first to erect temples to the gods.

TEMPLE OF MARDUK In the Babylonian temple of Marduk, there were reproductions of the Chambers of Fate, where the Sun daily received the Tablets of Destiny.

TEMPLE OF THE SOUL In Egyptian religion, part of the sky that was the abode of the gods. Its counterparts on earth were Heliopolis and Mendes.

TEMPLE OF THE SUN In Cuzco, Peru, this was the principal sanctuary of the Incas.

TEMPLE OF THE SUN The principal temple dedicated to the sun god of the Toltecs of Mexico.

TEN ABODES In Egyptian religion, ten locations were associated with Osiris and other deities. These localities were:
1. Anu,
2. Busiris,
3. Sekhem,
4. Pe-Tep,
5. The Rekhti Lands,
6. Abtu,
7. The Place of Judgment,
8. Mendes,
9. An-rut-f,
10. Re-stau.
The gods attached to these places were, correspondingly,

1. Shue, Tem, Tefnut
2. Osiris, Isis, Nephthys, Heru-netch-hra-teff
3. Thoth, Heru-khenti, An-Maati
4. Isis, Horus, Imset, Hapi
5. Isis, Horus, Imset
6. Isis, Osiris, Ap-uat
7. Osiris, Thoth, Anubis, Astennu
8. Three deities not named
9. Osiris, Ra, Shue, Bebi
10. Osiris, Isis, Horus

TENAT In Egyptian religion, the Tenat festival was held on the seventh day of the month. It was dedicated to Osiris.

TENGA One of the principal divinities of the Mossi, a Negro tribe of west central Sudan. She is considered the goddess of the carth and white of Winnam, the supreme deity.

TENOCHCA A variant name for the Aztecs of ancient Mexico. The name stems from Tenoch, a mythical progenitor.

TEOCALLI These were the temples of the ancient Aztecs.

TEOTIHUACAN Pre-Columbian religious site near Mexico City. Includes the Pyramids of the Sun and Moon.

TEPITOTON In ancient Mexico, they were minor household gods.

TERAPHIM Idols, images, or other objects representing the primitive household gods of the ancient Semites. Their cult survived into the early centuries of Christianity. They may once have been associated with ancestor worship. Later they were used in divination and as talismanic figures cabalist practices. According to a legend from a collection of twelfth-century *midrashim* (exegeses), they were idols made from the head of a first born male whose hair had been plucked out. The head was sprinkled with salt, rubbed with oil, and set up in a room behind lighted candles. A small plaque, inscribed with the name of an idol and placed under the tongue, enabled the head to speak.

TERMINUS In Roman religion, the deity who presided over boundaries. His cult was initiated by Numa.

TESCALIPUCA Among the pre-conquest Mexicans, a deity whose festival was held in May. At this time the priests remitted all sins.

TESHUB A Hurrian weather god, corresponding to the god Zeus (Jupiter). He was the supreme ruler.

TETHYS In Greek mythology, a Titaness, sister of Cronus, daughter of Uranus, and wife of Oceanus, to whom she bore the river gods and the Oceanids.

TEUTATES One of the gods of the Gauls, akin to Mercury.

TEUTONIC RELIGION Information about Teutonic religion is derived largely from the ancient Romans — Julius Caesar, and the historian Tacitus. Extant inscriptions also add to this knowledge of Teutonic deities.
The goddess Nerthis was Mother-Earth. Tanfana and Baduhenna were goddesses whose functions are not known. Other obscure goddesses were Garmangabis, Vihansa, Harriasa.
Teutonic gods were equated with Roman counterparts, as: Mercurius Channinus, Hercules Magusanus. Fertility cults were in vogue, while oracles and prophecy formed part of the sacred practices.

TEZCATLIPOCA In Aztec religion, the god of the upper air who watched over the affairs of men. Originally the chief god of the Nahuas, he was later identified with many gods of conquered tribes. Each year a youth who had imitated him was sacrificed on his altar at Tenochtitlan. He was also known as Yaotzin ('The Enemy'), and was worshipped by the Mexican witches at their sabbat.

THALASSIUS A Roman god of marriage.

THALNA In Etruscan religion, a deity whose functions are obscure.

THANGAWALU A giant god among the Fijians.

THE COMMON MAN In Assyro-Babylonian religion, when the common man died, he did not pass into the Lower Regions. The Lower Regions were reserved for rulers and priests. The common man's 'share' in the divinity was so much smaller than those who had status and prestige.

But, to increase this 'share', the common man enlisted the services of magic, or he used charms, or made a personal appeal to some particular deity.

No one except the Assyrian king could approach the deity in prayer and hope for a response.

THE GREAT ABOVE In Sumerian religion, the descriptive term for Heaven.

THE GREAT BELOW In Sumerian religion, the descriptive term for the Nether Regions.

THE GREAT DEEP In Egyptian religion, the reference is to the heavenly Nile.

THE GREAT EGG In Egyptian religion, the Great Egg was created by Geb, the earth-god, and thrust through the earth in the city of the Great Cackler. In the Other World, the deceased identified himself with the Great Egg. The life of the deceased was conditioned by the life of the Egg, and the deceased grew old as the Egg grew old.

THE LIVING DEITY In Assyro-Babylonian religion, the deity was considered to be anthropomorphically alive. It was therefore necessary to supply it with food and drink daily. After a meal was offered to the god, it was distributed among the temple attendants.

The living image had also to be clad, perfumed, and decked out with appropriate jewelry. Hence the equipment of the temple, the daily preparations, the personnel attached to the various rituals and festivals of the divinity, created a dominant economic institution.

THEMIS In Greek religion, a form of the earth goddess, viewed in moral terms as the harmony or order of natural phenomena. She was also a prophetic deity, daughter of Uranus, wife of Zeus, and mother of Prometheus.

THEODOSIUS AND EGYPTIAN RELIGION With the advent of Christianity in the second century A.D., the Egyptian religion began to lose its hold on the people. Its practice ceased in 391, when the Emperor Theodosius I closed the ancient temples of Egypt.

THEOPHAGY In ancient mystery religions, this denoted the eating of a sacred animal or the sacramental consumption of the god in animal form.

THEOSOPHY Knowledge of God and the universe achieved by direct mystical insight, philosophical speculation, or both. A modern Theosophical Society was founded in New York in 1875 by Mme. H. P. Blavatsky and others, with the avowed aims of promoting the brotherhood of man, advancing the study of the ancient world-religions, and developing the latent divine powers in man. A second theosophical organization was established in the United States after the death of Madame Blavatsky (1891).

THERIOLATRY This is the cult of animals, particularly in ancient Egypt. A variant name for the cult is Zoolatry.

THESMOPHORIA In Greek mythology, an agricultural festival associated with autumn sowing. Only women could participate in the celebration.

THE TERRIBLE ONE In Egyptian religion, the Terrible One denotes Osiris' heart. It devours all things that have been slaughtered.

THE TWO COMBATANTS In Egyptian religion, this expression denotes the gods Horus and Set.

THETIS Greek goddess of the sea. Married to Peleus, a mortal. Her son was Achilles, the Homeric hero.

THIALF In Norse mythology, the swift messenger of the god Thor. He was also Thor's squire.

THIASOI In ancient Greece these were brotherhoods composed of initiates in the Orphic mystery cult.

THOERIS In Egyptian religion, a deity with the feet of a lion, arms and breasts of a woman, the belly of a hippopotamus, and a crocodile head. She presided over childbirth and was a protector against evil spirits.

THOR In Norse religion, Thor was the son of the supreme god Odin. He was the god of thunder and lightning, storms and springs. His abode was Bilskinrir. He is represented as a mighty swashbuckling adventurer. Thursday, that is, Thor's day, is derived from his name.
Thor breaks up the winter snow and ice and revives fertility. The oak is his tree. He protects sailors, and is the protector of ships. His image on a ship brings good luck. Winter sacrifices to Thor bring back spring and fruitfulness. As a god of fertility his worship persisted in Europe into the eighteenth century. His day, Thursday, is propitious for weddings. He is represented as wearing red hair, a long beard. He carries a hammer. Thunder symbolizes the sound produced when he plays ninepins with the other gods.

THOTH Egyptian moon-god and god of wisdom and writing. He is identified among the Greeks with Hermes. He invented arts and crafts and writing. He is represented in human form with the head of the ibis.

THRACIAN RELIGION In early centuries, before contact with Greek influences, the religion of Thrace was barbaric, marked by human sacrifices, orgiastic rituals, animal worship, and magic.
The gods of Thrace were chiefly chthonic, associated with the earth. Dionysus, the principal deity, symbolized fertility, and was worshipped with passionate ceremonies. He was virtually identified with Sabazius, whose cult was popular in Phrygia as well. As Dionysus was represented in animal form, his votaries devoured animals raw, thus acquiring Dionysus' divine attributes. In addition, many Greek gods of the pantheon were worshipped along with Dionysus.

THRAETAONA The Persian Michael. He struggled with Zohak, the destroying serpent.

327

THREDDE (THRIDI) In Norse mythology, 'the third,' one of the three members of the Norse triad.

TI In Chinese mythology and religion, the Supreme Lord, the world honored deities, and mythological sovereigns whose virtues resembled those of heaven and earth.

TIAMAT In Semitic-Babylonian religion, this expression denotes Primeval Waters, the source of god and men, heaven and earth. Tiamat is the primal Mother. Her consort is Apsu. They constitute the parents of the gods. Tiamat is overcome by Marduk, who cuts up her body. Marduk then becomes the god of life, while Tiamat symbolizes darkness and chaos.
Tiamat is represented as chaotic waters, as a raging serpent, as a monstrous dragon. Together with Apsu, Tiamat created the universe.

TIBETAN BOOK OF THE DEAD The *Bardo Thodol*, or Book of the Dead, like its Egyptian counterpart, is a Tibetan book of instructions for the dead and dying. It is a guide for the dead man who must spend forty-nine days awaiting his rebirth. The first part of the text, called *Chikhai Bardo*, describes the psychic aspect of the moment of death. The *Chonyid Bardo* describes the dream state which follows death. The third part, *Sidpa Bardo*, reveals the secrets of the birth instinct and prenatal events. The instructions are intended to fix the dead man's attention on the possibility of his liberation and to clarify the nature of his visions.

TIBETAN RELIGIONS The indigenous animistic Bon cult of Tibet is based on superstition, witchcraft, and ancestor-worship. The older religion survives in Eastern Tibet, but its temples and priests have been absorbed by Lamaism, the dominant religion. Lamaism represents a fusion of Buddhism, imported from India in the seventh century, and Shamanism. See Shaman.

T'IEN In Chinese, the word mean's 'heaven.' It refers either to the physical heaven or to the Supreme Lord who is purposive and personal. It may also designate the creative process, the principle of excellence or perfection, or nature.

TIKAL A cultural center of the classic Maya civilization, similar to centers established at Palenque and Copan. Tikal, in the Department of Peten, in Guatemala, is the greatest of the ceremonial centers dating from the classic period of Maya civilization (300 A.D. to 900 A.D.). One of its temples rises to a height of 229 feet. The ceremonial nucleus of the sanctuary ruins covers an area of more than 220 acres. Beneath the pyramid of Temple I, on the east side of the great plaza of Tikal, was a tomb containing pottery, jade, and some delicately engraved bones.

TINIA In Etruscan religion, the supreme god. Along with Uni and Minrva (Minerva), he was one of the members of the divine triad represented in Etruscan art. Tinia (Tin, Tina) may have been known as Voltumna (Veltha, Veltune) by one of the twelve Etruscan tribes.

TITAN In Greek mythology, one of the primeval deities. Hesiod, in his *Theogony,* lists the twelve Titans, children of Uranus and Gaea: six sons, Oceanus, Coeus, Crius, Hyperion, Iapetus and Cronus; and six daughters, Theia, Rhea, Themis, Mnemosyne, Phoebe, and Tethys. Zeus and the Olympians were descended from Cronus and Rhea; Atlas, Epimetheus, Prometheus, Dione, and Maia from Iapetus and Themis; and Leto from Coeus and Phoebe. The great event in Titan history was their defeat in the *Titanomachy,* or war against the Olympian gods in Thessaly.

TIU In Norse mythology, the god of conflict. He was identified with the Roman god Mars, the war-god. His name is commemorated in Tuesday.

TIV (TIUV) In Etruscan religion, the deified moon.

TLALOC In Aztec religion, he was the god of rain, sacrifices of children were offered to him. He is identified with the Mayan god Chac.

TLALTECUHTLI In Aztec religion, the lord of the earth. He takes the shape of a male monster, half toad and half alligator, and is eaten by Tlaltecuhtli when the sun sinks below the horizon.

TLAZOLTEOTL In Aztec religion, the mother of the gods, goddess of procreation, carnal sin, and confession. She is also called Tlaelquani ('Filth Eater') and is supposed to devour the sins of those who confess.

TLOQUE NAHAUQUE The supreme deity of the Aztecs of Mexico. He cannot be represented in any way. He is also called Ipalnemohuani ('Him by Whom All Live').

TOBO In Gnostic writings, a mysterious being who carries the soul of Adam from Orcus to the place of life.

TOCI In Aztec religion, the goddess of the earth and harvest, associated with the moon, childbirth, and medicine. She is the mother of Cihuacoatl. Victims were thrown from a high place on to a pile of stones, then their hearts were removed in sacrificial rites performed in her honor.

TOLTECS They were the indigenous inhabitants of ancient Mexico who were subjugated by the Aztecs. The Aztecs absorbed the religion of the Toltecs, which included sun-worship and human sacrifices.

TON A word used by the Dakotas to designate the undefined but elemental power or force possessed by particular persons or objects. It is comparable to the *Mana* of Melanesia, *Orenda* of the Iroquoians, and *Hashina* of the Madagascans.

TONACATECUTLI One of the supreme deities of the Aztecs.

TONATIUH Among the Aztecs, the sun god. He must be fed on blood to renew his youth. From sunrise to midday he is escorted by the souls of sacrificial victims and of warriors killed in battle. From midday to sunset he is escorted by

Cihuateteo. He is also called Cuauhtemoc, Nauhollin, Piltzintecuhtli, Tlachitonatiuh, and Xiuhpiltontli. He is related to Huitzilopochtli and Tezcatlipoca.

TOPHET A word of uncertain meaning and etymology, now used to designate the sacred pit in which sacrificial victims were placed and burned, as in Tyre and Carthage. The word occurs several times in the Old Testament.

TORNAIT Also called Torngrat, Tartat, Tungat. Among Eskimos, these are spirits that help a shaman. They are almost human, male and female, and can change form and disappear at will.

TORNASSUK Among the Eskimos, the deity that presides over beneficent spirits.

TORNGARSUK In Greenland, a deity consulted in spirit by the angakok on matters such as sickness and the weather, but rarely worshipped.

TOSHIGOHI In Shinto, the *Toshigohi* ('praying for harvest') is an agricultural festival. It was celebrated in the imperial palace by a Nakatomi (priest) who represented the Mikado.

TOTEM ANIMALS The primitive belief that a person and his totem were of the same flesh and blood is exemplified in the sacredness in which many animals, insects, reptiles, birds were held. Among such totems were the wolf, owl, serpent, hyena, lobster, tapir, deer, especially among the tribes of Canada, in New Guinea, in the Punjab, Africa, and Assam. The totem implied such sanctity that to kill it was punishable by death.

TOTEMS A totem is defined by J. G. Frazer as "a class of natural phenomena or material objects — most commonly a species of animals or plants — between which and himself

the savage believes that a certain intimate relation exists."
Of Algonquian origin, the word denotes a species or class
of animals, plants, or objects with which a family or clan
is identified.

Australian aborigines, linked with some particular animal
as a totem, conceive the totem, the animal, as of the same
flesh as members of the family. Hence the Aborigines do
not kill or eat the animal, except in extremities.

TOVODUN The gods of the ancient Dahomans. The name contains the root of the word *vodun* (voodoo).

TOYO-UKE-BIME In Japanese religion, the food goddess. She
is also called Uke-mochi ('food possessor'). She is a goddess
of cereals, a provider of game, and a provider of clothing
and housing. Her worship dates from ancient times. After
the goddess of the sun, she is the most important goddess
in the Shinto pantheon.

TRANSITIONAL RITES Ritual acts, rather than abstract ideas,
seem to have given expression to primitive man's confrontation with the mysterious fact of death and the destiny of
human beings. Crises such as birth, death, and the hope of
immortality gave rise to emotions which shaped the cult
of the dead. A series of transitional rites, also called by
the French name *rites de passage,* have been called forth at
critical junctures to insure a fresh outpouring of life and
power. These ritual acts relieve the tension generated by
crises through which all must pass.

TRANSMIGRATION The belief that the soul passes at death
into another body figures prominently not only in Buddhism,
Jainism, among the Ajivikas, and other great sects, but
also in the Orphic mysteries.

One of the basic tenets of the mystery cult of Orpheus was
a belief in the transmigration of the soul. The Orphic cult
promised union with the divine agent and a permanent
liberation from the prison-house of the body.

TREES Trees, as manifestations of fertility, were worshipped
among the ancient Slavs and the Teutons. The Greeks and

Romans assigned a particular deity to each species of tree. The Maypole and, in Buddhism, the hanyan tree are associated with ancient religious rites.

TRETA YUGA In the Hindu cosmogony, the second age of the world, embracing a period of 1,296,000 years.

TRIAL BY ORDEAL In Zoroastrian sacred literature, the legal system on which religious and social laws were centered. Magas used fire and molten metal to judge avengers and criminals. Atar controlled the Ordeal and separated the Ashavants from the Dregvants with the aid of Spenta Mainyu.

TRIBHUVANA (TRILOKA) In Hinduism, the three worlds: Svarga (Heaven), Bhumi (Earth), and Patala (Hell).

TRICKSTER The myth of the trickster, who is at once creator and destroyer, affirmer and negator, exists among widely divergent tribes and probably has its roots in the oldest expressions of mankind. The mythical trickster is a grotesque individual with huge digestive and sexual organs, bereft of moral or social values, and marked by the traits of both gods and human beings, yet he is primarily an inchoate being who foreshadows the shape of man. He appears in various guises among the ancient Greeks, Chinese, Japanese, and Semites; in the figure of the medieval jester and the modern Punch-and-Judy shows; and in the tribal lore of the American Indians.

TRIGLAV A three-headed Slavic deity associated with the city of Stettin. His functions are obscure.

TRIPITAKA In Buddhism, the three baskets or divisions of the canon: the doctrine, the rules and laws for the priesthood and ascetics, and the philosophical dissertations and metaphysics.

TRITON In Greek mythology, a sea demigod, the son of Poseidon (Neptune) and Ampritrite. Later mythology made him one of the lesser divinities who served as attendants on the sea gods.

TRIUNE GOD In Egyptian religion, Ptah-Seker-Asar was the triune god of the resurrection of the dead.

TRIVIDHA DVARA Literally, the three gates. Purity of body, purity of speech, and purity of thought are the three virtues that one must practice in order to become a Buddha.

TRIVIA A name given by the Romans to Diana, whose temples were often erected where three roads met.

TROBRIAND ISLANDERS The natives of Kiriwina, in the Trobriand Islands, believe that when an individual dies, his *baloma* (soul) leaves the body and leads a shadowy existence in another world. The baloma which is the main form of the dead man's spirit, goes to a neighboring island; but the *kosi,* an offshoot of the spirit, remains near the usual haunts of the dead man and may be seen or heard for a few days after his death. The kosi soon vanishes forever, but the baloma confronts and pays the Topileta or headman of the villages of the dead, and enters the village where he will live forever.

TROLL In Teutonic religion, an earth demon or a personified nonhuman power.

TROPHONIUS In Greek mythology, an oracular god of Boeotia.

TSUKI-YOMI In Japanese mythology, the god of the moon. He was washed from the filth that filled the left eye of Izanagi.

TSUMA Among Arawakan Indians, an anthropomorphic white god.

TU A primal god worshipped by the inhabitants of central and marginal Polynesia. Other gods of the same general type are Tane, Rongo, and Tangaloa.

TU In Tahunaism, one of the three sons of Tane. He was god of the north and one of the 'Four Major Pillars of Creation.'

TUAMUTEF In Egyptian religion, one of seven deities linked with funerary rites.
Also one of the gods of the four cardinal points, he watched over the stomach of the dead. Also called Duamutef.

TUAT In Egyptian religion, a region far from heaven and from the earth. Here dwelt the dead. During the night Ra, the sun-god, passed through this area.

TUATHA DE DANANN In Celtic religion, they were the gods of Ireland who lived in the hills and underground.

TUCHULCHA In Etruscan religion, an ancient deity whose functions are obscure.

TUISCON An obscure Teutonic deity whose functions are unknown.

TUPUA Among the Samoians, the *tupua* was a family god.

TURAN In Etruscan religion, a goddess who was identified with Aphrodite.

TURIN PAPYRUS An Egyptian papyrus discovered in the mid-nineteenth century. It describes how the goddess Isis secured the secret name of Ra, the sun god.

TURIPID A Baltic deity whose functions care obscure.

TURMS In Etruscan religion, a deity who was identified with the Greek god Hermes.

TUMURIPO The Hawaiian epic of creation, composed in commemoration of the god Rono and transmitted orally through the centuries by the priests of the Rono cult. Of obscure origin, it traces the evolution of the Mu, the progenitors of the people known today as the Hawaiians. Dedicated to the 'Exalted Goddess of the Sun,' it combines two genealogies, the Ra'i Ra'i and the Paritu.

TUSHITA In the Hindu pantheon, a class of gods of great purity.

TUTELARY DEITIES In the Hittite religion, Karzi, Zitharim, and Hapantali were male tutelary divinities. Among the goddesses who performed the same function were Inar, Telepinu, Hatepinu, Halmasuit, Kamrusepa.

TUTELINA Also called Tutulina. A Roman goddess who presided over reaped corn.

TWILIGHT OF THE GODS In Norse mythology, the last conflict between the gods and their enemies the giants.

TWIN GODS In Egyptian religion, they are Heru-netch-hra-teff and Heru-khent-an-maati.

TWIN MAINYU Twin Spirits used by Zarathustra to explain the origin of evil and the dual nature of the human mind.

TZAR MOSKOY A Slavic god whose function was similar to that of the Roman sea-god Neptune.

TZITZIMITL In Aztec religion, deities who preside over the stars and evil. They take the shape of monsters and descend from the sky to devour mankind whenever an eclipse occurs.

TZURAH In the Cabala, the divine prototype.

U

UBOZE A Polish deity who presided over the home.

UGAR In Canaanite religion, a personification of the fields; messenger of the god Baal.

UGARITIC A language closely related both to biblical Hebrew and to Phoenician. Texts written in the language and discovered in Syria, particularly at Ras Shamra, record the religious and mythological heritage of the Canaanites. The city of Ugarit flourished as early as the second millenium B.C. Its two great temples, one dedicated to Baal and the other to Dagon, were separated by a library which housed the Ugaritic documents, comprising hundreds of tablets dating from the fifteenth and fourteenth centuries. These texts employ wedge-shaped signs and one of the earliest known specimens of an alphabet.

UGARITIC POEMS The most important of the poems discovered at the ancient site of Ugarit is the epic cycle of Baal and Anat, which begins with the struggle between Baal and Yam and ends with Baal's victory. Subsequently Baal is slain, brought down to the kingdom of the dead, and imprisoned by Mot, the god of death. Life on earth comes to a standstill until Anat rescues Baal and returns fertility and plenty to the earth.

UI-KASANG A god of war to whom sacrifices are made by the Apa Tanis. Ui-Kasang and Nia-Kasang are supposed to receive the animal sacrificed at the *ropi*-rite that follows a successful raid.

UJI-GAMI In Shinto, the Uji-gami are pseudo-ancestral deities who eventually became local deities of the districts where they were born.

UKKO In the religion of ancient Finland, he was the supreme god.

UKUPANIPO In the Hawaiian religion, he is the shark-god who presides over the fisheries.

ULLER One of the twelve principal gods in the Norse pantheon. he was represented as a hunter; also skilled in the use of snow shoes.

UMA A Hindu goddess, she was one of many of Shiva's consorts.

UNGAMBIKULA The Arunta believe that men were created long ago by the Ungambikula, two beings who descended from the western sky with large stone knives, discovered some undeveloped creatures called the Inapertwa, and shaped them into human beings.

UNI One of the divine triad appearing in Etruscan representations. Along with Tinia, Minrva, and nine other deities, he made up a celestial council of twelve.

UNKULUNKULU Among the Zulus, the 'Old-Old-One,' conceived as the first man, merged with the notion of creator and thunderer.

UPANISHADS Mystic teachings ('Sessions under a Teacher') representing one of the earliest serious attempts to grasp the meaning of life and deal with the problems of the great unseen powers. Atman is the ultimate truth of the All of existence and Atman (Soul or Self is Brahma, 'the Beginning of all, the End in which all things dissolve.' These teachings are a part of Sanskrit Brahmanic literature and a record of the human mind's struggle to understand human destiny.

UPEKSHA In Yoga, a state of absolute indifference attained by complete mastery over one's mental and physical faculties.

UPUAUT A wolf-headed or jackal-headed Egyptian god who presided over the dead.

URAEUS In Egyptian religion, the representation of the sacred asp, rearing or coiled. The symbol of divine protection, the asp was revered as a god. The uraeus is found on the pschent (royal headdress) of the pharaohs.

URANIA An epithet of Aphrodite. Also, in Greek mythology, the Muse of astronomy.

URANUS In Greek mythology, the son of Gaea (earth), personification of the sky, and father of the Titans, the Hecatoncheires, the Cyclops, and the Furies.

URI URI In Tahunaism, the divine name of Teave's daughter, Na Vahine.

URKISH The religious center of the ancient Hurrians (Horites).

UROBOROS The tail-eating serpent, used by Greek alchemists to symbolize the unity of sacrificer and sacrificed.

USHAS (USAS) The only goddess of importance in the Vedic pantheon, she is the goddess of dawn, celebrated in twenty-one hymns in the Rig-Veda. She is sometimes regarded as the mother of Surya, the sun god, sometimes as his husband.

USHEBTIS In Egyptian religion, these were figurines of human shape. They were placed in the tomb along with the deceased. These statuettes were required to work for the deceased in the Nether Regions.

USIL In Etruscan religion, the deified sun.

USOUS A Phoenician god whose functions coincide with those of Neptune.

UTCHAT Another name for the amulet worn by Egyptians as a protection against evil forces, commonly called the Eye of Horus.

UTGARD In Norse religion, the outer rim of the cosmic ocean, the home of the giants, also called Jotunheim.

UTNAPISHTIM In Sumerian religion, a pious king of Shuruppak who achieved immortality. In the Gilgamesh myth, he is the sage to whom the hero, represented as king of Uruk, goes to learn the secret of life and death. The name means 'I have found life.' Survivor of the Flood in Mesopotamian tradition, a figure akin to the biblical Noah.

UTU The Sumerian sun god. He was also a judge and a warrior and a law-giver.

UVASI In the Rig-Veda, a divine nymph whose beauty set the heavens ablaze. Cursed by the gods, she settled on earth.

V

VACERRI The name of the priests of the Druids.

VACUNA A Sabine godess. She is identified variously with the Roman deities Victoria, Bellona, Minerva, Venus.

VAGITANUS A Roman deity who presided over crying children.

VAINAMOINEN In ancient Finnish religion, he was the god of poetry and music. In his functions, he corresponds to the Greek Apollo.
A Finnish bard, hero of the epic *Kalevala,* and inventor of the harp. He is supposed to have visited the land of the dead, as did Orpheus and Dionysus.

VAISHESHIKA One of the six schools of philosophy founded by Kanada.

VAISHNAVA A follower of any group worshipping Vishnu as the supreme god.

VAIVASWATA In Hindu mythology, the name of the seventh Manu. The son of Surya (the Sun), he built an ark in obedience to a command of Vishnu. After the flood, he became the founder of the solar race of kings.

VAJRA In Hindu mythology, the scepter of Indra, similar in use to the thunderbolts of Zeus.

VALA In Norse and Teutonic mythology, a prophetess.

VALHALLA In Norse mythology, Valhalla is the abode of the slain. The Valkyries, daughters of the chief of the gods, Odin, brought the dead warriors to Valhalla, where they served these heroes.

VALI One of the twelve principal deities in the Norse pantheon.

VALKYRIES In Norse legend, they were the messengers of the supreme god Odin. The function of these divine warrior-maidens was to choose the bravest of those warriors who had died on the battlefield and to conduct them to Valhalla, where they would serve the heroes with mead for eternity.

VALLONIA In Roman mythology, a goddess who presided over valleys.

VAMANA In Hindu mythology, the fifth avatar of Vishnu, in the form of a dwarf.

VANADIS In Norse mythology, the goddess of Hope. An appellation also of Freyja.

VANIR In Norse mythology, divinities of the air. This group consisted of Frey, Freyja, and Njord. Their dwelling-place was Vanaheim. They were also deities presiding over wealth, commerce, productivity. They had quarreled with the other gods who were led by Odin.

VARA In Norse mythology, she was the goddess who punished unfaithful lovers and other oath-breakers.

VARAHA In Hindu mythology, the third avatar of Vishnu, in the form of a boar.

VARUNA In Hinduism, the supreme cosmic deity and guardian of the cosmic order. Called an asura in the earliest Vedic period, he is described as the origin of the tree of life. The corresponding female power is the mother goddess and earth-goddess Aditi. Varuna is the vedic equivalent of the Avestan Ormazd. Horse sacrifices and the soma were originally offered to him.

VASHISTA In Hinduism, one of the primitive seven Rishis. He was a very famous Vedic sage.

VASUDEVA In Hindu mythology, the father of Krishna.

VASUS In Hindu mythology, the eight evil deities who attended Indra. They are personified cosmic phenomena.

VATEA In the Hawaiian pantheon, a member of the fourth heavenly trinity, mate of the goddess Papa.

VAYU In Vedic mythology, god of the air. In the Ramayana, he is the father of Hanuman.

VE In Norse religion, Ve is the brother of the supreme god Odin. He participates with Odin in shaping men and women out of Askr and Embla.

VEDANTA The dominant religious thought of India developed on the basis of the Upanishads and systematized by Shankara about 800 A.D. Brahman is the one, eternal reality. The phenomenal world is illusion. Ignorance of the oneness of the self with Brahman is the cause of reincarnation.

VEDAS The four collections of the sacred literature of the Aryans. These hymns, prayers, and liturgical formulas are the foundation of Vedic Hinduism. The Rig-Veda is the oldest and most important. The Yajur-Veda includes liturgical and ritual materials, written in prose and verse. The Sama-Veda, contains hymns with musical notations. The Atharva-Veda contains charms, spells, curses, and prayers. The Brahmans and Upanishads are included in the Vedas.

VEDIC HINDUISM Dravidian or pre-Aryan Hinduism was largely displaced for several centuries by the Aryan invaders who entered India about 1500 B.C., with their optimistic, life-loving religion. The prayers and hymns of the

343

Vedas, the source books of Vedic Hinduism, reflect the needs and aspirations of the Aryans: material and martial success, and a long life on earth.

VEL In Etruscan religion, a deity who was associated with a particular Etruscan city.

VELCHAN In Etruscan religion, a god about whom little is known. He may have become the Roman Vulcan.

VELES A Slavic deity who presided over the flocks.

VELTUNE In Etruscan religion, a deity who was associated with a particular Etruscan city.

VENDIDAD A priestly code in Zoroastrian religion. It comprised part of the Zend Avesta. It contained directions regarding purificatory rites, punishment, and expiation.
It also deals with creation, the Golden Age, the Flood, agriculture, civil and penal law.

VENTH In Etruscan religion, a deity whose functions are obscure.

VENUS In Roman religion, the ancient Italian goddess of beauty, protectress of gardens, and mother of love. Her worship was introduced into Rome at an early date. Identified with the Greek Aphrodite, she figured prominently in mythology as well as in religion. The famous cult of Aphrodite at Eryx, Sicily, was the source of the worship of Venus Erycine, to whom a temple in Rome was founded in 217 B.C.

VENUS FIGURINES Female figurines in bone, ivory, or stone, characterized by grossly exaggerated maternal organs and belonging to the Upper Paleolithic period. These sculptured Venuses are an integral part of the cult of the Great Mother in advanced stages of civilization. The cult probably entered Europe from east. Many examples of these figurines, marked with the outward signs of fecundity and personified in the Earth Mother and her counterparts in various localities, have been found in the valley of the Don.

VERTUMNUS In Roman religion, a god of change. Probably of Etruscan origin, he was variously regarded as god of the changing season, of the manifold productions of the vegetable world, etc. He changed himself into a beautiful youth in order to persuade Pomona to marry him.

VESDRI Also *Westri*; means 'the West'. In Norse mythology, one of the four dwarfs who support the vault of heaven on their shoulders.

VESTALS Priestesses who served the Roman goddess Vesta, who presided over the domestic hearth. They were trained from an early age. At first there were four Vestals, then the number was increased to six in historical times. They service last for thirty years, during which time they were forbidden to marry. If they were found guilty of unchastity, they were entombed alive. As their prerogatives, in public thorough fares the highest magistrates had to make way for them. At public games they had reserved seats. If a criminal on his way to execution encountered a Vestal, he was set free.

VIBHAVASU In Hinduism, a mystic fire connected with the beginning of the dissolution of the universe.

VIBILIA A Roman goddess who directed travelers on their way.

VICA POTA An Italic goddess associated with Victory: or perhaps with food and drink. Her Latin name admits of either interpretation: otherwise, she is obscure.

VIDAR In Norse mythology, he is the son of Odin and the god who presides over forests. He participates with the other gods in killing Fenrir. He avenges his father Odin. His descriptive appellation is 'the silent god.'

VIDDUS A Roman deity. At the moment of death he separated the soul from the body.

345

VILCAPAMPA An ancient shrine of the Incas of Peru. It may have been built by the first Inca, Manco Capac, to honor his ancestors. The name means 'pampa where the *huilca* grows.' The huilca is a subtropical tree. It is also a medicine or purgative, according to Quechua dictionaries. When its powdered seeds are inhaled, the narcotic snuff (*cohoba*) produces a hypnotic state supposedly accompanied by supernatural visions. The ruins of the shrine lie in the shadow of Machu Picchu.

VILI In Norse religion, he is the brother of the supreme god Odin. With Odin he participates in shaping men and women out of Askr and Embla.

VINGOLF The palace of friendship. This was the abode of the Norse goddesses.

VIPRACHITTI In Hindu mythology, the chief of the Danavas, the giants who warred with the gods.

VIRACOCHA The Omnipotent Creator worshipped by the ruling class of the Incas.

VIRBIUS In Roman religion, a primitive deity of childbirth. In mythology, he is the son of Hippolytus.

VIRGIN BIRTH In the writings of ancient religions, accounts of unusual, miraculous, or supernatural births are widespread. In primitive cultures, conception sometimes occurred through the influence of an amulet, image, or fetish. Early rulers of the Mediterranean area often claimed divine parentage. Legends of such births are frequent in Egyptian, Zoroastrian, Greek, and Roman religions.

VIRGINS OF THE SUN The Chosen Women of the Incas of Peru. Apparently they were the residents of Macchu Picchu. They were associated with the sanctuaries where the sun was worshipped.

346

VIRIPLACA A Roman goddess who reconciled disputes between husband and wife.

VISHNU One of the Adityas in the Vedas, he became the supreme god of the great Vishnuite sect of Hinduism. He is the Preserver in the great triad in which Brahma is Creator and Shiva is Destroyer.

VISHNUISM (VAISHNAVISM) One of the two major theistic sects of Hinduism centering around the worship of Vishnu as a personal god or on one or more of his incarnations (Krishna, Rama, Buddha, etc.).

VISHVAKARMAN A Vedic god, a personification of the creative force. He is described as the all-seeing god who is beyond the comprehension of mortals.

VITULA A Roman goddess of mirth.

VITZIPUTZLI He was the principal deity among the ancient inhabitants of Mexico.

VODUN (VOODOO) A complex polytheistic system with elements taken from African cults and Catholicism. Formerly, in some rites, it included human sacrifice and cannibalism. The word voodoo may derive from the Dahoman term for gods, *tovodun*. The cult is now found chiefly among the Negroes of Haiti.

VOHUMANAH In Zoroastrian religion, one of the six Amesha Spentas, who aided the Supreme Deity in governing the universe.

VOLTUMNA One of a group of divinities who ruled over heaven and earth, according to the Etruscans. He may be the Volsinii designation of Tinia, the supreme Etruscan divinity. His sanctuary, near the lake of Bolsena, was the site of an annual convention at which a king was probably chosen by the twelve tribes of the Etruscan federation.

VOLUMNA A Roman goddess who made men want to pursue what was good.

VOLUMNUS A Roman god who made men willing to pursue what was good.

VOLUSIA Among the Romans, a minor goddess who was in charge of the blades of wheat.

VOR A Scandinavian goddess noted for her wisdom.

VRITRA In the Vedas, the demon of drought and a foe of Indra.

VULCAN In Roman religion, a fire god whose cult was brought to Rome by the Sabine king Titus Tatius. Originally a local divinity who had to be propitiated in order to avoid destructive fires, he was worshipped as the consort of the goddess Maia. In classical times, he was identified with the Greek Hephaestus and thereafter was regarded as the consort of Venus and the patron of metalworkers.

VYASA The term (literally, 'one who expands or amplifies') is applied to the highest gurus of India.

W

WAB In Egyptian religion, a body of priests who offered sacrifices to the gods. The priests were usually called the 'divine fathers.' Egyptian priests were often granted semi-hereditary privileges and fuctions. They wore white linen, shaved the head, and abstained from fish and beans as food.

WADD In Arabian religion, the god of the moon, known also as Sin, Ilumquh, and Amm.

WADJET In Egyptian religion, another name for Buto, cobra-goddess of the Delta, and protector of the pharaoh.

WAINAMOINEN See *Vainamoinen*.

WAKANDA Among the Sioux Indians, this was the universal principle of life.

WALKYRIES See *Valkyries*.

WALPURGIS NIGHT The eve of May Day was, by Teutonic and Nordic tradition, the night on which a witches' Sabbath took place on the Brocken or some other high mountain.

WANAX A deity worshipped by the ancient Anatolians.

WANINGA A sacred symbol in Central Australia. Usually made of two crossbars tied at the center with human hair, it may not be looked upon by women.

WAQLIMI The title given by the Zanj to their king, considered to be the son of the great god. Notwithstanding his divine kingship, he could be deposed whenever he exercised a tyrannical power and departed from the rules of justice. He may have been the forerunner of the Shilluk kings, who are believed to descend from Nyikang.

WARRIOR-GODS In Hittite religion, warrior-gods included Sulikatti, Shuwaliyatta, Wurunkatti, Yarris, 'Lord of the Bow.'

WAUWALAK A cult practiced by the Australian aborigines of Arnhem Land, similar in some respects to the Djanggawul cult. Both cults stress fertility and focus attention on sexual functions, particularly the female functions. The main difference stems from the fact that the Djanggawul are concerned with procreation (they are supposed to have given birth to the Wauwalak), while the Wauwalak symbolically reenact the myth of bringing all being into life, in order to maintain the status quo.

WEATHER GOD In Hittite religion, the weather god was represented as a bull. The lion was associated with his consort. He was the main God of the Hittites, but since his name was always written with one of the ideograms of the Mesopotamian Adad, its Hittite form is unknown. In Protohattic he was called Taru, in Hurrian Teshub, in Luwian Datta. The hieroglyphic ideogram corresponding to the Hittite weather god is read Tarhund.

WEKUFE Evil spirits to whom the Mapuche Indians attribute the death of their kinsmen.

WINNAM The supreme god of the Mossi, a Sudanese tribe. He is the sun god and husband of Tenga, the earth goddess.

WERET HERA In Egyptian, this expression means *great in magic*. It is a descriptive term applied to Isis in her aspect as goddess of magic.

350

WEST The ancient Egyptians held that the West was the abode of the dead. The dead were hence called The Westerners. The goddess Isis, for instance, was the First of the Westerners.

WHITE DOG SACRIFICE A ceremony elaborated in response to a dream of the god Teharonhiawagon, the personification of life. To celebrate the New Year, the Iroquois immolate a White Dog.

WIELAND A Teutonic deity who is identified with the Roman Vulcan.

WIND-GODS In classical mythology these were the deities who presided over the movements of the winds. The most notable of such divinities was Aeolus. The Romans considered four winds to have divine attributes: Boreas, the North Wind; Eurus, the East Wind; Notus or Auster, the South Wind; and Zephyrus, the West Wind.
The worship of the winds was common to the Persians as well.

WIRADJURI An Australian aboriginal tribe. Their medicine-men are initiated by entering a tomb and then being led before the crystal throne of the god Baiame.

WODEN In Teutonic mythology, he was equivalent to the Norse god Odin. His temple is probably the only pagan Teutonic temple of which ruins exist in Britain. Augustine purged the temple and consecrated it for Christian worship. The ruins may be seen in the grounds of the abbey at Canterbury.

WORLD OF GODS In Norse religion, the world of the gods is made from the skull of the giant Ymir.

WORSHIP OF ANIMALS Animal worship has been interpreted in various ways. Man's effort to ally himself to some animals, or to protect himself against others, may have contributed to animal worship. Various animals became identified with the concept of fertility. The snake received worship as the source of vegetation. Mystery cults conceived the souls of the dead as reappearing in animal form. An animal, attached to a particular region, became identified with the god, and the deity assumed part of the animal attributes and form, as occurred in so many instances in Egyptian religion.

WORSHIP OF TREES Pagan religions revered trees as divinities. To the Celts the oak was sacred. The Greek oracle at Dodona responded through rustling of oak leaves. In Rome a fig-tree, associated with Romulus, was worshipped.

WURUNKATTI In the Hittite pantheon, one of two famed warriors.

WURUSEMU In Hittite religion, the consort of the weather god Taru. She was the sun goddess of Arinna, the Queen of Heaven, and protectress of the king when he went into battle.

WOVOKA The Indian Messiah who taught that the Indians, recently deprived of their food supply as a result of the slaughter of the buffalo herds that roamed the West, would soon be reunited on a regenerated earth. He made the Ghost Dance, previously a part of a popular religious movement, the chief rite of the new movement. He initiated the Ghost Dance religion in 1889.

X

XIBALBA Among the Quiché Indians of Central America, this term denotes the Lower Regions.

XILONEN In Aztec religion, the Goddess of young ears of corn and sister of Tlaloc. She was also called Chicomolotzin.

XIPE-TOTEC He was the Aztec god of the West. His color was red. He was the god of spring and vegetation.

XIUHCOATL One of the Plumed Serpent cults of the Aztecs. Its center was Tenochtitlan.

XIUHTECUHTLI In Aztec religion, the god of fire. He is accompanied by Xiuhcoatl, the fire serpent, and is also called Ixcozauhqui.

XOCHIPILLI In the Aztec religion, he was the god of flowers. He presided over sports, gambling, and dancing.

XOCHIQUETZAL In the Aztec religion she was a goddess of flowers. Her function coincided with that of the Roman goddess Venus. At certain sacred periods, young women, generally harlots, were offered to her as sacrifices.

XOCHIYAYOTL This expression means 'War of the Flowers.' Among the Aztecs of ancient Mexico, this was a method of securing human sacrifices to the sun-god by capturing victims for the immolation.

XUDAM An Etruscan deity who was identified with the Roman Mercury.

Y

YACATECUHTLI In Aztec religion, the god of commerce and patron of merchants and travelers.

YACHU A deity of the Apa Tanis. Himalayan tribesmen sacrifice a fowl to Yachu and Pila, expecting in return the release or escape of a prisoner of war.

YADAVA In Hindu mythology, a descendant of Yadu, the son of King Yayati of the Somavansa or lunar race.

YAKSHA In popular Indian folklore, a class of demons who devour men.

YAKU In the shamanistic religion of the Veddas, a diminutive Stone Age group living on the island of Ceylon, the *yaku* or spirits were considered to be dangerous. A yaka could possess a shaman during a dance and cause him to fall to the ground.

YAM In Canaanite religion, Yam is the Sea. He is in charge of the ocean, rivers, lakes, springs. His variant names are Ruler of the Stream and Leviathan. He is depicted as a dragon of hydra form.

YALO Among the Apo Tanis, the word means soul. The members of this Himalayan tribe believe that the yalo of everyone who dies a natural death goes to Neli, the region of the dead, where he will complete a second life similar to the first before dying once more and entering another region of the dead. A sick man's yalo may leave him and enter Neli, where it will remain until ransomed by a shaman.

YAMA AND YAMI In the Vedas, they are twins who become

355

parents of the human race. Another tradition makes Manu the first parent. Yama is the first to discover a pathway from earth to heaven and become king of the blessed dead, although he is also known as ruler of hell and, most frequently, as the god of the dead.

YANG In Chinese thought, yang is the male, positive, light, beneficent, active principle of the universe, in contrast to yang. Yin and yang are terms in a dualism which runs through much of Chinese philosophy, religion, medicine, science, and magic.

YAREAH In Canaanite religion, the moon god. His consort was Nikkal, the Queen. The city of Jericho stems from the name of the god.

YASHTS In Zoroastrian religion, these were Avestan hymns of praise, glorifying the divine Zoroastrian beings. Some of these deities, particularly Tishtrya, Mithra, and Anahita, were ancient Iranian divinities.

YASNA In Zoroastrian religion, the chief liturgies, consisting of seventy-two chapters, comprising part of the Zend Avesta. Included were invocations to the gods, particularly to the supreme Ahura Mazda.

YAZATAS In Zoroastrian religion, the divine powers of lower rank than Ahura Mazda and the Amesha Pentas.

YENGI-SHIKI The *Yengi-shiki* ('Institutes of the Yengi Period') is a valuable source of information concerning the ceremonies of Shinto. It includes some prayers and describes the ritual of the Yengi Era (901-923).

YESZA An ancient Polish deity whose functions are obscure. Sometimes identified with Jupiter.

YETZIRAH In the Cabala, the third of four worlds, the abode of all the ruling angels who control planets, worlds, and spheres.

YEZIDIS A sect of demon worshippers in Armenia and the

Caucasus. Their religion is an admixture of ancient Mazdean and Christian elements. They consider themselves to
be the descendants of Adam alone. Their sacred books are
The Book of Revelation and *The Black Book.* Their supreme being is a passive transcendent god whose seven
angels rule the world. The chief angel, Melek Taus, represented as a peacock, is apparently the author of evil.
He must therefore be propitiated as co-creator. The sect
claims descent from Adam alone.

YGGDRASIL In Norse mythology, the world-tree. Its leaves are
perpetually green and its roots are in the Underworld. In
the twilight of the gods the tree will be destroyed.

YGGR In Norse religion, this is a variant name for the supreme
god Odin.

YIMA (YAMA) In Persian mythology, Yima is an A Avestan
demigod, the first mortal to die. After his death, he was
deified and made king of the dead. *Yima* corresponds to
the Vedic *Yama.*

YIN In Chinese thought, yin is the female, negative, dark, evil,
passive principle of the universe, as contrasted to yang.

YMIR In Norse mythology, he was the first Giant. Ymir's son
was Odin's father. Ymir was killed by Odin and his two
brothers. The myth is akin to the Greek myth of Cronos
and the Titans.

YOGA In Hinduism, mental discipline directed toward the identification of consciousness with its object. The yogi (prac-
titioner) may seek to attain union with the universal spirit,
Brahma. The main yogas are the devotional, intellectual,
and work, or, physical, yoga. The three stages of trance are
fixed attention, contemplation, and concentration.

YOK Among the Tlingit, the divine essence indwelling in all
things, all animals, and all spirits.

YUAN-SHIH T'IEN-CHUN The Chinese expression means 'The

Heavenly Honored One of Origin and Beginning.' In Taoism, it designates the highest deity, also called Yuan-shih T'ien-Wang, 'The Heavenly King of Origin and Beginning.' He is the first member of the Taoist Triad or the Three Purities, Essence, Vital Force, and the Spirit.

YUGA The thousandth part of a Kalpa. One of the four ages of the world. Each Yuga is preceded by a transition period (Sandhya) and followed by another period of like duration (Sandhyansa). The four Yugas are computed by divine years, totalling 4,320,000 years of mortal men, known as a Mahayuga or Manvantara. Two thousand such Mahayugas make a Kalpa, equivalent to a day and a night of Brahma.

YUM KAAX In Maya religion, the god of corn and the harvest and patron of husbandry.

Z

ZAGREUS In Greek mythology, a god of the Lower Regions. In the Orphic mystery cult, Zagreus was a variant name for Dionysus.

ZALMOXIS A deity of the Getae. He was a god of the dead. Some ancient authorities identified him with Cronos (Saturn). The Getae lived in Dacia (modern Rumania).

ZAMAMA An Assyro-Babylonian deity associated with the city of Kish. Her worship was extremely popular.

ZAMPUN The Tibetan sacred tree of life.

ZANDIKS A name applied to the followers of Mani, the founder of Manichaeanism.

ZANJ The name given by Arabs of the ninth and tenth centuries A.D. to the Negroes living on the eastern coast of Africa. They were probably forerunners of present Swahili, Hamitic, and Bantu-speaking populations, who have preserved many of the elements of the Zanj religion. Though not codified, it was animistic and comprised a divine kingship. Everyone worshipped what he pleased, animal, vegetable, or mineral. Waqlimi, meaning son of the great god, was the title given to the king, who ceased to be recognized as divine as soon as he departed from the rules of justice.

ZAOTAR Among the ancient Persians, this term means *a caller.* He was the priest-magician who invoked the gods by reciting certain ritualistic formalities and chants.

ZARATHUSTRA His Greek name was Zoroaster. He was the reformer of Iranian religion who flourished in the sixth century B.C. His life and the exposition of his doctrines appear in the sacred writings known as the Zend-Avesta. While still young, Zarathustra was subject to visions and began to preach. He was assassinated by the people of Balkh in Bactria. His tomb was believed to be at Persepolis.

His religious system was based on a dualism that postulated an everlasting conflict between good, represented by light, and evil, symbolized by darkness.

In modern times the descendants of the Zoroastrians are the Parsees, most of whom are to be found in Bombay. They still profess the main tenets of Zoroastrianism. They pray in their temples to Ahura Mazda. A notable feature of their funerary customs is the procedure of exposing the dead to vultures, in a Tower of Silence, in order to avoid pollution of the elements.

ZARPANIT In Assyro-Babylonian religion, she was the consort of the god Marduk.

ZCERNOBOCH An obscure Baltic deity.

ZEHUT In Egyptian religion, this is an early form of the name of Thoth.

ZEN BUDDHISM A Buddhist sect popular in Japan. This sect was established in Japan, by way of India and then China, in the twelfth century. It teaches a possible way to attain a Buddha-state principally by means of meditation.

ZEND The sacred language of the Zoroastrians. It was the earliest form of Indic.

ZEND AVESTA The sacred writings of Zoroastrianism. They consisted of hyms and invocations to Zoroaster, texts, injunctions to votaries, dialogues between Ahura Mazda and Zoroaster. The original Avesta was largely destroyed by Alexander. Five parts of the remnants were taken to India: Yasna, Vispered, Vendidad, Yashts, and Khorda Avesta.

ZERTUR In Sumerian religion, the mother of Tammuz. The appellation means 'young maiden.'

ZERVAN AKARANA An expression that appears in the Zoroastrian *Vendidad*. It denotes *Eternal Time*. Zervan or time was either a primeval deity or fate itself.
In Zoroastrian religion, Zervan is the father of Ahura Mazda, and of Ahriman, the Spirit of Evil.

ZERVANISM A heretical sect known to the Greeks as early as the fourth century B.C. and later partially incorporated by nascent Mithraism. According to the Zervanite heresy, infinite time is the originating principle of existence. It is prior to the dual principles of good and evil.

ZEUS (JUPITER) The supreme god in Greek and correspondingly in Roman mythology.

ZEUS' FLEECE In ancient Greek folk legend, Zeus' fleece — *Dios kodion* — was used in the initiatory rites of the Eleusinian mysteries.

ZEUS HERKEIOS In ancient Greek religion, Zeus (Jupiter) in his aspect as a protector of houses and fences.

ZEUS MYODES In Greek mythology, Zeus, the supreme god, in his function as a hunter of flies. Flies were often a pest during the performance of divine sacrifices.

ZEUS XENIOS In ancient Greek religion, the supreme god Zeus in his function as a protector of foreigners.

ZHYWIE An ancient Polish deity whose functions are not known. Sometimes known as the god of life.

ZIGGURAT An ancient Mesopotamian temple tower. The tower of Babel is the best known, but that of Ur is the best preserved. Many great shrines were equipped with ziggurats, of which many bear names identifying them as mountains, supposedly the center of the mysterious potency of the earth and therefore of all natural life. Frequently the deities associated with ziggurats clearly personify chthonic forces.

ZILHARIYA In Hittite religion, he was a tutelary deity.

ZITHARI A tutelary god in the Hittite pantheon.

ZIU In Teutonic mythology, he was god of the sky.

ZIUSUDRA In the Sumerian religion, this is the counterpart of the Biblical Noah. Ziusudra too is involved in a universal Flood.

ZOGOTES Among the Malu tribesmen, sacred performers who participate in the initiation rites culminating in the revelation of the secret name of the god.

ZOHAK In the Zend Avesta, the personification of evil in the shape of a serpent.

ZOHAR A compendium of Jewish Cabalistic lore introduced into Spain in the thirteenth century by Moses de Leon, who ascribed the book to Simeon ben Yohai, a second-century rabbi. It is reputed to be the oldest extant treatise on the Hebrew esoteric religious doctrines. It contains a complete theosophy, treating of God, the cosmogony and cosmology of the universe, and other matters such as the soul, sin, and redemption.

ZOMBIE In the vodun (voodoo) cult, a human whose soul has been possessed by another person through evil magic and whose body is at the disposal of the magician.

ZOOGONOI In Greek religion, these were the deities who were animal-born. They were credited with the prolongation of life.

ZOROASTRIAN SACRED LITERATURE The Zoroastrian canon of sacred literature established in the fourth century A.D. is only part of the original Avesta. It included the Yasna, records on morality, theology, ceremonial invocations, hymns, litanies, and the priestly code known as the Vendidad.

Of later origin are the Dinhart, the legends and philosophy of Zoroastrianism, the Bundahish and the Arda Viraf Nameh, dealing with cosmology and the afterlife. In addition, there were the Sayast la-Sayast, dealing with what was proper and improper. The Datistan-i-Dinik, a body of opinions on religious questions, and the Shikand Gumanik Vigar, the Double-dispelling Explanation, which was composed with reference to Zoroastrianism, Islam, and Christianity.

ZOSIMOS OF PANOPOLIS A third-century alchemist and non-Christian Gnostic. He was probably an adherent of the Poimandres sect and a follower of Hermes. In his treatises, he relates a number of visions combining pagan and Christian elements. He is the author of an encyclopedia of alchemy.

ZOTZILHA CHIMALMAN In Maya religion, the god of light and darkness. He lives in a cave and struggles against Kinich Ahau, symbolizing the eternal conflict between day and night.

ZWIMBGANANA In African voodoo cults, a creature raised from the dead to do a witch's evil work. Natives use a plant, the *mbanje,* for protection. After seeing a zwimbganana or a witch, they quickly set fire to the herb and inhale the fumes.

DATE DUE

REFERENCE